Neil Jackm

IREL
ANCIENT EAST

A Guide to Its Historic Treasures

The Collins Press

For Róisín

First published in 2016 by
The Collins Press
West Link Park
Doughcloyne
Wilton
Cork
T12N5EF
Ireland

Reprinted 2018

A CIP record for this book is available from the British Library.

Paperback ISBN: 978-1-84889-270-5
PDF eBook ISBN: 978-1-84889-560-7
EPUB eBook ISBN: 978-1-84889-561-4
Kindle ISBN: 978-1-84889-562-1

Design and typesetting by Burns Design
Typeset in Chaparral Pro
Printed in Poland by Białostockie Zakłady Graficzne SA

Photograph on p.i: Clogh Oughter Castle, County Cavan.

VISITING THESE MONUMENTS

Although a monument may be in the care or ownership of the State, some are not easily accessible. Some of the sites featured in this guidebook lie in the middle of agricultural fields, or on the summit of mountains, without a public pathway that provides easy access. In such cases, it is recommended that you ask permission from the landowners to cross their land. This often brings benefits, as they can tell you exactly where the monument is located. Take particular care when crossing fields with livestock and heed any warning notices. Please do not climb on walls or on top of the monuments: despite their robust appearance, many are in a very fragile condition.

Readers should note that this is an information guide and does not act as an invitation to enter any of the properties or sites listed. No responsibility is accepted by the author or publisher for any loss, injury or inconvenience sustained by anyone as a result of using this book.

CONTENTS

ACKNOWLEDGMENTS

My first thanks must go to my family, especially my wife Róisín Burke, who was of immeasurable help with this publication; it simply would not have been possible without her unceasing support and forbearance. Thanks are also due to Róisín's parents, Bartley and Philomena, whose keen interest and enthusiasm are a constant source of inspiration and energy. I am very grateful to Dr Conor Ryan who assisted with the research and who compiled the maps used in this volume. I would also like to thank The Collins Press for their support throughout this project.

I am also deeply grateful to the various landowners, private and state, who allowed me access to these incredible places. Particular mention must be given to the kind support of the Office of Public Works (OPW), especially the OPW tour guides who surely must rank as the most accomplished in the world for their ability to weave a story. Thanks are also due to the National Monuments Service, National Museum of Ireland and Fáilte Ireland for all their assistance and inspiration.

To compile a guidebook such as this, particularly one focused on Ireland's archaeological and historical sites, involves standing on the shoulders of a myriad of giants. To all the archaeologists, historians, academics, writers, geographers, scientists, bloggers, storytellers, *seanchaithe*, recorders, researchers, guides and enthusiasts who compiled all of the bedrock of information upon which the story of Ireland is built, I am eternally grateful for all of your work and genius. Any errors or omissions in this work are entirely my own.

The head of the southern high cross at Castledermot, County Kildare

INTRODUCTION

The tomb of Pierce Fitz Óg Butler, Kilcooley Abbey, County Tipperary

A round practically every corner on Ireland's eastern coast you can discover millennia of history and archaeology, dating back to the first days after the glaciers released their frozen grip on the country at the end of the last Ice Age. Fáilte Ireland's new concept, Ireland's Ancient East, helps visitors to explore counties Louth, Monaghan, Cavan, Longford, Westmeath, Meath, Kildare, Offaly, Laois, Carlow, Wicklow, Kilkenny, Tipperary Wexford, Waterford and the eastern parts of Limerick and Cork. Each of these counties has its own unique story to tell. From the wild majesty of the Wicklow Mountains, to the plains of Kildare, the bogs of the midlands and the lush green pastures of Tipperary, you can discover the fascinating story of the people who shaped these landscapes and who, in turn, were shaped by the land. This region holds some of the world's finest examples of prehistoric ingenuity and religious practice. Ireland is also internationally famous for the wealth of early Christian monasteries that are so prevalent across this region, with their intricate high crosses and soaring round towers. Ireland was altered by successive waves of peoples arriving from across the seas, from the farmers who brought agriculture to these shores and forever changed the landscape over 5,000 years ago, to the Vikings who arrived as raiders before going on to establish Ireland's first secular towns and cities, and the Anglo-Normans who constructed massive castles and sprawling abbeys. Ireland's story is soaked with drama and intrigue, not least in the tumultuous years of the seventeenth century, when a series of wars, famines and rebellions tortured the land. The years that followed saw the great estates of Ireland established by the new power in the country, the Protestant Ascendancy. The sense of injustice in the years that followed would lead to further hardship that eventually led to the road to independence and the modern state of Ireland.

Ireland is a landscape imbued with unique stories and tales, where you can encounter an authentic cultural experience and be inspired by the landscape, life and people of the island. This guidebook suggests 100 archaeological and historical places to visit to help you to explore the story of Ireland. The sites are numbered according to their geographic location, with Site 1 (Carlingford) being the most northerly, and Site 100 (Blarney Castle) being the most southerly. I have further broken Ireland's Ancient East into sub-regions for ease of navigation, and each entry has a table containing practical information and coordinates about the sites. The great difficulty when compiling a book such as this is choosing which sites to include and which to omit, as there are thousands of incredible places waiting to be discovered in Ireland's Ancient East. These sites are some of my personal favourites, and are a mix of large, well-known attractions like the Rock of Cashel (Site 73) and hidden gems such as Gaulstown Dolmen (Site 90). These ancient ruins, mighty fortresses and great houses in all their splendour still resonate with echoes of the past.

1 | CARLINGFORD
COUNTY LOUTH

Nestled between Slieve Foye and the majestic beauty of the Mourne Mountains, Carlingford in County Louth is an atmospheric town that still retains its medieval character. Carlingford was founded at the beginning of the thirteenth century by Hugh de Lacy (the younger son of the Hugh de Lacy who constructed Trim Castle). He began by constructing a strong castle on an outcrop of rock that overlooked the Carlingford Lough, and soon afterwards a settlement began to flourish in the shadow of the fortress.

The town developed rapidly during the fourteenth, fifteenth and sixteenth centuries, and many of the striking buildings listed here date to that period. The town entered a steep decline, however, throughout the seventeenth century, a turbulent time in Irish history of war, famine and plague. The town was overshadowed by

The Tholsel in Carlingford

near neighbours Dundalk and Newry, which quickly developed into bustling urban centres, while Carlingford stagnated. This decline, however, served to protect the historic structures of the town, as there was little development here, ensuring that today it is a wonderfully atmospheric place to visit.

King John's Castle at Carlingford was established by Hugh de Lacy around 1200. It was later named after King John who took the castle

A view across the harbour to King John's Castle at Carlingford

in 1210. It is essentially a D-shaped enclosure with a large curtain wall and projecting towers. It appears to have undergone regular alterations throughout the later medieval period, but by the late sixteenth century it seems the castle had already become derelict as it was described as being 'in a wretched condition'. The Office of Public Works (OPW) began conservation works on the castle in the 1950s and more renovation works are currently ongoing.

The remains of Carlingford's Dominican friary date back to the early fourteenth century. The Dominicans were invited to establish a foundation in Carlingford by the powerful Richard de Burgo. The friary followed the usual convention of a Dominican establishment, with a cloister, church, dormitories, refectory and kitchen, and a small mill on the stream that runs alongside the site. Today you can still see the nave-and-chancel church with a fine tower. The friary reflects the turbulent times during the late fourteenth and early fifteenth centuries when raids on such monastic sites were common: the buildings were fortified and battlements were added to make the site more defensive, including a machicolation above the entrance. The site was dissolved during Henry VIII's reign in 1540, but Dominicans returned to the site in the late seventeenth century. You can access the interior of the site and explore the nave-and-chancel church, and the partial remains of the residence block.

The Tholsel is the only surviving medieval gateway into Carlingford, and probably dates from the fifteenth century. Originally this would have been a three-storey structure, but it was modified in the nineteenth century and is now two storeys with a modern slate roof. This gateway would have given access to the main street at the eastern end of the town, with a levy being paid at the gateway before any goods could be brought in. There is very little of the medieval town walls left today. There is a short section just south-east of the Tholsel, and another at Back Lane at the north-west end of Carlingford.

The Mint is located on the main street, a short walk from the Tholsel. It is a fortified townhouse that dates to the fifteenth–sixteenth centuries. The name 'The Mint' presumably derives from a 1467 charter that granted Carlingford permission to strike its own

Carlingford's Dominican friary

coins; however, it is more likely that this structure is simply the well-built and defended townhouse of one of Carlingford's prosperous merchants during the late fifteenth or early sixteenth century. The decorated limestone windows are a notable feature of this building. Each one bears a unique design.

Taaffe's Castle is another good example of a fortified medieval Irish townhouse. As it is positioned close to the harbour front, it was probably the home of a wealthy merchant, and is likely to have also served as a well-protected warehouse for their goods. The usual layout of a fortified townhouse from this period is to have all the public business conducted on the bottom and lower floors, with the upper floors as the residence. The name is likely to derive from the powerful Taaffe family, who became Earls of Carlingford in the middle of the seventeenth century.

The Church of the Holy Trinity is an early nineteenth-century Church of Ireland place of worship that has many clues of medieval structures that may have originally been on the site. The pointed doorway on the south wall appears to be from the seventeenth century or perhaps slightly earlier, and the church is attached to a tall three-storey crenellated tower that may originally date back to the fifteenth or sixteenth century. The eighteenth- and nineteenth-century renovations make the origins of this site a little unclear, but it is still well worth dropping in as the church was leased to the Carlingford Lough Heritage Trust and is now a visitor centre, which hosts concerts.

Carlingford is certainly worth a trip to enjoy the atmospheric medieval streets and breathtaking scenery. There are a number of superb heritage sites nearby, particularly Castleroche (Site 3).

CARLINGFORD   SITE MAP 1

Coordinates: Lat: 54.040754, Long: -6.186731

Grid reference: J 18753 11915

Opening times: Open all year round

See: www.carlingford.ie for details about events and festivals that may be taking place in the town.

Entry fee: Free

Facilities: Tourist office, toilets, cafes and restaurants

Car parking: Parking in town

Directions: Carlingford is located on the coast in north Louth on the Cooley Peninsula. Exit the M1 motorway at Junction 18 and continue east on the R173 for about 22km. Turn left onto the R176, which leads into the town. Carlingford is well signposted.

Nearest town: Dundalk, about 27km to the west

2 | PROLEEK MEGALITHIC TOMBS
COUNTY LOUTH

Within the golf course of Ballymascanlon House Hotel are two iconic reminders of County Louth's ancient past. The dolmen has two large portal stones, each measuring over 2 metres (6.5 ft) tall, and a back stone supporting a massive capstone that is estimated to weigh over 40 tonnes. This monument dates to the earlier part of the Neolithic period, and is likely to be over 5,000 years old.

Local folkloric tradition suggests that you will be married within the year if you can throw a small pebble back over your head and it lands on top of the capstone without rolling off.

Proleek Portal Tomb, County Louth

Just a short distance away is a fine example of a wedge tomb. This is a later monument than the portal tomb, and was probably constructed towards the end of the Neolithic period, some time around 2,500 BC.

PROLEEK MEGALITHIC TOMBS SITE MAP 1

Coordinates: Lat: 54.037185, Long: -6.348246

Grid reference: J 08203 11047

Opening times: Open all year round

Entry fee: Free

Facilities: The site is located close to Ballymascanlon House Hotel

Car parking: Car parking available at Ballymascanlon House Hotel

Directions: Exit the M1 motorway at Junction 18 and continue east on the R173. Turn left into the entrance for Ballymascanlon House Hotel and park at the hotel. Follow the signs along the path to the site, approx. 10 minutes or so, but look out for low-flying golf balls!

Nearest town: Dundalk, about 9km to the south-west

---

3 | CASTLEROCHE
COUNTY LOUTH

Castleroche is arguably the finest example of a thirteenth-century castle in Ireland and it is the only one of its period to have been commissioned by a woman. It was commissioned by Lady Rohesia de Verdun in 1236 to serve as a bastion of defence for the Anglo-Norman colony in Louth against the Gaelic tribes of Ulster. Lady Rohesia was a formidable individual: legend has it that she had the castle's architect thrown from one of the tower windows so he could never reveal the castle's secrets.

The castle is nearly triangular in shape, with a projecting tower at the north-east angle. It is protected on three sides by the precipitous slope that surrounds it, with the entrance on the eastern side guarded by a deep rock-cut ditch. A wooden drawbridge would have led to the interior of the castle through the two massive D-shaped

The gate towers of Castleroche

towers. The drawbridge may once have had additional protection from outworks or a barbican gate but no clear above-ground remains of that can be seen today.

The towers are rounded at the front in the defensive style of the time with a number of arrow loops at varied levels to allow the archers defending the gateway to loose murderous volleys on the attacking enemy. The towers also have four storeys at the rear, which would have provided accommodation and living space for the garrison of Castleroche.

When you look at the outside of the castle you may notice there are a number of rectangular cavities regularly spaced along the wall near the top. These are 'putlog' holes, and are evidence that wooden battlements or hoardings once hung over the side of the castle walls, similar to those that once surrounded the mighty keep of Trim Castle, in County Meath (Site 20). From these wooden hoardings, defenders would have been able to fire arrows and throw stones down onto anyone attacking the walls, adding to the castle's already formidable defences.

Like Dublin Castle and Kilkenny Castle, Castleroche seems to have been a 'keepless' castle, so there was no central defensive tower to retreat to in the event of the walls being breached. This appears to have become the defensive fashion of the mid thirteenth century, and instead of a keep there would have been a great hall. In the case of Castleroche, the great hall was located on the southern side of the castle (to the left as you enter through the towers).

Above: Castleroche and surrounding landscape
Facing page: The gate towers

This castle still exerts a power and dominance over the landscape today. It has to be one of the most impressive heritage sites in Ireland.

CASTLEROCHE SITE MAP 1

Coordinates: Lat: 54.046436, Long: -6.488667

Grid reference: H 98998 11877

Opening times: Open all year round. Please be aware that the site is on farmland and always seek landowner's permission when entering private land. Please watch your footing on uneven surfaces and close all gates behind you.

Entry fee: Free

Facilities: None

Car parking: Parking on side of road, please do not block any gateways

Directions: To find Castleroche from Dublin, head north on the M1 and exit at Junction 17. Take the first exit off the roundabout, following signs for the N53/Castleblayney. Continue on this road until reaching a right-hand turn signed for Castleroche and Forkhill; take this turn and follow the road. The site is on the right-hand side up a laneway. Park on the roadside. Be aware that the site is on farmland, so please do not block any gateways and ensure all gates are closed behind you. Simply walk up the slope through the field to access the castle. There is an interpretation panel on the right as you enter through the gateway.

Nearest town: Dundalk, about 8km to the south-east

4 | MELLIFONT ABBEY
COUNTY LOUTH

The lavabo of Mellifont Abbey

Mellifont Abbey was the first Cistercian abbey in Ireland, known to the Cistercians in Ireland as the 'mother house', a base from which the community expanded, adding more and more institutions (known as 'daughter houses') across Ireland. The name Mellifont comes from the Latin *Fons Mellis*, meaning 'Fount of Honey'.

The Cistercian Order was founded by St Bernard of Clairvaux in Burgundy, central France, in 1098. St Bernard believed that the other monastic orders had become dissolute and undisciplined, and he founded the Cistercians as an austere and hard-working order who focused on a life of prayer. Inspired by his zeal, St Malachy of Armagh, the Irish saint and friend of St Bernard, founded Mellifont Abbey in 1142 with a group of Irish and French monks.

The surviving section of the cloister at the rear of the lavabo

The abbey was extremely successful from its earliest stages and it developed rapidly. Monks from Mellifont were dispatched to found 'daughter houses' around Ireland. Within just five years of the foundation of Mellifont, in 1147, a daughter house had already been established at Bective in County Meath (Site 21) and within twenty years the Cistercians also had establishments in Connacht, such as the one founded at Boyle, County Roscommon in 1161. It is recorded that at least twenty-one abbeys were founded by monks from Mellifont.

The Cistercian community in Ireland faced a grave crisis following the Norman invasions in the late twelfth century. Irish Cistercian institutions such as Mellifont became embroiled in a power struggle with the Cistercian establishments that came from England following the invasion. The outcome of what became known as 'The Conspiracy of Mellifont' was a dramatic reduction in the powers and number of monks allowed for Mellifont. Despite these restrictions, Mellifont remained one of the richest monastic institutions in Ireland due to its huge holdings of rich agricultural land in Meath and Louth.

It was probably due to this vast ownership of prime land that Mellifont was one of the first of the Irish monastic sites to be dissolved in 1539 during the Dissolution of the Monasteries. Mellifont became the private fortified home of Sir Edward Moore, and it was here that the famous Treaty of Mellifont, which ended the bloody Nine Years' War, was signed in 1603. Later, Mellifont played host to William of Orange, who established his headquarters here during the Battle of the Boyne in 1690.

On the site there is not much of the original abbey left standing. However, excavations have revealed the foundations of many of the buildings, so it is easy to get a good sense of the size and layout of this important abbey. Mellifont became the standard format for all Cistercian abbeys in Ireland, and many other monastic orders were influenced by the layout. The cloisters were positioned at the south, and were surrounded by a range of domestic and spiritual buildings, with a cruciform church to the north. The site is certainly worth visiting for its famous lavabo. This building dates to the early thirteenth century. Octagonal in shape, it served as the ritual washroom, where the monks would wash their hands before entering the refectory for meals. Excavations have revealed fragments of lead pipe that brought the water into the central fountain. The interior was decorated with delicate images of plants and birds. A number of fragments of the fine architectural features are on display in the visitor centre.

MELLIFONT ABBEY   SITE MAP 1

Coordinates: Lat: 53.721211, Long: -6.412437

Grid reference: O 01202 780990

Opening times: Old Mellifont Abbey is open to the public all year round but the visitor centre is open only from end May to end August

Entry fee: Please visit www.heritageireland.ie/en/midlands-eastcoast/oldmellifontabbey/

Facilities: Toilets, exhibitions and guided tours of the site available in the visitor centre

Car parking: Large car park at site

Directions: Old Mellifont Abbey is located off the R168 (Drogheda–Collon Road). When travelling on this road towards Collon, turn left onto the L6314 (Old Mellifont Road). Continue on this road for about 2km, then continue straight through the crossroads. Old Mellifont Abbey will be directly in front of you.

Nearest town: Drogheda, about 10km to the east

5 | MONASTERBOICE
COUNTY LOUTH

The round tower at Monasterboice

The name Monasterboice derives from *Mainistir Bhuithe* ('Buithe's Monastery'), as a monastery is thought to have been founded here by St Buithe in the sixth century. Over time it flourished and grew in both size and prominence. However, today all that is visible is the very heart of the monastery, with a fine round tower and three high crosses, one of which is arguably the finest high cross in Ireland.

As well as the early medieval high crosses and round tower, there are the remains of two small stone churches. These probably date to the late medieval period. Within one of the churches is a small bullaun stone. This stone with a circular hollow may have been used as a rudimentary holy water font during the early days of the monastery, or perhaps as a large version of a pestle and mortar, maybe to grind herbs, ore for metallurgy, or pigments for manuscript illustration.

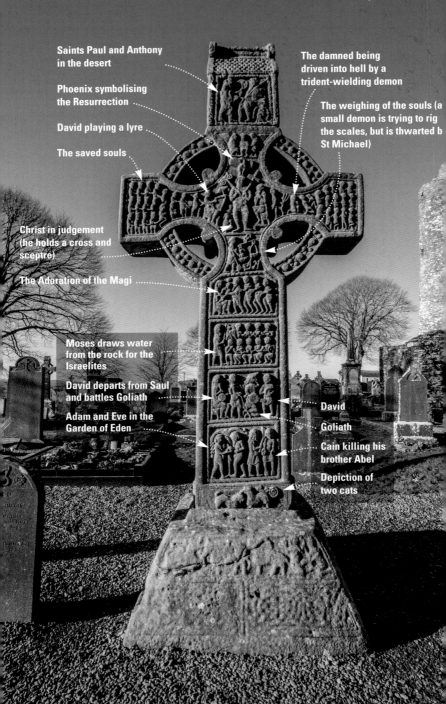

Saints Paul and Anthony in the desert

Phoenix symbolising the Resurrection

David playing a lyre

The saved souls

Christ in judgement (he holds a cross and sceptre)

The Adoration of the Magi

Moses draws water from the rock for the Israelites

David departs from Saul and battles Goliath

Adam and Eve in the Garden of Eden

The damned being driven into hell by a trident-wielding demon

The weighing of the souls (a small demon is trying to rig the scales, but is thwarted b St Michael)

David

Goliath

Cain killing his brother Abel

Depiction of two cats

The round tower is approximately 28 metres (92 ft) tall. The iconic Irish round towers are thought to have been primarily constructed as bell towers as they are known as *cloigh teach* in Irish, which translates as 'bell house'. They would have been visible for miles around, and as such would have acted like a signpost to pilgrims on the route to Monasterboice. The round tower here is said to have housed the monastery's library and other treasures; unfortunately, records state that it was burned in 1097.

The South Cross is arguably the finest example of a high cross in Ireland. It probably dates to the early tenth century, as it is very similar to the West Cross at Clonmacnoise, which has been dated to *c.* 904–916. Like the Clonmacnoise example, the South Cross at Monasterboice also bears an inscription, asking for 'a prayer for Muiredach'. It seems likely that this refers to a Muiredach who died in 924. He was the abbot of Monasterboice, and the vice-abbot of Armagh. He was also the chief steward of the powerful southern Uí Néill dynasty, making him an important and influential figure in both religious and secular Ireland. The cross is simply one of the

Above: Detail of one of the panels of the South Cross. On the left, Eve tempts Adam in the Garden of Eden; on the right, Cain slays Abel

Facing page: Annotated image of the eastern face of the South Cross, known as Muiredach's Cross

most important and visually stunning examples of early medieval sculpture in the world.

The West Cross is the tallest high cross in Ireland, standing at an imposing 6.5 metres (21 ft) tall. Thanks to its size, it also has the largest number of figure sculpture panels of any high cross. As on the South Cross, these panels are beautifully carved with depictions of biblical stories from both the Old and New Testaments.

The North Cross stands within a small fenced area at the very northern boundary of the site. It is much plainer than the South and West Crosses, though it is still worth a look as it has some lovely carvings. Next to it is an interesting sundial, which would have marked the passing of time for the monks of Monasterboice, indicating the canonical hours of 9 a.m., 12 noon and 3 p.m. In this fenced area, some other architectural fragments from the site are on display.

It is a short (ten-minute) drive from here to Mellifont Abbey (Site 4), another beautiful and fascinating site.

MONASTERBOICE   SITE MAP 1

Coordinates: Lat: 53.777761, Long: -6.417839

Grid reference: O 04303 82055

Opening times: Open all year round

Entry fee: Free

Facilities: Toilets

Car parking: Large car park at site

Directions: Monasterboice is located a short distance off the M1 motorway. Exit at Junction 10 (signposted Drogheda North/Collon/Navan) and travel east on the N51 to the next roundabout. Take the first exit onto the R132. Continue on the R132 and take the first left after the bridge over the motorway. Bear left at the fork in the road and the site will be on the right.

Nearest town: Drogheda, about 8km to the south-east of Monasterboice

6 | DROGHEDA
COUNTY LOUTH

The streetscape of Drogheda, looking towards Millmount Fort

The town of Drogheda was founded in the late twelfth century by the Norman Lord of Meath, Hugh de Lacy. He chose to locate it at the narrowest part of the River Boyne to allow easy development of both banks of the river. Drogheda spans two dioceses, as the northern bank of the Boyne is in the Diocese of Armagh and the southern bank in the Diocese of Meath. De Lacy founded a church on each bank, St Peter's north of the river and St Mary's to the south. Situated near the mouth of the River Boyne, Drogheda was perfectly placed to become one of Ireland's most important ports during the medieval period, and the town grew wealthy through trade.

Drogheda's walls were built between 1234 and 1424, and enclosed a total area of 113 acres. These walls were most severely tested in the seventeenth century. The year 1641 saw a large rebellion in Ireland. In November that year a large rebel army besieged Drogheda, though it was eventually repulsed. The walls were strengthened following the siege, but in 1649 Drogheda faced a far greater threat. After the English Civil War, Oliver Cromwell brought his veteran New Model Army to Ireland to smash the Irish rebels. The first town he attacked was Drogheda, as he needed a secure port to ensure his army could be supplied through the winter. The town was defended by four regiments made up of soldiers of the Irish Catholic Confederation and English Royalist soldiers who had fled to Ireland following their defeat in England. Cromwell commanded a force of approximately 12,000 men, and his naval forces blockaded the harbour. Instead of surrounding the town with his army in an attempt to starve the defenders into surrender, Cromwell chose to concentrate his forces on the southern side of the town to unleash a swift and savage attack in one place. His artillery pounded the walls at two points near the Duleek Gate (near St Mary's Church) and opened two breaches in the walls. He sent a message to the commander of the defending garrison, Sir Arthur Aston, demanding his surrender.

Aston refused, in the hope that the Earl of Ormond, who was stationed nearby with 4,000 troops, would come to their rescue. His hopes were not to be realised. At 5 p.m. on 11 September, Cromwell launched simultaneous assaults on both the breaches. Though the defenders fought bravely, they were short of gunpowder and ammunition. They were pushed back and eventually their defence collapsed. The remnants took refuge in Millmount Fort while Cromwell's forces quickly pushed into the town. Cromwell was enraged at the sight of the corpses of so many of his men and ordered that no quarter be given to the defenders. The 200 or so in Millmount Fort were persuaded to surrender on the promise of their lives. However, when they were disarmed they too were butchered. Sir Arthur Aston was horrendously killed, reportedly beaten to death with his own wooden leg. Other defenders who sought refuge in the steeple of St Peter's Church were killed when Cromwell's men set fire to the steeple. The last of the defenders were either killed or taken prisoner and transported to Barbados. The Massacre of Drogheda still resonates today as one of the darkest days in Irish history.

You can discover more of the story of the siege and its aftermath in the excellent Millmount Museum, located within the old fort. This was originally the site of a Norman motte and bailey. During the Napoleonic Wars in the early nineteenth century, a Martello tower was constructed on the site to protect Drogheda from French ships.

Drogheda has a wealth of other fascinating historical buildings, including St Laurence's Gate. This was originally a thirteenth-century barbican gate with an arched entrance flanked by rounded towers. The enormous five-storey-high gate towers over the eastern side of town. A twin gate on the west side of town was demolished in 1808. St Laurence's Gate is the sole survivor of the thirty towers and gates that once lined Drogheda's walls.

St Peter's Church (now the Church of Ireland parish church) was originally founded by Hugh de Lacy and given to the Augustinian canons of Llanthony Prima in Monmouthshire, Wales. The church flourished, along with the town, through the medieval period, and by the sixteenth century it contained six chapels. After the siege of Drogheda, Cromwell's forces contributed funds for the repair of the church. However, by 1747 the old medieval church had become dilapidated and was demolished to make way for a new church. There are a number of fascinating gravestones and effigies in the churchyard. Perhaps the most striking is the remarkably ghoulish tomb of Sir Edmund Goldyng and his wife, Elizabeth Fleming. This tomb effigy dates from the earlier half of the sixteenth century. It is known as a 'cadaver tomb' and depicts the decomposing bodies surrounded by their burial shrouds. Rather than simply being slightly gruesome and terrifying, it is intended to make the observer consider his or her own brief mortality.

The 'cadaver tomb' of Sir Edmund Goldyng and his wife Elizabeth Fleming

St Peter's Roman Catholic Church in the town was built in the nineteenth century and it contains the shrine to the Catholic martyr St Oliver Plunkett. He was born at Loughcrew near Oldcastle in County Meath in 1625, during the penal times. He trained abroad to become a Catholic priest and returned to Ireland to become Primate of Ireland and Archbishop of Armagh. He established a number of schools and a Jesuit college in Drogheda, as the Penal Laws had begun to relax. However, King Charles II grew increasingly paranoid about a possible Catholic plot to assassinate him and demanded that the Penal Laws be once again strictly enforced. St Oliver went into hiding, as he was accused of conspiring with the French, but was arrested and taken to England, where he was tried for treason. King Charles II ignored many pleas for leniency, and St Oliver was found guilty. He was taken to Tyburn where he was executed by being hanged, drawn and quartered. He was the last Catholic martyr to die in England. His head became a sacred relic. In the twentieth century, it was placed in a shrine within the church, where it remains a revered, if somewhat grisly, reminder of his sacrifice.

DROGHEDA   SITE MAP 1

Coordinates: Lat: 53.713527, Long: -6.349191

Grid reference: O 08781 75181

Opening times: Open all year round

Entry fee: Free

Facilities: Walking tours of Drogheda take place from May to September. See drogheda.ie/boyne-valley/tours/walking-tour.html for more information. The tourist information office is located at The Tholsel, West Street, Drogheda.

Car parking: Car parking available throughout the town

Directions: Drogheda is located at the mouth of the River Boyne on the east coast of Ireland. To get to Drogheda from Dublin, travel north on the M1. Exit at Junction 8 onto the R152. Continue on the R152 and follow signs for Drogheda.

Nearest town: Dublin, about 48km to the south

7 | CLONES
COUNTY MONAGHAN

The round tower of Clones, with the stone shrine in the foreground

The market town of Clones in County Monaghan developed from an early monastery founded by St Tighearnach in the sixth century. The monastery became an Augustinian foundation after around 1140. Though much of the original monastery has been lost, echoes of Clones' early roots can still be discovered in the town. An early medieval high cross stands in the 'Diamond', at the centre of the town. This cross is unusual in that it is actually fragments of two different tenth-century crosses mounted together, hence its distinctive look. The shaft that comprises the lower section is intricately carved with biblical scenes on its faces and geometric ornament on its sides. Though weathered, some of the depictions can still be discerned: Old Testament scenes adorn the western face, and New Testament the eastern face. The head of the cross depicts more Old Testament scenes on the western face, with the Crucifixion on the eastern face.

In the old graveyard there is more evidence of the early monastery: a 23-metre (75-ft) round tower stands proudly amidst the tombs. The round tower is thought to date to some time between the tenth and twelfth centuries. An unusual gabled stone shrine, shaped like a miniature church, stands nearby. It is carved from a single block of sandstone, with a very worn figure wearing a mitre on the eastern 'gable'. This shrine may have originally housed the relics of St Tighearnach himself, though it dates to at least 500 years after his time. It was moved to its current position in the eighteenth century to cover a burial vault. The graveyard has many fascinating tombstones from the seventeenth, eighteenth and nineteenth centuries. Many bear a depiction of a skull on the reverse, known as a memento mori: a grisly reminder of our mortality and fleeting time on earth.

Other monuments in Clones include the remains of a medieval church known as 'The Wee Abbey'. This stone church is likely to date from the twelfth century, and it was originally dedicated to Ss Peter and Paul. More evidence of Clones's medieval past is to be found in the large motte-and-bailey castle on the western side of the town. Historical records state that it was built in 1212 as part of the Anglo-Norman campaigns in the region.

CLONES SITE MAP 1

Coordinates: Lat: 54.179492, Long: -7.232563

Grid reference: H 50151 25722

Opening times: Open all year round

Entry fee: Free

Facilities: Visitor Information Point in the Monaghan County Library

Car parking: There are a number of parking options in the town

Directions: Clones is located in western County Monaghan close to the Northern Ireland border. It is located on the busy N54 road which links Cavan and Monaghan. The sites (high cross, old graveyard and round tower and 'The Wee Abbey') are all within walking distance of each other in the town.

Nearest town: Cavan, 25km to the south, and Monaghan, 20km to the north-east

8 | THE CAVAN BURREN
COUNTY CAVAN

The wooden walkways
of the Cavan Burren

This remarkable upland limestone plateau is part of the Marble Arch Caves Global Geopark. The Cavan Burren has a visitor information point, leading to a number of superb walks along well-made paths and boardwalks offering stunning views over the landscape. Here you will encounter an array of megalithic tombs, including the Giant's Grave, a large and well-preserved wedge tomb that dates to around 2500 BC. The tomb has two burial chambers and, interestingly, has a large amount of cup-and-ring rock art. It is said to be aligned with the rising sun at the winter solstice. The remains of other monuments, including a small promontory fort and later eighteenth- and nineteenth-century settlements, mean that the Cavan Burren is an absolutely perfect blend of breathtaking scenery and heritage.

The source of the River Shannon at the Shannon Pot can be visited nearby. This deep pool is formed by the confluence of a number of underground streams. In legend, the Shannon was formed when Sionnan, a granddaugher of the God of the Sea, Manannán Mac Lír, travelled to the Shannon Pot to catch the Salmon of Knowledge. The salmon didn't take kindly to this and in outrage it caused the waters of the pool to spring up and overwhelm her, drawing her down into the depths of the pool to drown. Once unleashed, the waters of the pool continued to flow and created the mighty river that still bears the doomed Sionnan's name. Recent water-tracing experiments have shown that several of the streams that sink on Cuilcagh Mountain flow underground to join the

The wedge tomb known as the Giant's Grave

Shannon Pot, the furthest of which is a stream that sinks into the Pigeon Pots in County Fermanagh, making that arguably the true geographical source of the River Shannon.

The Cavan Burren is well signposted from the village of Blacklion and it is free to access. The Shannon Pot is also well signposted from the Cavan Burren, and can be found at coordinates 54.23693, -7.92216.

CAVAN BURREN SITE MAP 1

Coordinates: Lat: 54.26519, Long: -7.88745

Grid reference: H 06514 34637

Opening times: Open all year round

Entry fee: Free

Facilities: Toilets, interpretative panels and waymarked walks

Car parking: Large car park at site

Directions: From Blacklion follow the N16 west towards Sligo. Take the left fork after about 400 metres (signposted Cavan/Glangevlin). Take the next left (signposted Cavan Burren) and follow this road for about 3.5km. The Burren entrance will be on your left; continue through the gate towards the interpretative centre and car park.

Nearest town: Blacklion, about 3km to the north

Clogh Oughter Castle

Lough Oughter (from the Irish *Loch Uachtar*, meaning 'Upper Lake') is a beautiful patchwork of water separated by small islands and drumlins. It is a spot much loved by fishermen, but it is also home to a wonderful array of archaeological and historical gems. Perhaps most famous of these is the stunning Clogh Oughter Castle. It was originally constructed in the early thirteenth century – around 1220 – by William Gorm de Lacy, son of Hugh de Lacy (of Trim Castle) and Rose O'Connor (daughter of Ruaidrí Ua Conchobair, King of Connacht). He chose the site at Lough Oughter to dominate the region and overshadow the local O'Reilly clan. When the de Lacy family fell foul of the Crown, Clogh Oughter Castle was captured by William Marshal's forces, who joined with the O'Reillys. The O'Reillys controlled the castle for the next four centuries, until the turbulent seventeenth century. The castle became a prison for a number of years; it is where Owen Roe O'Neill died in 1649. He had been the key figure of the Confederate Wars of 1641, and won a vital victory at the Battle of Benburb in 1646, where he routed a Scottish Covenanter army under the command of General Monro. There are conflicting stories surrounding his death at Clogh Oughter. Some say he died from an illness or as the result of infections in an old wound; others say that he was poisoned by a priest. Local tradition suggests that he was buried nearby at the church on Trinity Island. Clogh Oughter Castle was the very last Irish stronghold to fall to Cromwell's forces. It was bombarded by cannon until the garrison finally surrendered. Archaeological excavations in the late 1980s revealed some grisly evidence of the siege, as the remains of some of the victims were discovered. One unfortunate was found buried where he fell under a pile of rubble from the bombardment. The castle is accessible by boat, which can be hired locally in Killeshandra. For a great viewing point for the castle, park in the small car park at the end of a narrow road at 54.01687, -7.45851, and then walk through the forest track to the shore.

Another monument on the shores of Lough Oughter is the Gartnanoul Court Tomb. Set within the lovely Killykeen Forest Park, this ancient tomb was constructed over 5,000 years ago. The tomb is located at 54.0148, -7.49200. To get there, travel north from Killashandra on the R201. After a series of sharp bends on the road take the right turn onto the L1509. Continue down this small road

Gartnanoul Court Tomb

and stay right to come to a large sign for the Coillte Forest Park. Go past this and continue on the track for a couple of hundred metres until reaching a small lay-by on the right. Park here and follow the track for around 50 metres to the tomb.

LOUGH OUGHTER SITE MAP 1

Coordinates: Lat: 54.016014, Long: -7.529116 (Killashandra)

Grid reference: H 35755 07858

Opening times: Open all year round

Entry fee: Free

Facilities: None

Car parking: Car parks at fishing spots around the lake

Directions: Lough Oughter can be explored by renting boats from Killashandra. The R201, R199 and R198 are the main routes around the lake.

Nearest town: Belturbet, about 14km to the north

10 | SHANTEMON STONE ROW
COUNTY CAVAN

When I visited the ancient stone row of Shantemon, the land was shrouded in thick mist and countless spiders had woven a tapestry of webs across every branch and tree. It was the perfect atmosphere in which to visit a 3,000-year-old place of ritual and ceremony that is soaked in legend and folklore.

The stone row at Shantemon consists of five stones aligned north-west to south-east. They are graded in height, with the smallest at the north-western end (approximately 50cm or 19½ inches tall) and the tallest at the south-east (approximately 2 metres or 6.6 ft tall).

Though there is a significant number in Ulster, stone rows and alignments are more common in the south-west of Ireland, particularly in counties Cork and Kerry. They generally date to the Bronze Age, between 1700–800 BC, and are occasionally found in association with stone circles. They may have had an astronomical function because, like the example at Shantemon, they tend to be sited on prominent slopes or hilltops; unfortunately, however, the true purpose for these enigmatic monuments remains unknown. Similar monuments are found across Britain as well as in parts of Scandinavia and northern France.

This site is imbued with folklore and tales of the legendary warrior Fionn Mac Cumhaill. It is said that the four tall stones are Fionn's fingers and the low stone his thumb (indeed, the site is signposted 'Finn's Fingers').

The cobweb-strewn path to Shantemon Stone Row

Shantemon Stone Row, shrouded in mist

SHANTEMON STONE ROW

SITE MAP 1

Coordinates: Lat: 54.017467, Long: -7.291443

Grid reference: H 46466 07400

Opening times: Open all year round

Entry fee: Free

Facilities: None

Car parking: Car park at lay-by opposite sign for 'Finn's Fingers'

Directions: To find Shantemon Stone Row from Cavan, take the R188 north through Drumalee Cross. Continue on this road for about 10 minutes, turning right at Coratober (the third right turn after going under the N3). At the crossroads, turn left and continue on this road until reaching a small car park on the left at 54.02054, -7.29423. Park here; opposite there is a sign pointing up a track to Finn's Fingers with interpretation of the 'Castletara Millennium Trail'. Walk along the track for approximately 350 metres, where a smaller, rougher track disappears into the gorse on the right. Follow this track to the stone row.

Nearest town: Cavan, less than 15km to the south-west

11 | GRANARD MOTTE AND BAILEY
COUNTY LONGFORD

In the Longford town of Granard, you can discover one of Ireland's finest examples of a motte and bailey. This was a standard form of Norman fortification, as it was quickly constructed and extremely effective as a defensive position. To build one, the Normans would raise the motte, a large steep-sided earthen mound with a wooden or stone tower on the flattened surface at the summit. The mound was surrounded at the base by the bailey, an area enclosed by more earth and timber ditches and palisades. The bailey housed buildings such as a hall, barracks, stores, forges, workshops and all the other key ancillary buildings necessary for maintaining the garrison.

This example at Granard is thought to have been constructed by the Norman Lord Richard de Tuite *c.* 1199 to fortify the north-west frontier of the Anglo-Norman lordship of Meath. It is one of the largest in Ireland, standing approximately 11 metres (36 ft) high. As it is over 160 metres (534 ft) above sea level, it offers superb views over the surrounding landscape. From the summit, five lakes, parts of nine counties and even the distant Slieve Bloom Mountains can be seen on a fine day. The D-shaped bailey is on the south-west side

The Granard motte and bailey

A statue of St Patrick stands sentinel above Granard

of the motte and would have also been protected by ditches and palisade fences. It stands on the site of an earlier Irish fortification. It was relatively common for the Normans to reuse the sites of existing Irish forts both for practical purposes (they were generally in strategic locations) and as a way of demonstrating their subjugation of the region. However, later in its history Granard once again became a place of importance and power for the Gaelic Irish. The motte became an inauguration place of the O'Farrell clan in the later Middle Ages. In more recent times, a statue of St Patrick was erected on top of the motte in 1932 to mark the 1,500th anniversary of St Patrick's arrival in Ireland in 432.

Located less than 4km to the south of Granard in the village of Abbeylara are the remains of a Cistercian monastery that was also founded by Richard de Tuite. All that is visible today is the tall ruin of the crossing tower, which was remodelled in the fifteenth or sixteenth century. Most of the church and surrounding abbey buildings were demolished following the Dissolution of the Monasteries in the sixteenth century, and it is likely that the tower was converted into a domestic dwelling around this time.

The fourteenth-century monks of Abbeylara appear to have been far from peace-loving holy men. In 1318 they were accused of

The ruined crossing tower of the Cistercian monastery of Abbeylara

hunting the Irish with spears by day, to be followed by vespers (prayers) in the evening. The monastery can be easily accessed from the R396 just south-east of the village of Abbeylara.

GRANARD MOTTE AND BAILEY   SITE MAP 2

Coordinates: Lat: 53.775341, Long: -7.500610

Grid reference: N 32921 80758

Opening times: Open all year round

Entry fee: Free

Facilities: None

Car parking: Car park at the church

Directions: If travelling from Dublin/west of Ireland, leave the N4 at Edgeworthstown and travel north on the N55. This road goes to Granard. In Granard, turn left towards the church. Park at the church and walk up the small lane beside it to the site.

Nearest town: Located in the town of Granard, approximately 25km east–north-east of Longford town.

GRANARD MOTTE AND BAILEY

12 | THE CORLEA TRACKWAY
COUNTY LONGFORD

The Corlea Trackway, County Longford

Ireland's bogs have always had a sense of otherworldliness. They often formed the natural boundaries and borders between ancient kingdoms, and were seen as 'liminal' spaces where the natural order of things was different and sometimes dangerous. Archaeological and accidental discoveries over the years of votive offerings, including human remains, have enforced the otherworldly aspect in the national consciousness. However, somewhat paradoxically, bogs have also had an entirely practical aspect to Irish lives over the centuries. Though today they are chiefly exploited for peat-turf fuel, in the past they would have been hunting grounds for wildfowl, places noted for their preservative qualities for goods like butter, and important sources of useful plants and building materials like reeds for thatch, and more.

However, the bogs were, and still are, undoubtedly highly dangerous to traverse without proper roads. From the time of the earliest settlements in Ireland to the present day, the difficulty of

The bog that was once traversed by the Corlea Trackway

constructing safe routes through the bog has challenged communities. One of the most remarkable solutions is the Corlea Trackway. This trackway (also known as a togher) is over 2,000 years old, dating to 148 BC. It was made of oak planks laid transversely on large parallel runners that were laid lengthways. It stretched for over 2km (1.25 miles), crossing into the neighbouring townland of Derraghan.

The Corlea Trackway was excavated by Professor Barry Raftery in 1984, and was found to be the widest such trackway ever discovered. Intriguing evidence of the people who built it was also identified by the archaeologists: a number of tub-shaped wooden containers were found, perhaps the refuse of prehistoric packed lunches. A large section of the trackway from Cloonbreany townland was excavated and conserved. It is now on display in the Corlea Visitor Centre, which was constructed on the exact axis of the trackway.

THE CORLEA TRACKWAY SITE MAP 2

Coordinates: Lat: 53.612260, Long: -7.844691

Grid reference: N 10280 62514

Opening times: Open from April to end September. Please see: www.heritageireland.ie/en/midlandseastcoast/ CorleaTrackwayVisitorCentre for specific opening hours

Entry fee: Please visit www.heritageireland.ie/en/midlands-eastcoast/ corleatrackwayvisitorcentre/

Facilities: Toilets, audiovisual presentation, guided tours and exhibitions

Car parking: Car parking at site

Directions: The Corlea Trackway is located close to the village of Keenagh in County Longford. To get to the visitor centre (opening season: April–September) from Ballymahon, take the R392 north-west. The site is signposted off this road.

Nearest town: Corlea Trackway is 3km from the village of Keenagh and 15km from Longford

13 | ST MUNNA'S CHURCH
COUNTY WESTMEATH

St Munna's near Taghmon in County Westmeath is a fortified church dating to the middle of the fifteenth century. St Munna is said to have established a monastery on the site in the early seventh century. A well-respected saint in early medieval Ireland, Munna met several of the leading saints and was one of the first people in Ireland to hear of the death of St Colmcille. After that, he was chosen to be the recipient of news of holy deaths. When he heard the news of the death of Molua of Kyle, it is said he was struck with leprosy seven days later. He was cured seven years later by Mochua of Timahoe. Today, the only visible hint of an early monastery can be seen in the

St Munna's Church

subcircular shape of the boundary wall of the churchyard, as it may follow an original enclosing element for the early site.

The unusually fortified church was originally constructed as a parish church. It is a single-celled building with a barrel-vaulted roof. The large tower would have provided strong protection for the clergy who worshipped at the church. The highly defensive nature of the building, with its crenellations, arrow loops, base batter and machicolation, indicates how dangerous life was in Ireland in the mid fifteenth century. There are a number of other fascinating medieval features, like a Sheela-na-gig on the window of the northern wall. This one is carved in a seated position with a wide-open mouth (in a somewhat pained expression). Somewhat less exhibitionist are the stone heads that can be seen. These may represent ecclesiastical figures or perhaps a wealthy benefactor. Extensive restorations were carried out on the church in 1843 by the noted architect Joseph Welland (1798–1860). He was solely

The Sheela-na-gig above a medieval window of St Munna's Church

responsible for Church of Ireland building projects in Ireland from 1843 until his death in 1860. It was intended for the church to act as a new place of worship for the local Church of Ireland community.

ST MUNNA'S CHURCH SITE MAP 2

Coordinates: Lat: 53.601052, Long: -7.266730

Grid reference: N 48520 61529

Opening times: Open all year round

Entry fee: Free

Facilities: None

Car parking: Limited parking at the site

Directions: St Munna's Church is approximately a 15-minute drive from Mullingar. From Mullingar, head north on the R394. After around 8km, take the right-hand turn marked L1618 (signed for St Munna's Church). The site is on the right after about 2km.

Nearest town: Taghmon is about 2km east of Crookedwood and 11km north of Mullingar

14 | FORE ABBEY
COUNTY WESTMEATH

Fore Abbey, County Westmeath

Located in the village of Fore in rural Westmeath, this wonderful example of a medieval monastic complex was founded by St Féichín around 630. The small monastery quickly grew in size and importance, and received many mentions in the Annals of Ireland. Although there are no visible remains of this initial seventh-century monastery (indeed, the exact location of the earliest foundation has still not been conclusively proven) there is still a fine tenth- to eleventh-century church located on the slopes directly above the main part of Fore Abbey. This is St Féichín's Church: the main part probably dates to the tenth century, with a later chancel added in the thirteenth century to extend the church. The huge lintel above the doorway is said to be one of the Seven Wonders of Fore (see below).

Most of the structures forming the main part of Fore Abbey date to the period following the Norman invasion of Ireland. Hugh de Lacy ruled the Lordship of Meath (which, roughly speaking,

Fore Abbey viewed from the car park

incorporated today's Meath and Westmeath) from his fortress at Trim Castle. De Lacy would have appreciated the value of the monastery and the population growing around it. He had a priory established *c.* 1180 and gave the site to the Benedictine Order.

The Benedictine movement was extremely popular across Europe, but there were not many Benedictine monasteries established in Ireland, and there can be few examples as well preserved as Fore. It was constructed around a central cloister, with a church to the north, the dormitory for the monks to the east, and the refectory to the south with its adjacent kitchen to the south-west.

By the fifteenth century Fore Abbey had become vulnerable to attack by the Gaelic chieftains because it was located outside of the area known as The Pale. It was attacked in 1423 and 1428, and remained vulnerable enough that gates and walls were built to surround the monastic settlement. Despite these raids Fore Abbey was still a wealthy place, and new towers and a revamped cloister area were added in the fifteenth century.

Fore Abbey is steeped in history. Its stunning ruins can easily occupy you for an afternoon's wandering around. Fore is also known for the Seven Wonders of Fore. These are:

- The anchorite in a stone
- The water that will not boil

- The monastery built on a bog
- The mill without a millstream
- The water that flows uphill
- The tree that will not burn
- The stone lintel raised by the saint's prayers

FORE ABBEY   SITE MAP 2

Coordinates: Lat: 53.683898, Long: -7.227242

Grid reference: N 51049 70724

Opening times: Open all year round

Entry fee: Free

Facilities: Café where you can find more information about the abbey.

Car parking: Car parking at the site

Directions: To get to Fore, travel east from Castlepollard on the R195. After about 3km, turn right at L5756 and travel on this road for about 2km. The abbey will be on your left.

Nearest town: Castlepollard, 5km to the west, and Mullingar, about 26km to the south-west

15 | THE HILL OF UISNEACH
COUNTY WESTMEATH

Like the Hill of Tara (Site 22), Uisneach is another site where archaeology and mythology are entwined and almost inseparable. It was one of the great ceremonial sites of late prehistoric Ireland. Located almost perfectly in the centre of the island of Ireland, in mythology Uisneach is the meeting place of the five ancient provinces (Ulster, Leinster, Munster, Connacht and Mide or Meath).

The site is imbued with legend, and it is associated with many of the pre-Christian gods of Ireland, including Ériu, the personification of Ireland, who is said to have been buried at Uisneach, and the god

A depiction of the goddess Ériu on the Hill of Uisneach

The Cat Stone

Lugh, who tradition states is also buried on the hill at Carn Ludach. The god Dagda was also closely associated with Uisneach, and is said to have stabled his horses here. Geoffrey of Monmouth's *Historia Regum Britanniae* (History of the Kings of Britain) claims that the stones of Stonehenge were brought to Britain from Uisneach.

It is said that Uisneach was the site of the first great fire in Ireland, and this tradition has been rekindled in the present day. Fires were put out across the country in anticipation of the Uisneach Bealtaine fire, which welcomed the first day of summer (Bealtaine is celebrated on 1 May). Every year the fire at Uisneach was said to be the biggest and brightest and lit up half the country. When the fire of Uisneach was spotted, the great fire at Tara was lit. Later legends associate St Patrick with Uisneach. He is said to have founded a church on the hill, though no evidence of a Christian church site has yet been discovered.

There are remains of over two dozen archaeological monuments, including a megalithic tomb, burial mounds, standing stones, enclosures and ringforts, on the Hill of Uisneach today, and traces of many others have been identified beneath the ground surface by archaeological survey. This indicates the importance of the site, with a history spanning over 5,000 years. Some of the features of Uisneach were partially excavated in the early twentieth century by Macalister and Praeger, who discovered artefacts such as a Roman-style key and a Roman coin.

One of the more famous features of Uisneach is the Cat Stone, so called for its appearance from a distance of a cat about to pounce.

A view of Lough Lugh on the Hill of Uisneach. Lough Lugh is named after the sun god Lugh, who is said to have been drowned in the lake.

This glacial erratic has five faces, each looking towards one of the ancient provinces of Ireland. It was known historically as *Ail na Mireann* (the Stone of Divisions). The Norman chronicler Giraldus Cambrensis referred to it as the *Umbilicus Hiberniae* (the Navel of Ireland). Recent survey work carried out by Dr Roseanne Schot of the National University of Ireland, Galway, identified an embanked enclosure surrounding the Cat Stone, and a large enclosure on the eastern summit of the hill. The most visible monument is the large bivallate ringfort known as Rathnew. It was the seat of the powerful southern Uí Néill kingdom in the eighth century. Recent reappraisal of Macalister's excavation has determined that there was an earlier Iron Age ceremonial enclosure beneath the ringfort, showing that the Uí Néill kingdom wanted to appropriate what was likely to have been a powerful site symbolic of national identity.

THE HILL OF UISNEACH

Coordinates: Lat: 53.4831, Long: -7.55606

Grid reference: N 29493 49041

Opening times: Open all year. Please see www.usineach.ie for details about festivals, events and guided tours of the site.

Entry fee: Please visit www.uisneach.ie

Facilities: None

Car parking: Limited car parking

Directions: The Hill of Uisneach is located between Mullingar and Athlone on the R390

Nearest town: Mullingar is about 14km to the east

16 | ATHLONE CASTLE
COUNTY WESTMEATH

Athlone Castle was built to defend a strategic crossing point of the River Shannon, forming a well-guarded gateway into Connacht. It is likely that the original Norman castle was constructed on the site of an earlier Gaelic fortification established by the Ua Conchobair (O'Connor) kings of Connacht, as the Annals of the Four Masters record that a castle and bridge were built at Athlone by Toirrdelbach Ua Conchobair in 1129. The present castle began to take its shape in 1210, when John de Grey was ordered by King John of England to build three castles in Connacht. However, just one year after it was constructed, the stone tower collapsed, killing nine men, including Richard de Tuite, the Lord Chief Justice of Ireland. The castle was quickly rebuilt, and historical records show significant sums were spent on its maintenance and upkeep through-out the late thirteenth and early fourteenth centuries.

During the chaos that engulfed Ireland in the wake of the Bruce invasion of 1315, the King of Connacht, Ruaidrí Ua Conchobair, seized the opportunity to attack the Anglo-Norman lands, and

The keep of
Athlone Castle

The striking representations of key figures from the siege on display in the castle's visitor centre

launched an assault on Athlone, burning the town and attacking the castle. The castle changed hands between the English and Gaelic Irish many times during the fourteenth and fifteenth centuries, until it was finally recaptured by Crown forces in 1537, as it is recorded in the Carew Manuscripts that the 'Castle of Athlone, standing upon a passage betwixt Connaught and these parts, is recovered, which has long been usurped by the Irish'. The castle was repaired and became the residence of the presidents of Connacht after 1569. It endured its greatest test during the Williamite Wars at the end of

the seventeenth century. King William himself led his army against Athlone in 1690 but was unsuccessful. However, there was only a brief moment for the garrison to savour its victory, as William's forces returned the following year. For over a week in June 1691, 18,000 Williamite troops, commanded by General Godard de Ginkel, battled to capture the town, which was held by 23,000 Jacobite soldiers. The castle withstood what is thought to be one of the heaviest bombardments in Irish history: over 60,000 cannonballs and mortar bombs blasted the walls. A survivor of the siege recorded that 'with the balls and bombs flying so thick, that spot was hell on earth'. Both sides fought with incredible valour; the Jacobites repelled attack after attack, until de Ginkel identified another crossing point and sent 2,000 of his elite grenadier soldiers across the Shannon to attack the Jacobites from the rear. When the Jacobites saw their defence of Athlone was doomed, they retreated from the town only to fight again nearby at Aughrim, a battle that would become a key victory for King William.

The siege left Athlone Castle in ruins. It was in a dilapidated condition until the end of the eighteenth century, when it was largely reconstructed to defend against the possibility of a French attack during the Napoleonic Wars. The castle was considerably rebuilt

The walls of Athlone Castle

following a survey by Lt Colonel Tarrant in 1793 and further modifications took place during the nineteenth century. Today, Athlone Castle has a fine visitor centre that immerses you in the story of the siege. Close by to the castle you can enjoy another fine historical experience, a pint in Sean's Bar, an atmospheric pub that claims to be the oldest in Ireland.

ATHLONE CASTLE   SITE MAP 2

Coordinates: Lat: 53.423114, Long: -7.942714

Grid reference: N 03798 41444

Opening times:

November to February

Wednesday to Saturday: 11 a.m. – 5 p.m.

Sunday: 12 p.m. – 5 p.m.

Last admission 1 hour before closing: 4 p.m.

Closed Monday & Tuesday

September, October & March to May

Tuesday to Saturday: 11 a.m. – 5 p.m.

Sunday: 12 p.m. – 5 p.m.

Last admission 1 hour before closing: 4 p.m.

Closed Monday

June to August

Monday to Saturday: 10 a.m. – 6 p.m.

Sunday: 12 p.m. – 6 p.m.

Last admission 1 hour before closing: 5 p.m.

Open seven days

Athlone Castle & Visitor Centre open on bank holidays for seasonal Sunday hours, except on Christmas Day and St Stephen's Day

Entry fee: Please visit www.athlonecastle.ie

Facilities: Cafe, toilets, visitor information point

Car parking: Parking available around the castle

Directions: Located on the western side of the River Shannon in the town of Athlone

Nearest town: In the centre of Athlone

17 | LOUGHCREW CAIRNS
COUNTY MEATH

Cairn T at Loughcrew

The incredible passage-tomb cemetery of Loughcrew is located near the village of Oldcastle in County Meath. The most striking features of the archaeological landscape of Loughcrew are the three large cairns that dominate the summit of three steep hills, Patrickstown, Carnbane West and Carnbane East. The most visited is Carnbane East because it has the largest of the tombs, Cairn T, the focal point of the whole cemetery.

Cairn T dates back to approximately 3000 BC. On the summit of Carnbane East, Cairn T is surrounded by a number of smaller tombs. The large cairn measures around 35 metres (115 ft) in diameter, and this passage tomb has a cruciform chamber and some of the finest examples of Neolithic art in Ireland. Visit during the autumn or spring equinox to witness sunlight entering the chamber to illuminate the inside of the tomb (cloud cover permitting).

Entering the tomb itself is an atmospheric experience: the passageway is lined with large orthostats that display intricate carvings of spirals, lines, lozenges, zigzags, circles and cup marks.

The passageway to the burial chamber at Loughcrew

The Hag's Chair is one of the kerbstones that surround Cairn T; it displays megalithic art but unfortunately the carvings are very difficult to make out today, except near the base, if the light is strong enough. The cross inscribed on the seat is clearer. It possibly represents the use of the stone as a Mass Rock during penal times. It was also thought to have been used as a ceremonial or inauguration chair during the early medieval period.

The Irish name of Loughcrew, *Sliabh na Calliagh*, is thought to derive from *Sliabh na Caillí*, 'The Hill of the Witch'. Folklore has it that the monuments at Loughcrew were formed when a witch called *An Cailleach Bhéara* was challenged to drop an apron full of stones on each of the three Loughcrew peaks: if she succeeded she would be proclaimed the ruler of all Ireland. She was successful on the first two peaks, but missed the third and fell to her death.

Loughcrew is one of the most rewarding sites to visit in Ireland, and a true must-see for anyone who visits the Boyne Valley. In comparison to Newgrange, Loughcrew is rarely visited, and offers perhaps a more intimate experience with the Neolithic passage-tomb builders. There are free guided tours by OPW staff between 30 May and 28 August. At other times of the year, the key must be collected from Loughcrew Gardens Coffee Shop (a deposit and identification

The highly decorated Equinox Stone

are required). Please note that the walk up to the site is quite steep so suitable footwear should be worn.

The site affords some spectacular views of County Meath as well as a truly wonderful archaeological experience.

LOUGHCREW CAIRNS   SITE MAP 3

Coordinates: Lat: 53.744677, Long: -7.112322

Grid reference: N 58549 77595

Opening times: Open all year round. An OPW guide is at the site from 30 May to 28 August. For the rest of the year, a key can be obtained from Loughcrew Gardens Coffee Shop. A deposit must be left to get the key and is refundable when the key is returned.

Entry fee: Free

Facilities: None, but there is a coffee shop, as well as toilets and gardens, close to the site. Please see www.loughcrew.com for more information.

Car parking: There is a small car park at the site

Directions: To get to Loughcrew from Oldcastle, travel south on the R195 for about 2km. Turn left onto the L2800 and continue on this road for another 3km, keeping left at the fork to reach the car park.

Nearest town: Oldcastle, about 6km to the north

18 | KELLS
COUNTY MEATH

St Colmcille's House in Kells, County Meath

Kells has a treasure trove of superb heritage sites to discover. Kells, or *Ceanannas Mór* (meaning 'Great Fort'), was associated with legendary figures from the Irish sagas like Conn of the Hundred Battles and Cormac Mac Airt. Evidence of the importance of the area during the prehistoric period can be seen in the enormous hillfort on the Hill of Lloyd to the north-east of the town. Legend has it that Queen Medbh and her armies camped on the hill on their way to steal the Brown Bull of Cooley in the *Táin Bó Cúailnge* saga. More recently, Edward Bruce, brother of Robert the Bruce, also camped on the hill, following his victory over the Anglo-Normans at the Battle of Kells in 1315. Today the Spire of Lloyd, a wonderfully quirky inland lighthouse constructed in 1791, stands at the summit of the hillfort and gives outstanding views over the landscape.

The town of Kells rose to prominence in the early medieval period. The High King Diarmuid Mac Caroll is said have granted the *dún* (fort) of *Ceanannas* to St Colmcille (also known as St Columba) in

The round tower and South Cross in Kells   The Market Cross in Kells

the sixth century to establish a monastery. Little remains to be seen of the earliest phases of this once great monastery. Excavations behind St Colmcille's House (see p. 57) in the late 1980s uncovered some seventh-century activity; however, the clearest evidence comes from the ninth century onwards. St Colmcille's community on the island of Iona (off the western coast of Scotland) had been repeatedly raided by the Vikings, and in 804 the monks were granted land at Kells. By 878 the raids on Iona had become so frequent that the relics of Colmcille were moved from Iona to Kells (presumably including the famous Book of Kells now on display at Trinity College Dublin).

By the early tenth century, Kells became an important monastery. One of the key features remaining from this period is the remarkable round tower. It probably served as a bellhouse and would have been an obvious marker in the landscape to weary pilgrims travelling to visit the sacred relics of St Colmcille. This tower also has a darker story, for it is within it that Murchad Ua Máel Sechnaill, King of Mide and High King of Tara, was murdered in 1076.

Close to the tower is one of the early medieval high crosses at Kells. This, the South Cross, was crafted in the ninth century. It was the only high cross to have borne the name of its maker, having once borne an inscription in Latin (now sadly worn away) that read 'Muirdeach made this'.

Two other early medieval high crosses are within the walls of the monastic site: the North Cross, which has biblical depictions, and the so-called 'unfinished cross', which is located just to the side of the eighteenth-century church.

Perhaps the finest high cross at Kells is now located just outside the Old Courthouse. It originally stood in the centre of the crossroads in the town but was moved to its present location to protect it from damage from traffic. The cross is ninth-century and stands almost 3.5 metres (11.5 ft) tall. It depicts stories from the Bible, but also displays some more unusual designs, like the Celtic spirals, which may have drawn their influence from the tombs of the Boyne Valley. It also displays wrestling figures, horsemen with shields, centaurs and a wonderful depiction of a deer hunt.

Along with the monastic site, Kells also boasts a rare example of an early Irish church known as St Colmcille's House, located on Church Lane. The stone-built church possibly dates to as early as the ninth century, and local tradition has it that it was in this building that the Book of Kells was completed.

KELLS   SITE MAP 3

Coordinates: Lat: 53.727175, Long: -6.877011

Grid reference: N 58549 77595

Opening times: Open all year round

Entry fee: Free

Facilities: Coffee shops and toilets located in the town. See: www.visitingkells.ie for more information about facilities.

Car parking: Car parking throughout Kells

Directions: Kells is located just off the M3 motorway and all the sites in the town are within walking distance

Nearest town: Trim, about 27km to the south

19 | RATHMORE CHURCH
COUNTY MEATH

Rathmore Church, County Meath

Rathmore Church is situated outside the town of Athboy in rolling Meath pastureland. The church at Rathmore was founded in the fifteenth century by the Plunkett family and was dedicated to St Lawrence. The Plunketts resided at Rathmore Castle, which is in one of the fields adjacent to the church but of which now very little remains above ground. The castle and church were held by the Plunketts for generations until the seventeenth century when they passed to the Bligh family. There are records of rectors present at the church until the late seventeenth century when the parish became united with Athboy. The church probably began to fall into ruin after that time.

The church is surrounded by a graveyard within which are the remains of the shaft of a decorated cross that was probably erected for Sir Christopher Plunkett and his wife, Catherine, in the early sixteenth century. The figures on the shaft of the cross have been identified as St Patrick grappling with a snake, St Lawrence and an abbess or female saint, which, it is thought, might be a representation of St Brigid.

Within the church there are more superb medieval carvings, including one of a labyrinth on the wall of the church. It most likely dates to the fifteenth century and is a motif found across Europe. The labyrinth design is a maze, with carved lines leading to the centre.

The church has an L-shaped plan and there is a small room to the left of the chancel as one looks east: this was the sacristy. Steps lead up above it to a room that was once the living room of the sacristan, or resident priest. There is a fireplace in the wall and steps lead up to another floor that would have served as a bedroom, though that no longer exists. The sacristy on the ground floor contains a tomb and effigy of Thomas Plunkett and his wife, Marion Cruise. The

The labyrinth at Rathmore

The tomb effigy of Sir Thomas Plunkett and Marion Cruise

A view across the earthen banks and ditches of Tlachtga

carving has been defaced and it is difficult to make her out, but the carving of Sir Thomas is in a better state of preservation. He is in full armour with a dog at his feet, a symbol of his loyalty and fidelity. This tomb originally stood in the church but was moved to the sacristy in the 1980s to protect it from the elements.

The altar, which stands at the top of the chancel, has a range of figures carved into its surface, of saints and ecclesiastical figures. This probably dates to the mid or late fifteenth century. It also has carvings of the Plunkett coat of arms. At the end of the nave is a doorway leading into what would have been the belfry. There are now no floors within this part of the church, but the exterior of the belfry, or bell tower, is quite well preserved.

Another beautiful feature of this site is the east window. It is a fine example of medieval art and probably dates to the fifteenth century. On the external wall of the church, there are three carved stone heads around this window, depicting quite jolly-looking people: a king, queen and ecclesiastical figure. A similar carving depicting another church figure is on the western external wall at the opposite end of the church.

Not far from Rathmore, and just to the east of Athboy, you can find Tlachtga (known as the Hill of Ward), another monument well worth exploring. The site is a quadrivallate earthwork (meaning it has a series of four ditches and earthen banks). It is one of a very few known quadrivallate enclosures, along with The Rath of the Synods on the Hill of Tara and Rathra near Rathcroghan in County Roscommon. These complex sites are thought to have been of extremely high status, and possibly originated in the Late Bronze Age or Early Iron Age as ceremonial enclosures.

The enigmatic site of Tlachtga is full of mythology and folklore. It is believed by some to be named after a druidess, the daughter of the mythical sun-god figure Mog Ruith (named in other sources as the executioner of John the Baptist). Alternatively, Tlachtga is often translated as 'earth spear'. The word 'lacht' appearing within the name may also derive from a term for an ancient burial place.

Through the seventeenth-century historian Geoffrey Keating, Tlachtga has become associated with the festival of Samhain, the precursor to modern Halloween. On Samhain Eve, it is believed that a great fire was lit on the site, summoning all 'the priests, augurs and druids of Ireland to consume the sacrifices that were offered to their pagan gods'. It was decreed that all the fires within the kingdom were to be extinguished, and rekindled using the sacred flame of Tlachtga.

RATHMORE CHURCH SITE MAP 3

Coordinates: Lat: 53.643207, Long: -6.872623

Grid reference: N 74563 66527

Opening times: Open all year round

Entry fee: Free

Facilities: None

Car parking: Very limited car parking on the side of the road. Please try and avoid blocking gates with your car.

Directions: To get to Rathmore, travel on the N51 towards Athboy. Take the first left-hand turn after the village of Rathmore and park on the verge. The church and graveyard are located in fields on the right-hand side of the road. The site is on private land so please make sure to seek landowner's permission and always close all the gates behind you.

Nearest town: Athboy, about 5km to the south-west

Trim Castle, County Meath

Trim Castle is the largest and undoubtedly one of the most impressive Norman castles in Ireland. It stands at an important crossing point on the banks of the River Boyne, which gave the town its name, *Áth Truim*, or 'the Ford of the Elder Trees'. Trim Castle was constructed by the powerful Norman lord Hugh de Lacy in the 1170s.

Hugh was described by the Norman chronicler Giraldus Cambrensis as 'dark with sunken eyes and flattened nostrils. His face was grossly disfigured down the right side as far as his chin by a burn, the result of an accident. His neck was short, his body hairy and sinewy'. Giraldus's rather unflattering description does not seem to have held Hugh back as he appears to have had no shortage of romantic success. As Giraldus further remarks, 'after the death of his wife he was a womaniser and enslaved by lust, not just for one woman, but for many'. His ambitions in the bedroom and politics combined when he wed Rose, the daughter of the Irish High King, Ruaidrí Ua Conchobair. This was interpreted as a grave threat by King Henry II, who had feared that de Lacy was positioning himself to become an independent king in Ireland.

Soon after his marriage, in 1186, Hugh de Lacy went to Durrow in County Offaly (Site 27) to construct a castle to fortify the area. As he inspected the works, he bent down to show an Irish labourer how to use a pickaxe properly. Seizing this opportunity, one of his retinue, a young Irish noble called Gilla-gan-inathair Ua Miadhaigh, struck de Lacy down with an axe he had hidden under his cloak, decapitating the mighty Lord of Meath. Gilla-gan-inathair (whose name literally means 'youth without bowels', probably reflecting his skinny frame) fled the scene and managed to escape. King Henry II was overjoyed to hear of the demise of this powerful but troublesome magnate, and as Hugh's eldest son, Walter, was not of age to inherit, he incorporated all de Lacy's vast and hard-won estates as Crown lands and ensured the revenues filled his own purse.

Walter finally inherited Trim and his father's lands in 1189, but he too fell out of favour with the Crown. He joined forces with John de Courcy in attacking the lands of Prince John, who was in rebellion against King Richard the Lionheart. John never forgot the insult,

The keep (or donjon) of Trim Castle

and after he became king following Richard's death, he punished Walter by seizing his lands, and eventually forced him to flee to France. It was only after King John signed the Magna Carta along with a general reconciliation with the barons that Walter was allowed to resume control of his estates, though he remained in chronic debt to the Crown. It was during Walter's time at Trim that the castle was refortified and an extra storey was added to the keep. Walter died in 1241, outliving both his son and grandson. What was left of his estates was divided between his two granddaughters, Maud and Margery. Maud was granted Trim, and she married the wealthy noble Geoffrey de Geneville. They brought prosperity to Trim, redeveloped the keep and added new buildings, such as a fashionable great hall, and refortified the walls of the town. Eventually the castle passed to their eldest daughter, Joan, who married Roger Mortimer. He would become notorious in English history as the man who had an affair with Queen Isabella, wife of King Edward II, and who allegedly contrived the death of the king by using a red-hot poker in a manner not conducive to good bowel health.

During the fifteenth century, Trim Castle became a Yorkist stronghold during the Wars of the Roses but, by the end of the seventeenth century, it had fallen into disrepair and decay. It passed into state ownership in 1993, and featured prominently in Mel Gibson's film *Braveheart*. As the castle was never converted into a grand house in the eighteenth and nineteenth centuries, unlike Kilkenny Castle for example, it remained largely unaltered from medieval times. Today it is one of the best places to get a really good sense of the architecture of a medieval fortress, and you can enjoy one of the finest guided tours in the country from the excellent OPW staff.

After the guided tour, take time to do the River Walk to Newtown Trim. Simply cross the wooden bridge that leads from the car park and follow the path alongside the Boyne. The walk takes no more than 20 to 30 minutes, and passes through several beautiful medieval ruins before ending up close to a rather nice old pub, Marcie Regan's, on the banks of the river. The perfect reward after all that exploring! As you cross the wooden bridge, take a moment to look at the stone bridge on the left. This bridge was constructed some time between 1330 and 1350. The tall stone tower opposite

The Yellow Steeple of St Mary's Augustinian abbey

the castle is known locally as the Yellow Steeple. It too dates to the fourteenth century (thought to be constructed around 1368–70). It was the bell tower of the Augustinian abbey of St Mary's, which once stood opposite the castle. At 40 metres (131 ft) tall, the Yellow Steeple is said to be the tallest medieval building still standing in Ireland. There are little visible remains of the other buildings of St Mary's, though Talbot's Castle, the fine fortified townhouse to the left of the Yellow Steeple, is thought to have incorporated abbey buildings. Talbot's Castle was built shortly after the Dissolution of the Monasteries in the middle of the sixteenth century. It was said to have once been the home of the famous satirist Jonathan Swift, author of *Gulliver's Travels* and vicar of Laracor on the outskirts of Trim in 1670.

The stone gate that straddles the path is called the 'Sheep Gate'. Like the majority of medieval towns, Trim was surrounded by a defensive wall. As well as providing extra fortifications to protect the townspeople at times of conflict, the wall also served as a clear boundary between the town and countryside, where people entering the town could expect to be under different rules and regulations. The gateways served as control points, where tolls and taxes could be easily collected. The low stretch of stone wall running up the slope from the Sheep Gate is what remains of the once strong defensive walls, and the Sheep Gate itself is the only surviving medieval gate into Trim.

After a walk of around 15 minutes, you will come to the Cathedral of Ss Peter and Paul at Newtown. The cathedral was founded by the Norman bishop Simon de Rochfort around 1206. Although only parts of the nave and chancel survive today, it is easy to get the impression of just how large this cathedral once was. Many of the fine decorative flourishes in the stonework are still visible, and it has lovely lancet windows. The piscina, where the priest used to wash the holy vessels during Mass, is also still well preserved.

Just beyond the cathedral remains is a small parish church that probably dates to the later fifteenth century. This site is famous for the remarkable sixteenth-century tomb of Sir Lucas Dillon and his wife, Lady Jayne Bathe. The two stone effigies on the tomb are separated by a ceremonial Sword of State. The tomb is known locally as 'The Tomb of the Jealous Man and Woman', and it is believed that instead of signifying the sword of state, the sword actually represents Sir Lucas' displeasure at his wife for having an affair, forever separating the two. Folklore has it that the tomb possesses a cure

The Priory and Hospital of St John the Baptist at Trim

for warts and skin complaints. Rub your wart on a pin and leave the pin on top of the tomb; as the pin rusts, the wart withers and falls off.

Further along the path and just over a small medieval bridge, you come to remarkable ruins of the Priory and Hospital of St John the Baptist. The priory was founded in the early thirteenth century by Simon de Rochfort for the Order of the Crutched Friars (*Fratres Cruciferi*). As well as being a monastery and guesthouse for pilgrims, the site also served as a hospital. The Order of the Crutched Friars were just one of a number of religious orders that were brought to Ireland by the Normans following their invasion. They also brought the Knights Templar, the Hospitallers and Trinitarians, as well as strongly supporting the expansion of religious orders like the Augustinians, Benedictines and Cistercians who already had a foothold in Ireland. The site was excavated in 1984. Archaeologists discovered the remains of a fifteenth-century rood screen, which separated the nave from the choir, and a doorway in the gable end of the nave. They also found the remains of a tower leading to a room over the sacristy, and part of the original domestic range to the north-east of the choir. Today, the nave and chancel and a striking three-light window in the eastern wall can still be seen. The large rectangular three-storey tower is fifteenth-century, and is likely to have housed domestic quarters. Sections of the later sixteenth-century enclosing walls that surround the site can be made out, and

one small corner turret still stands in the western side of the field. The priory was dissolved during the Reformation in 1541, and was converted to a private residence. Across the river is our last historical destination, Marcie Regan's Pub.

TRIM CASTLE SITE MAP 3

Coordinates: Lat: 53.554623, Long: -6.790007

Grid reference: N 80221 56727

Opening times: Trim Castle is open all year. From November to mid February, it is open at weekends only; from mid February to end October it is open daily from 10 a.m. to 6 p.m. Last admissions are 1 hour before closing. The other sites on the River Walk are open all year.

Entry fee: Please visit www.heritageireland.ie/en/midlands-eastcoast/trimcastle/

Facilities: Guided tours of the site, tea rooms, exhibitions, toilets

Car parking: Large car park (paid parking) beside the castle

Directions: Trim Castle is located in the centre of Trim town

Nearest town: Located in the town of Trim

Sunset on the River Boyne

21 | BECTIVE ABBEY
COUNTY MEATH

Bective Abbey, County Meath

Bective Abbey is a superb heritage site located in the valley of the River Boyne. It was founded in 1147 by the King of Meath, Murchad Ua Máel Sechnaill and given to the Cistercian Order. Bective was the 'daughter house' of Mellifont (Site 4), the first Cistercian foundation in Ireland. Unlike many other Cistercian foundations, which typically sought out wilderness and isolation, Bective was positioned on fertile agricultural land, and quickly rose to prominence as an important ecclesiastical centre. Indeed, Bective was of such high status that the powerful Norman Lord of Meath Hugh de Lacy had his body interred at Bective for a while before he was eventually reburied with his wife's remains at the (now demolished) St Thomas's Abbey in Dublin.

By the sixteenth century, the Cistercians of Bective Abbey had become wealthy from rents, tithes and donations. At the time that Bective was dissolved during the Dissolution of the Monasteries in the middle of the sixteenth century, it was recorded that the estate of Bective contained 1,580 acres, valued at £83 18s 8d. The abbey and its possessions were purchased in 1552 by Andrew Wyse, but he seems to have come into financial difficulties soon after and Bective changed hands a number of times, before being transformed into a manor in the early seventeenth century. It came into the hands of the Bolton family, and was eventually donated to the state in 1894.

The extensive ruins that one can explore today at Bective tell the story of both the Cistercian monastic site and the private home. The cloisters are superbly well preserved (and featured in the Mel Gibson film *Braveheart*).

The site is well worth a visit and is part of a densely packed medieval landscape, close to Trim Castle (Site 20). It is free to enter all year round and is well signposted from the R161 between Trim and Navan in County Meath.

BECTIVE ABBEY　　　　　　　　　　　　　　　　SITE MAP 3

Coordinates: Lat: 53.582562, Long: -6.702612

Grid reference: N 85940 59932

Opening times: Open all year round

Entry fee: Free

Facilities: None

Car parking: Large car park at site

Directions: The site is well signposted between Trim and Navan. To get to Bective Abbey from Navan, travel south on the Trim Road (R161) for approximately 7km. Turn left onto the L4010 and the abbey will be on the left.

Nearest town: Navan, about 9km to the north, and Trim, 8km to the south

22 | THE HILL OF TARA
COUNTY MEATH

The Hill of Tara is one of the most iconic archaeological landscapes in Ireland. As the majority of Tara's buildings would have been constructed from timber, the site appears today as a series of undulating earthworks and grassy banks and ditches. It can be a little difficult on first viewing to get a true sense of the phenomenal concentration of archaeology at Tara, and the site certainly requires the visitor to use their imagination. However, at such an evocative and atmospheric place, it is not hard to conjure visions of ancient temples, palaces and tombs.

The name Tara derives from either the Irish word *temair*, meaning 'a great height', or the Greek *temenos* or Latin *templum*, meaning 'a sacred space'. Both of these meanings perfectly suit Tara, once described as 'probably the most consecrated spot in Ireland'. From Tara on a clear day, hills in all four of Ireland's provinces can be seen. With such a vista, it is no wonder that it became the ritual centre of kingship and ceremony in Ireland. Tara is deeply imbued with legend and folklore, and is associated with the goddess Medb, 'the one who intoxicates'. Legend has it that any man who wished to establish himself as King of Tara would have to symbolically wed himself to her. It is also associated with many of the other pre-Christian gods of Ireland, such as Lugh.

Many of the names of the monuments at Tara come from *Dindshenchas Éireann* ('Lore of the Place Names of Ireland'), which

The curving bank of *Ráith na Ríg* (Fort of the Kings) at Tara

The nineteenth-century church at Tara

was compiled in the eleventh century. As they were recorded centuries after the initial use of the monuments, these descriptions must be taken with a pinch of salt, however they add to the folkloric mystique of this most enigmatic of Irish landscapes.

Inside the nineteenth-century church (now the visitor centre), there is a beautiful stained-glass window by artist Evie Hone, and an informative audiovisual presentation that tells the story of Tara. Guided tours are available from May to September. The churchyard has a number of historic features, including two standing stones, known in legend as Bloc and Bligne, which are said to have played a part in the royal inauguration ceremonies. The taller stone, Bligne, has a Sheela-na-gig near the base, though it can be difficult to see due to weathering and lichen growth. Just outside the churchyard, the statue of St Patrick reflects the legend of Patrick lighting the Easter Fire on the nearby Hill of Slane (Site 23) in 433.

By heading north from the churchyard, one of the first monuments encountered is the Banqueting Hall (*Tech Midchúarta*). This is thought to be one of the later monuments on the hill, and is believed to be of early medieval date. Legend recounts that these long parallel lines of earthworks were originally the foundations for the great feasting hall of Tara, where warriors, nobles and kings would drink, feast and boast as part of lavish banquets. However, this feature is more likely to represent a processional route, perhaps used during ritual or inauguration ceremonies. The twin earthworks block the view as one walks up the slope, with occasional gaps that appear to focus on key features in the landscape. As you reach the top of the slope, Tara's oldest monument, the Mound of the Hostages, appears in view.

Before reaching the Mound of the Hostages, the remains of *Ráith na Ríg* (the Fort of the Kings) must be passed. Though now it appears

Duma na nGiall (the Mound of the Hostages)

merely as a shallow depression with a slight bank, at the time it was first dug *Ráith na Ríg* was cut nearly 3 metres (9.8 ft) into the underlying bedrock. Unusually, it has its earthen bank on the outside of the ditch rather than the inside, which goes against usual practice and defensive function, and, as such, hints at the ritual and ceremonial nature of the enclosure. *Ráith na Ríg* measures approximately 320 metres (1,045 ft) north–south by 264 metres (866 ft) east–west, and encloses the majority of the key monuments of Tara.

One of the first monuments inside the *Ráith na Ríg* is the uneven ground that marks the Rath of the Synods (*Ráith na Senad*). According to medieval lore this is again described as a ceremonial feasting hall. Excavations revealed fragments of high-status imported fine glass goblets, lending some credence to the mythology. Unfortunately, the site was badly damaged when a group that called themselves the British Israelites roughly dug the site in their futile search for the Ark of the Covenant in the early twentieth century.

The Mound of the Hostages (*Duma na nGiall*) is a Neolithic passage tomb, and is over 5,000 years old, though it continued to be an important place of burial and ritual for many centuries afterwards. When the Mound of the Hostages was excavated in the 1950s, the chamber of the Neolithic tomb with a rich assemblage of artefacts and human remains was discovered. The dig also revealed that the earthen mound was used as a cemetery in the Bronze Age. One of these burials, the very last to be inserted into the mound, was that of a young teenager. He was found buried with a necklace made of exotic stones and beads, and was, perhaps, one of the 'hostages' from whom the tomb takes its name.

Moving further south you will encounter the Forradh. This distinctive mound is one of Tara's most enigmatic monuments, as the date of its construction is uncertain. It is believed to have been the inauguration mound, which played a central role in the ceremonies of kingship during the early historic period. Today it is topped with a standing stone, said to be the *Lia Fáil* (Stone of Destiny), which legend said would cry out when the rightful King of Ireland placed his foot upon it.

The *Lia Fáil* (Stone of Destiny)

Adjoining the Forradh you can see the circular earthworks of Cormac's House (*Teach Chormaic*). This is a large bivallate ringfort that probably dates to the early medieval period. By conjoining the ringfort to the iconic Forradh within the sacred precinct of Tara, it is likely that the builder was sending a strident political message. It is linked with the legendary ruler Cormac mac Airt. Cormac may well have been an authentic historical figure, although he has become entwined with mythology and legend. He is said to have ruled from Tara during the Iron Age, for forty years. He was famous for his wisdom and generosity. In the Annals of Clonmacnoise, translated in 1627, he is described as 'absolutely the best king that ever reigned in Ireland before himself … wise, learned, valiant and mild, not given causelessly to be bloody as many of his ancestors were, he reigned majestically and magnificently'.

More monuments imbued with legend can be found west of the Banqueting Hall. These are large barrows, Bronze Age burial mounds. One is named Rath Gráinne, after the heroine of the great romantic story of Diarmuid and Gráinne. The other monument, the

Sloping Trenches (*Cloenfhearta*), was said to have formed when the house of King Lugaid MacConn collapsed along with the side of his face, as retribution by the gods for his bad judgement. Irish kings had to be perfect in every way – physically, morally and in judgment and deed; if they failed or became impaired, they fell from power.

Tara still held potent political power even centuries after its heyday. It is said that Hugh O'Neill rallied his troops at Tara before leading them south to the Battle of Kinsale in 1601. During the doomed rebellion of 1798, a group rebels made their last stand at Tara before being slaughtered and buried on the hill where a memorial stands today. Less than a century later, Tara was once again the setting for the struggle for Irish independence. In 1843 Daniel O'Connell addressed an audience of many hundreds of thousands at Tara, perhaps the most famous of his 'Monster Meetings' as part of his campaign to repeal the Act of Union.

Tara is place where there is only a thin veil between archaeology and mythology, history and legend.

THE HILL OF TARA SITE MAP 3

Coordinates: Lat: 53.580999, Long: -6.609526

Grid reference: N 91926 59775

Opening times: Open all year. The exhibition centre is open from mid May to mid September. Please see: www.heritageireland.ie/en/hilloftara for specific opening hours.

Entry fee: Please visit www.heritageireland.ie/en/midlands-eastcoast/hilloftara

Facilities: Tea rooms, gift shop and toilets are located close to the site. In the visitor centre there is an audiovisual presentation. Guided tours of the site are available.

Car parking: Large car park at the site

Directions: Tara is located off the M3 motorway. Exit at Junction 7 (signed Skyrne/Johnstown) and continue on the R147 for about 1km. Turn right (following signs for the Hill of Tara) and continue up this road. At the T-junction, turn right and the car park and site will be on the left.

Nearest town: Dublin, about 43km to the south, and Dunshaughlin, 11km to the south

The tall sixteenth-century bell tower on the Hill of Slane

Like its near neighbour Tara (Site 22), the Hill of Slane in County Meath is a place steeped in Irish myth, legend and history. The hill rises nearly 160 metres (525 ft) above the surrounding landscape, and offers commanding views of the surrounding land. This elevated position made it a strategic and desirable place for thousands of years. According to Irish mythology, this was the burial place of Sláine mac Dela, king of the legendary Fir Bolg. It is from *Dumha Sláine* (meaning 'burial mound of Sláine') that we get the modern name, Slane.

The Hill of Slane features in the legends that grew around St Patrick. The main pagan festivals of the time were *Imbolc*, marking the beginning of spring, *Bealtaine*, marking the beginning of summer, *Lughnasa*, the harvest festival usually set in late August, and *Samhain*, marking the beginning of winter. Of these festivals, the most important rituals surrounded *Bealtaine*. All the fires across the country would be extinguished to mark the end of the winter,

A view through the window of the Franciscan college at Slane

Statue of St Patrick on the Hill of Slane

and a great fire that could be seen for miles around would then be lit at dawn on the Hill of Tara, symbolising the dawn of a new year. Patrick sought to hijack this pagan practice by lighting a huge fire on the Hill of Slane. This burned throughout the night before the king's warriors managed to capture Patrick and bring him to Tara to answer to the king. Legend has it that Patrick then managed to perform many feats and miracles to prove to the king that the Christian God was far more powerful than the old gods, and in one of the most famous of the hagiographic legends that surround Patrick, it is said that he used a three-leaved shamrock to explain the mysteries of Christianity to the king. While the king had no wish to convert to Christianity himself, he allowed Patrick to continue on his mission to spread Christianity across Ireland.

Though the stories of Patrick at Slane are likely to be the product of later hagiographic legend, the Hill of Slane was undoubtedly important to the early Irish Church, as a monastery was founded on the hill by St Erc, who died in 514. This monastery is mentioned a number of times in the Annals of Ireland as an important centre of early Irish law. It is also mentioned for a number of Viking raids that struck the site, most notably in 948, when it is recorded that the 'abbot of Slane was taken prisoner and died in pagan hands', and two years later in 950 when the 'bell-tower of Slane was burned, together with a particularly fine bell and the crozier of the patron saint, and the lector and many people were burned after they took refuge with the monastery's valuables in the tower'.

Though nothing remains above ground of the early sixth-century monastery, today visitors to the Hill of Slane can find a superbly preserved sixteenth-century Franciscan church and college, which are fascinating to explore. Both are thought to date to 1512 when Sir Christopher Fleming, Baron of Slane, founded the site for the Franciscan order. The church has a particularly fine bell tower with a large Gothic window. Look for the stone head leering from above the windows of the tower on one side of the church. The college was established to serve the church and housed four priests, four choristers and four lay-brothers. It was constructed around an open quadrangle, with the priests' quarters on the northern side. It is possible to explore some of the original features, like the staircases (please do take extreme care in wet weather), and see the fireplaces, window mouldings and a double garderobe.

THE HILL OF SLANE   SITE MAP 3

Coordinates: Lat: 53.717352, Long: -6.543041

Grid reference: N 96175 75174

Opening times: Open all year round

Entry fee: Free

Facilities: None. Please make sure to take care (especially with small children) inside the ruins of the Franciscan college, as the staircases may be dangerous in wet weather.

Car parking: Large car park at the site

Directions: The Hill of Slane is well signposted from Slane: just head north up the hill on the N2 through Slane and take a left turn at Chapel Street/N2.

Nearest town: The Hill of Slane is 750 metres north of Slane.

24 | BATTLE OF THE BOYNE VISITOR CENTRE COUNTY MEATH

The Battle of the Boyne Visitor Centre

The Boyne Valley was the setting of some of the key events of the later medieval and post-medieval periods in Irish history, the most famous being the Battle of the Boyne, the story of which is told in the Battle of the Boyne Visitor Centre at Oldbridge.

In the 1690s Ireland became a theatre of war for international and religious politics. Catholic forces supporting James II fought with the Protestant supporters of William of Orange to decide who would become the King of England, Scotland, Wales and Ireland. For the Jacobite forces, the war was a struggle for Irish sovereignty, rights for Catholics and land ownership, and a revocation of the harsh laws imposed on Irish Catholics following the Cromwellian conquest decades earlier. By 1690, the Jacobites controlled nearly all of Ireland with the exception of Ulster. For the Williamite forces, the war was a struggle to maintain English (and Protestant) rule in Ireland. They deeply mistrusted the Jacobites and believed it would lead to the wholesale massacre of the Protestant population if the Irish were to gain supremacy, fearing a repeat of the bloody early days of the 1641 Rebellion. Though the majority of fighters on the Jacobite side were Irish Catholic, and a large proportion of the Williamite forces were Ulster Protestants, this was a truly European war and many nationalities were present on the battlefield.

The Battle of the Boyne took place on 1 July 1690 (according to the old Julian Calendar; by today's Gregorian Calendar it was on 12 July 1690) and became one of the pivotal moments of the war. Although relatively few casualties were suffered on either side (an

Cannon and ordnance on display at the Battle of the Boyne Visitor Centre

estimated 1,500 Jacobites and 500 Williamites) it still scared James II enough that he decided to flee the battlefield and Ireland, and exiled himself safely in France. The war continued in his absence and became far bloodier. The excellent Battle of the Boyne Visitor Centre gives the story of the battle and there are demonstrations of the weapons and equipment used.

By October 1691 Jacobite resistance ended and William of Orange became King of England, Scotland, Wales and Ireland. He introduced the severe Penal Laws that restricted life for Catholics by banning priests and putting strong limits on the amount of land or property a Catholic could own, as well as banning them from voting. This extensive and intricate legislation continued into the nineteenth century.

BATTLE OF THE BOYNE VISITOR CENTRE   SITE MAP 3

Coordinates: Lat: 53.721211, Long: -6.412437

Grid reference: O 04084 76000

Opening times: Open all year round.
See: www.battleoftheboyne.ie/VisitorInfo for specific opening hours

Entry fee: Please visit www.heritageireland.ie/en/midlands-eastcoast/battleoftheboyne/

Facilities: Tea rooms, toilets, walled garden, audiovisual exhibition, self-guided walks and visitor centre

Car parking: Large car park

Directions: Travelling north on the M1, exit at Junction 10 and take the slight left onto the N51. After about 3km, take the third left off the N51 onto the L16014. Continue on the L16014 over the bridge and turn right. The visitor centre entrance gates will be ahead

Nearest town: Drogheda, about 6km to the east

25 | BRÚ NA BÓINNE
COUNTY MEATH

Dawn over Brú na Boinne

The Brú na Bóinne (meaning Palace or Mansion of the Boyne) complex is a truly sacred and monumental landscape, and one of the most important prehistoric landscapes in the world. It is packed with an almost bewildering array of ancient tombs and monuments. In 1993, Newgrange and the tombs of Brú na Bóinne were declared a UNESCO World Heritage Site. The visitor centre gives a great overview of the archaeology and history of these important monuments, and it is solely from the visitor centre that Newgrange and Knowth may be accessed.

These sites are particularly important for their wealth of megalithic art. The rest of Ireland has sixty stones with megalithic art depicted, while in the whole of Britain there are only twelve stones with megalithic art, France has 200 and the Iberian Peninsula has fewer than 200. In County Meath alone there around 1,000 stones bearing megalithic art, with the great majority being found here in the Boyne Valley.

NEWGRANGE

One of the most iconic and popular sites in Ireland, Newgrange is a spectacular example of the ingenuity and ability of Ireland's first farmers. Built *c.* 3300 BC, Newgrange predates Stonehenge and the

Newgrange

The entrance into Newgrange. Note the elaborately decorated entrance
stone, and the roofbox above the passageway

Great Pyramid of Giza by centuries and, as it is aligned with the winter solstice, it is also one of the earliest structures known to have an astronomical function. This phenomenon was rediscovered by the archaeologist who conducted the main excavations at Newgrange, Professor M. J. O'Kelly. He identified the purpose of the 'roofbox' and its alignment with the midwinter sun. Each year at the winter solstice, light travels through the roofbox, and snakes its way along the passageway before illuminating the chamber. Imagine those who built this great tomb over 5,300 years ago standing in the dark in the cold winter air waiting for the beam of sunlight to show that from this point forward the darkness of winter would begin to recede and a new year had begun. You can experience the same phenomenon today if you are fortunate enough to win the annual lottery to access the chamber at the solstice, though you must be doubly fortunate and hope that the sun is not obscured by cloud. It is an incredible moment where it is possible to gain a true and tangible connection with our distant ancestors.

Newgrange is positioned on a ridge overlooking the Boyne Valley. To this day it remains a highly visible and potent symbol in the landscape. The main tomb measures approximately 11 metres (36 ft) high and almost 95 metres (312 ft) in diameter. The mound is made up of a cairn of stones covered with earth, and surrounded by ninety-seven kerbstones, many of which display impressively intricate megalithic art. The entrance stone in particular and one positioned on the opposite side of the mound are beautifully decorated and must be considered as some of the finest examples of Neolithic art from anywhere in the world. The striking façade of white quartz with round granite stones is still a controversial interpretation by O'Kelly based on his excavations; the quartz may have originally been laid out as a pavement (as interpreted at Knowth, see below). The passageway measures approximately 19 metres (62 ft) and leads into a cruciform chamber with a corbelled stone roof. A stone basin was found in each of the recesses. The excavations discovered the cremated remains of just four or five individuals. There is more intricate megalithic art throughout the tomb.

Newgrange continued to be a focus for ritual and ceremony throughout the Neolithic period and into the Bronze Age. A cursus monument (a long linear feature of parallel earthen banks) was constructed close to the tomb. This is thought to have had a role in ceremonial processions and rituals. A number of other smaller satellite tombs were also constructed nearby, perhaps in an attempt to share the same sacred space. Later, in the Early Bronze Age, people constructed timber and stone circles, again highlighting the religious importance of Newgrange.

Today Newgrange is one of Ireland's most visited heritage sites, but archaeologists discovered that tourism to Newgrange is not a recent phenomenon. Roman coins were discovered near the entrance of the tomb, deposited centuries ago by fellow travellers to this sacred space.

KNOWTH

Positioned near the western end of the Boyne Valley, Knowth is one of the largest of Ireland's passage tombs. It is best known for its kerb of 127 stones, many of which are highly decorated with megalithic art – a phenomenal assemblage. By sheer volume, Knowth alone boasts a quarter of all known megalithic art in Europe, with over 300 decorated stones.

The mound shelters two passage tombs, placed back to back, one facing east and the other west. The east-facing tomb has a passageway that measures approximately 35 metres (115 ft) leading to a cruciform chamber with a corbelled stone roof. The west-facing tomb has a passage that measures approximately 32 metres (105 ft). However, it does not open into a chamber as such; instead the passageway is simply slightly enlarged. Unfortunately, the interior

Knowth

of the great mound of Knowth is no longer accessible to the public as it is unstable.

There are also a number of smaller satellite tombs, spread in no discernible pattern from the main mound. Knowth continued to be an important place of activity and settlement for millennia. It eventually became the royal residence of the *Slí nAedo Sláine*, rulers of North Brega. A large settlement grew upon and around the ancient tombs, with a number of houses and souterrains constructed. In the medieval period, a large rectangular structure was constructed on top of the mound, possibly as part of an enclosed Anglo-Norman farmstead, but little of it remains today.

DOWTH

Dowth is located around 2km north-east of Newgrange. Unlike Newgrange and Knowth, Dowth has never been properly excavated by archaeologists so there is far less known about the site. However, in the middle of the nineteenth century, an extremely large hole was dug into the top of the mound by antiquarians seeking treasure.

Dowth is thought to date to around 5,000 years ago. It measures approximately 85 metres (280 ft) in diameter and is ringed by 115 kerbstones, some of which display megalithic art. Two tombs are known at the western side of the large mound at Dowth and the setting sun in winter seems to illuminate the southernmost of these. The more northerly tomb has an 8-metre (26-ft) passageway that leads into a cruciform chamber with an annexe leading off it. It also

Dowth

has an early medieval souterrain, probably dating to around the tenth century, leading off the passageway. This shows that the tomb was still an important place in the early medieval period. The southern passage has a circular chamber with a diameter of 4 metres (13 ft).

There are no satellite tombs immediately outside the great tomb at Dowth, but there are outlying tombs around 0.5km away, and a massive earth-embanked henge is located to the east, though there is no public access to that site.

Dowth was known in early literature as *Dubad* and *Sid mBresail* ('the otherworld mound of Bresal'). The medieval manuscripts known as *Dindseanchas* explain how Dowth (*Dubad*) got its name. They tell the story of how all the men of Ireland were commanded by the king to come together for just one day to build a tower that would reach the heavens. The king's sister secretly used magic and stopped the sun in the sky so that there would be an endless day. As time wore on the men of Ireland became exhausted and realised they had been tricked. However, the magic spell was broken when the king and his sister committed incest. Darkness swiftly covered the land and work on the great mound was abandoned. It was said that *Dubad* (darkness) would be the name of the place from that day.

BRÚ NA BÓINNE   SITE MAP 3

Coordinates: Lat: 53.695154, Long: -6.447025

Grid reference: O 02606 72787

Opening times: Open all year round. Please note that Newgrange and Knowth can be accessed only via the visitor centre.

Entry fee: Please visit www.heritageireland.ie/en/midlands-eastcoast/brunaboinnevisitorcentre/

Facilities: Tea rooms, toilets, exhibition centre, bus to sites

Car parking: Parking at site

Directions: The visitor centre is located on the south side of the River Boyne. From Slane, travel south on the N2. Turn left at Kentstown (signposted for Brú na Bóinne). Continue on this road for approximately 6km and the visitor centre will be on the left.

Nearest town: Slane, approximately 10km to the north-west

Fourknocks Passage Tomb

In a landscape packed with ancient monuments, one of the most spectacular is Fourknocks 1, a Neolithic passage tomb that is over 5,000 years old.

The tomb was excavated in the 1950s and subsequently reconstructed by the OPW with a concrete dome as a roof to protect the site. Enter the tomb through the doorway in the north-east of the mound, and pass through a short passageway into a large central chamber. Three small burial chambers are inserted into the walls, each roughly cruciform in shape. The remains of stone corbelling around the perimeter of the chamber are visible, though unusually for a passage tomb it appears that the roof of the structure was not corbelled all the way to the top; instead it is thought that there was a wooden-framed roof supported by a large timber post placed in the centre of the burial chamber. Some have suggested that this

One of the burial chambers inside the tomb at Fourknocks. Note the striking megalithic art.

unusual arrangement may be evidence that Fourknocks originally began as an open-air monument that was later converted into a passage tomb.

The excavation revealed that the people interred in the burial chambers of Fourknocks were predominantly adults who had been cremated, whereas the unburned skeletal remains of children were discovered in the passageway, along with a number of unburned adult skulls. Fourknocks also has a number of striking examples of megalithic art. Particularly eye-catching are the lintels above the burial chambers, which are embellished with geometric and angular motifs.

Long after the tomb was sealed it continued to be an important place of veneration and ritual practice. Bronze Age burials were placed in the mound, perhaps a way of reconnecting with ancestors who had died centuries earlier.

27 | DURROW ABBEY
COUNTY OFFALY

Durrow was one of Ireland's most important early monasteries. It is said to have been founded by St Colmcille at the end of the sixth century. It was positioned in an economically strategic location, near the geographic centre of Ireland and just to the south of the *Slí Mhór* ('The Great Way'), the key routeway that traversed Ireland from east to west. This made Durrow extremely accessible for pilgrims and traders, and helped to ensure that the monastery became wealthy. However, being well-known also came with danger. Durrow was raided numerous times between the ninth and twelfth centuries. From the time of its first founding, it had to prepare for external threats of raids and violence. In a poem ascribed to St Colmcille, he appointed Laisrenas as abbot of Durrow and instructed him to create a great boundary around the monastery 'so that there might not be a breach therein', then to cut down the brave forest of Dair Magh and to make stakes and place them 'in a comely row on every side around the monastery so that the congregation may have a protection against danger'. A faint ring of earthworks can still be seen from aerial photography, which provides evidence of the enclosure. It was not just opportunistic raiders seeking plunder against whom monasteries needed to protect themselves, however; occasionally monasteries would go to 'war' with other monasteries in bitter disputes over land and prestige. In 764, Durrow fought a pitched battle with the monastery of Clonmacnoise, and lost over 200 men. By this time, monasteries like Durrow and Clonmacnoise were not isolated places, but had large settlements around them, becoming Ireland's first large urban centres, bearing many similarities to later secular towns.

The earliest buildings of the monastery were of timber, so there are no visible remains of them today. However, a fine high cross, thought to date to the ninth century, can be seen in the nave of St Columba's Church on the site. This cross may have originally stood near the western end of the graveyard, but was moved inside to protect it against weathering. The cross stands some 3 metres (nearly 10 ft) tall, and it bears a number of biblical scenes and geometric design. The head of the eastern face of the cross depicts Christ in glory, holding a cross staff and sceptre. The interlacing ornament on which he stands may be a representation of clouds, perhaps suggesting he is in Heaven. Above his head is the Lamb of God, and he is flanked by two angels: the one on the left (Christ's right) plays a flute or pipe. David is pictured on both the arms of the cross: on the left he plays his lyre, on the right he is depicted fighting a lion. The panel below the head of the cross shows the Sacrifice of Isaac, below which is a panel of intricate knotwork. At the bottom of the shaft is the risen Christ with two angels and two apostles. The western head of the cross depicts Christ being crucified, with two soldiers visible. Above the Crucifixion scene is what is thought to be a depiction of Christ handing the keys of Heaven to Peter and Paul.

Facing page: The high cross in St Columba's Church

St Columba's Church at Durrow

The two depictions on the arms of the cross are difficult to discern, but may represent Peter's denial of Jesus, and Pilate washing his hands. The panel below the cross head shows the Roman soldiers casting lots for Christ's clothes, and below them is the mocking of Christ by Roman soldiers. The bottom of the shaft shows Christ in the tomb guarded by two soldiers. The south side of the cross has a depiction of Adam and Eve in the Garden of Eden at the bottom, above which is Cain slaying Abel. The unusual depiction of a warrior with two dogs may represent Flann mac Máel Sechnaill, then High King of Ireland, who may have been a key patron of Durrow. He became King of Tara in 846, and would have been broadly contemporary with the erection of this cross. There are fragments of other high crosses in the graveyard and five cross-inscribed slabs that are now housed inside the church. Sculpture was not the only art form associated with the monastery. The famous manuscript, The Book of Durrow, is said to have been compiled here. It was recorded historically that it was enshrined by Flann mac Máel Sechnaill, King of Ireland, in Durrow. By the seventeenth century the manuscript had changed ownership a number of times before finding a home at Trinity College Dublin. Many great nobles and kings were buried in the sacred ground of Durrow, amongst them Murchad Ua Briain, a grandson of the great Brian Boru.

By the middle of the twelfth century, St Malachy had begun his reform of the Irish Church to bring it in line with that of the continent and introduced some of the European religious orders. An Augustinian abbey was founded at Durrow at Malachy's instigation. This was attacked in 1175, and no visible traces remain of it. At the end of the twelfth century, the Norman Lord of Meath, Hugh de Lacy, ordered the construction of a motte and bailey at the site. It was while inspecting the works at Durrow that he was assassinated by an Irishman in his retinue. It is said that the prime motivation for the killing was de Lacy's perceived desecration of Colmcille's monastery. The remains of this motte can still be seen to the east of the walled garden and south of the present church. The Normans established another castle on the site in 1213, though it was recorded as being ruined by the sixteenth century.

The monastery was dissolved in 1541, and the building was converted into a parish church. This church was renovated and modified in the eighteenth and nineteenth centuries. Today the church has been conserved by the OPW and houses the high crosses and grave slabs that were discovered on the site. The church sits within the parkland of Durrow Demense with a nineteenth-century neo-Gothic revival house, also in state ownership.

DURROW ABBEY   SITE MAP 4

Coordinates: Lat: 53.325785, Long: -7.519741

Grid reference: N 32029 30709

Opening times: Open all year round

Entry fee: Free

Facilities: None

Car parking: Limited car parking available

Directions: To get to Durrow from Dublin, travel towards Galway on the M6. Exit at Junction 5 and travel south on the N52. Durrow Abbey is on the right, just after the village of Durrow. The site is accessed through the large wrought-iron gates of Durrow Demesne and is sign-posted High Cross.

Nearest town: Tullamore, about 8km to the south

The Cross of the Scriptures in front of the cathedral at Clonmacnoise

Clonmacnoise is undoubtedly one of Ireland's most iconic historical sites. The monastery was founded by St Ciarán in the middle of the sixth century. Unlike many of the other early Irish saints, who often came from privileged families, Ciarán was the son of a craftsman, but despite his relatively humble origins, he soon gained a reputation for his intelligence and holiness. After completing his education, Ciarán became the founder of a small monastery on Hare Island in Lough Ree, before choosing the site of Clonmacnoise to establish another monastery.

This choice of location was incredibly shrewd. Though today it seems like a peaceful and somewhat isolated place, in the early medieval period Clonmacnoise was at the crossroads of the two major routeways of Ireland: the mighty River Shannon and the *Slí*

Teampall Finghin, Clonmacnoise

Mór (meaning 'The Great Way'), the roadway that traversed the country from east to west over glacial eskers, offering easy passage over the wetlands and bogs of the midlands. Clonmacnoise was also situated on the border of two of the great kingdoms of early medieval Ireland – Connacht to the west, and *Mide* (Meath) to the east – and the site prospered from its close relations to both of the ruling dynasties.

The earliest church at Clonmacnoise would have been built from wood, known at the time as a *dearthach* (Oak House), but as Clonmacnoise grew in power and prestige these small wooden churches were gradually replaced with grander buildings made from stone, often founded by kings and nobles. In 909 King Flann of Mide commissioned the construction of the cathedral and the beautiful

The fifteenth-century doorway into Clonmacnoise cathedral

high cross known as the Cross of the Scriptures. The cross now on display in the excellent visitor centre bears an inscription marking the event. Not to be outdone, over the centuries more ruling dynasties like the O'Melaghlins (kings of Meath) commissioned churches at Clonmacnoise. The monastery grew wealthy as rulers and nobles clamoured to be buried within the same hallowed ground as St Ciarán, as it was believed that the saint would ensure entry into Heaven.

The spectacular Romanesque doorway of the Nuns' Church, Clonmacnoise

At its height the monastery was surrounded by a large bustling settlement, with markets, craftsmen, labourers and farmworkers. It was surrounded by one of the largest early medieval populations outside of the Viking cities of Dublin, Waterford, Limerick and Cork. The growing wealth and reputation did not go unnoticed, and Clonmacnoise was raided a number of times, mostly by warriors from rival Irish kingdoms like Munster, and in 842 and 845 by the Vikings. As the fortunes of the once mighty kingdoms of Meath and Connacht waned following the Norman invasions, Clonmacnoise too gradually declined over the centuries. The Normans left their mark on the site by constructing Clonmacnoise Castle to ensure they controlled the strategically important crossing point of the Shannon. Despite Clonmacnoise having a brief period of resurgence, by the mid seventeenth century the site had been largely abandoned. Its isolation has left us with a wonderfully atmospheric site that is a marvellous place to explore.

When you have finished exploring the main site, follow the Pilgrim's Path for 400 metres or so to the Nuns' Church. The Annals record that the Nuns' Church was completed for Derbforgaill in 1167. It is in a field to the east of the main monastic complex and is one of the finest examples of Hiberno-Romanesque architecture in Ireland. Serpents, plants and highly stylised animal heads are all represented on the arches of the west portal and the chancel.

Today Clonmacnoise is under the auspices of the OPW, and a visit to the site should be on everyone's bucket list.

CLONMACNOISE   SITE MAP 4

Coordinates: Lat: 53.325747, Long: -7.986734

Grid reference: N 00913 30668

Opening times: Open all year round (except 25 and 26 December) Please see: www.heritageireland.ie/en/midlandseastcoast/ clonmacnoise

Entry fee: Please visit www.heritageireland.ie/en/midlands-eastcoast/ clonmacnoise/

Facilities: Visitor centre, audiovisual presentation, guided tours of site, tea rooms

Car parking: Large car park at site

Directions: To get to Clonmacnoise, take the M6 motorway towards Galway. Exit at Junction 7 (signed Clonmacnoise/Moate/R446). Join the R446 and continue for about 2.5km. Turn left and continue for 4km to reach the junction with the N62. Turn left onto the N62 and after 1km, bear right at the fork. This road will merge with the R444. Continue on the R444 for 7km. Turn right at the T-junction and the site will be directly in front of you.

Nearest town: Athlone, about 20km to the north, and Ballinasloe, 20km to the west

The ruined medieval church at Lemanaghan

St Manchán is believed to have founded a monastery in Lemanaghan in the seventh century. He was a monk from the nearby monastery of Clonmacnoise (Site 28). Clonmacnoise had been given the lands of Lemanaghan as a reward for their prayers on behalf of Diarmuid, who won a battle against Guaire, the King of Connacht. When visiting Lemanaghan today you will experience a vastly different landscape to how it appeared in medieval times. When the site was first founded, it was on an 'island' within the bog, but through agricultural intensification in relatively recent times, the landscape has changed utterly to one of green pastures.

Little remains to be seen of the earliest phases of the monastery, apart from some cross slabs and a bullaun stone that sits beside a holy well, which is also dedicated to St Manchán. The waters of the well were believed to have curative properties for all manner of ailments. You can also see a 'rag tree' beside the well.

The two churches we can see today are known as St Manchán's Church and St Manchán's House. The architecture of St Manchán's Church is thought to reflect two phases, the twelfth and fifteenth centuries. Today, little remains of St Manchán's House apart from

St Manchan's Shrine

its foundations; archaeologists believe that it also dates to the fifteenth century. Approximately 350 metres along a roughly paved trackway are the remains of St Mella's cell. She is believed to have been Manchán's mother, and local folklore states that the depressions and indentations visible along the stones of the togher were caused by her cow. Mella is said to have lived and worshipped in the cell as an anchorite.

The name Lemanaghan reflects Manchán's early monastery, as it derives from the Irish *Liath Mancháin*, meaning 'the grey land of Manchán'. Manchán died in 665 during the *Mortalitas Magna* or Great Plague. His remains were kept as sacred relics, and the site became a place for medieval pilgrimage on his feast day (24 January). In the twelfth century, Toirrdelbach Ua Conchobair, King of Connacht, had a beautiful shrine carved from yew wood and bronze in the shape of a miniature church. The Annals record that his son, Ruaidrí Ua Conchobair, had the shrine 'embroidered with gold ... in as good a style as a relic was ever covered'. The shrine is a truly breathtaking example of early medieval Irish craftsmanship and is well worth a visit. It is on display nearby in the parish church at Boher (an exact replica is on display in the National Museum of

Ireland, Kildare Street, Dublin). The church at Boher also has a number of beautiful stained-glass windows by the renowned artist Harry Clarke.

LEMANAGHAN SITE MAP 4

Coordinates: Lat: 53.292908, Long: -7.743641

Grid reference: N 17069 27000

Opening times: Open all year round

Entry fee: Free

Facilities: None

Car parking: Limited car parking beside the site

Directions: From Dublin/Galway, exit the M6 motorway at Junction 6 (Moate/Clara). Continue south on the R420 and after about 2.5km, turn right onto the L2018. Continue for about 5.6km. At the T-junction, turn left onto Station Road and then turn right onto the R436. After about 900 metres follow the road left to stay on the R436. Continue on this road for about 5km to Lemanaghan. The site will be on your left.

Nearest town: Ferbane, about 5km to the south-west

---

30 | BIRR CASTLE
COUNTY OFFALY

Standing sentinel over the charming Georgian town of Birr is the Gothic splendour of Birr Castle, seat of the Parsons family, Earls of Rosse since 1620. The story of the castle begins with a Norman motte and bailey, established here in the late twelfth century. The castle became the stronghold of the O'Carroll family, until it was purchased by the Ormond Butlers in the 1580s. In 1620 the castle (by then ruined) and its estates were granted to the Parsons family, and the medieval tower house was incorporated into a larger mansion by Sir Laurence Parsons.

The castle withstood two attacks in the seventeenth century: when it was besieged in 1641 during the Irish Confederacy Rebellion,

Above: Birr Castle

Right: The great telescope of Birr Castle, known as the 'Leviathan of Parsonstown'

and again in 1689 during the Williamite Wars. Throughout its long history, the castle has been added to, adapted and remodelled to suit the personality of the particular earl, with each descendant and their family leaving their mark on the estate.

It was during the nineteenth century that Birr and the Earls of Rosse became synonymous with science. William, third Earl of Rosse, was fascinated with astronomy. He became famed for his academic achievements and skills, and was President of the Royal Society. He had the largest telescope of the time constructed in the grounds of the castle, and it attracted visitors from all over the world to see what became known as the 'Leviathan of Parsonstown'. His wife Mary, Countess of Rosse, was a pioneering photographer, and remarkably her darkroom, complete with equipment and chemicals, still survives intact in the castle. The room remained untouched from 1908 until its rediscovery in 1983. The scientific spark was strong in the family: the youngest son of the third Earl, Sir Charles Parsons, invented the steam turbine, transforming shipping and the world forever. The superb Science Centre, housed in the castle grounds, details more of the story of science at Birr. The grounds themselves are a beautiful place to enjoy a walk, and are filled with

an abundance of rare plants and trees that were collected by the Earls of Rosse on their travels around the world. You can follow winding paths to lovely waterfalls, rivers and lakes.

The town of Birr grew in the shadow of the castle, and its development was also influenced by the various Earls of Rosse. Amongst the handsome Georgian buildings, echoes of an earlier age can be discovered, in the form of a large block of Carboniferous limestone known as the 'Birr Stone'. It was referred to as the *Umbilicus Hiberniae* ('the Navel of Ireland') by Giraldus Cambrensis, the Welsh cleric who accompanied the Normans during their invasion of Ireland. This stone is thought to have possibly been part of a megalithic tomb that was located nearby, though according to legend it marked a meeting place of the legendary warriors, the Fianna.

BIRR CASTLE   SITE MAP 4

Coordinates: Lat: 53.095772, Long: -7.914639

Grid reference: N 05742 05108

Opening times: Open all year round

Entry fee: Please visit www.birrcastle.com

Facilities: Tea rooms, toilets, visitor centre

Car parking: Paid parking available close to the castle

Directions: Birr Castle is located at the edge of the town of Birr and access to the Castle is off William Street. The castle is well sign-posted.

Nearest town: Located in the town of Birr

31 | DONAGHMORE WORKHOUSE AND AGRICULTURAL MUSEUM
COUNTY LAOIS

Donaghmore Workhouse

At Donaghmore, you can see the rooms of an Irish workhouse almost exactly as they appeared in the late 1800s. The Donaghmore Workhouse was built to house the most poverty-stricken people of County Laois. It was completed in 1853 and was paid for by a tax on local property owners. Workhouses like this were built right across Ireland under the Poor Law Relief system as part of the government's response to rural poverty.

People who entered the workhouse suffered shame and degradation. Once inside, they gave up their clothes and put on rough workhouse uniforms. Families were divided upon entry and were not allowed to stay together. Children from the age of two were taken from their mothers and sent to live with either the boys or girls, as there were separate dormitories for boys, girls, men and women.

Living conditions were harsh. Inmates slept on rough mattresses of straw, covered with rags. The only toilet facilities were large buckets in the centre of the dormitories. Inmates worked at tasks during the day, then ate their meals in total silence. Food was scanty and of poor quality, consisting of thin gruel and bread. Workhouses were often overcrowded, which meant that disease spread rapidly and deaths were commonplace. There is a graveyard behind the workhouse where inmates were buried.

By the time the Donaghmore Workhouse opened, many of the poorest of the area had already perished or emigrated in the wake of the Great Famine. The workhouse was probably operational for only a few years before it closed in 1886.

In the early 1920s, during the War of Independence, British forces used the buildings as a barracks, and you can still see graffiti left by the soldiers. In 1927, the Donaghmore Co-Operative Society established a creamery to assist farmers with the production and sale of butter. By the following year, it was producing 400,000 gallons of milk. Some of this history is reflected in the displays of agricultural machinery and implements that help to tell the story of life in rural Ireland.

In 1988 a committee was formed to develop the former workhouse as a museum. Part of the building was leased to the community as a place to inform visitors about the history of the area, with poignant stories of the harsh life inside an Irish workhouse.

32 | AGHABOE ABBEY
COUNTY LAOIS

Nestled in a low-lying area and surrounded by fertile fields are the ruins of the monastic site of Aghaboe. The name Aghaboe means 'Field of the Ox', probably a reflection of the quality of the surrounding pastureland.

St Canice founded a monastery here in 560. He positioned the monastery close to one of the great ancient highways of early medieval Ireland, the *Slí Dála*. This routeway connected many early medieval monasteries and led from Munster all the way to the Hill of Tara. By locating his monastery close to this routeway, Canice ensured that it was easily accessed by pilgrims and could benefit from connections and trade links with other monasteries and settlements along the route.

Feargal, also known as Vigilius, was another abbot of Aghaboe who rose to prominence in both Ireland and Europe. He became abbot of Aghaboe *c.* 730. He resigned this post in 739 and set off on the long pilgrimage to the Holy Land. He then travelled around Europe and befriended Pepin, the first Carolingian king, who helped to establish Feargal in Salzburg. Feargal's links with Salzburg were celebrated during the church's restoration: a plaque commemorates the visit in 1984 of the Bishop of Salzburg, who officially launched the conservation works, and a second plaque commemorates the visit of the Austrian ambassador, who visited the site when the works were completed.

As many monastic establishments became increasing wealthy in the eighth and ninth centuries, raids became a part of life for the monks living in these foundations. However, with the arrival of the Vikings, these raids became increasingly ferocious. There are a number of historical references documenting the plunder of the abbey by the Vikings in 845 and 913.

In 1052 a new church was constructed on the site of the monastery, to hold the relics of St Canice. This church has not survived, unfortunately, as fire swept through the site in 1116, and a new programme of building works began in the late twelfth century. During this time, Aghaboe was the seat of the bishopric of

The church of the Dominican friary at Aghaboe, County Laois

Aghaboe Abbey viewed from the south

Ossory (a region comprising parts of Laois and Kilkenny). All changed for Aghaboe when Felix O'Dullany, the last bishop there, was compelled by an order from Henry II in 1190 to move the bishopric, the seat of power, to Kilkenny, where the cathedral for the bishopric of Ossory still stands at St Canice's.

There is evidence of the more unsettled side of medieval life at Aghaboe in the steep-sloped grassy mound covered in trees in the field to the north, which is all that remains of a motte and bailey, an early Norman fortification. The motte was a man-made earthen mound, with a strong wooden tower constructed on top of it. It would have had a bailey positioned to one side. This was a raised platform surrounded by a large fence to protect livestock and stores. Motte and baileys were very effective defensive fortifications that were cheap and quick to construct. It is believed that the motte at Aghaboe was built by a Norman knight named de Hereford who had been granted the lands around Aghaboe.

By the thirteenth century, continental monastic orders had established themselves in Ireland, and an Augustinian priory was founded on the site of the early medieval monastery (where the Church of Ireland church is located today). In 1346, Dermot MacGillaPatrick, leader of the Irish tribes from the surrounding area, burned the priory and adjacent town. Thirteen years later, the MacGillaPatricks came back and took the castle located near the site from the English settlers and claimed the land around Aghaboe as their own. This was not the end for Aghaboe. Decades later, Fingin MacGillaPatrick (Lord of Ossory), invited the Dominican Order to establish a friary on the ruined early medieval monastic site, perhaps as an act of repentance for the desecration carried out by his kinsmen some forty years before. The Dominican friary at Aghaboe continued in use until the time of the Reformation. It was disestablished in 1540, and in 1586 a lease was issued to Daniel Kelly for the monastery at Aghaboe and cottages associated with it.

The Church of Ireland church that Kelly presided over was built on the site of the early medieval monastery and Augustinian priory around 1818, and has incorporated some features from the priory into the fabric of the building, such as the belfry. Above the main door are three stone heads that also belonged to the medieval abbey, along with a large stone baptismal font located in front of the door.

AGHABOE ABBEY   SITE MAP 4

Coordinates: Lat: 52.921920, Long: -7.514051

Grid reference: S 32674 85797

Opening times: Open all year round

Entry fee: Free

Facilities: None

Car parking: Small car park off the road to the side of the abbey

Directions: Coming from Dublin or Limerick, exit the M7 at Junction 21 and follow the signs for Borris-in-Ossory. Drive through Borris-in-Ossory on the R445. After the village, turn right onto the R434. Continue on the road through crossroads and over the railway line. The abbey will be on the right.

Nearest town: Portlaoise, 24km to the north, and Abbeyleix, 15km to the east

33 | HEYWOOD GARDENS
COUNTY LAOIS

The lake at Heywood Gardens, County Laois

Located just north of Ballinakill village in County Laois, Heywood Gardens is the site of two historic garden types: the great park created by Frederick Trench in the late 1700s and the small interlocked formal gardens created by Sir Edwin Lutyens and Gertrude Jekyll in the early 1900s.

After Trench built Heywood House in 1773, he landscaped the area between his house and the village of Ballinakill. Inspired by his Grand Tour of Europe, Trench moved hills, dug lakes, planted trees and built follies. His results were considered to be the most exquisite romantic landscape of their time. Trench himself was a noted architect and engineer and was a friend of renowned architect James Gandon. He named Heywood after his mother-in-law, Mary Heywood of County Tyrone. Heywood passed through various families in the nineteenth century, eventually coming into the possession of the Poe family. It welcomed many visitors, including the Empress Elizabeth of Austria in 1870.

In the early 1900s, Colonel Hutchenson-Poe hired the eminent architect Sir Edwin Lutyens to create formal gardens around Heywood House. Lutyens is considered one of the greatest British architects of all time, as he was responsible for architecture on a truly epic scale, including the design of New Delhi in India. The gardens

The castle folly at Heywood

were probably landscaped by Gertrude Jekyll, who faithfully worked to Lutyens' design. Like many aristocratic families, the Poes left Ireland following political independence, and the house was acquired by the Catholic Salesian Order in 1941. Unfortunately it was destroyed by fire in 1950 and demolished. After the demolition, a modern secondary school, Heywood Community College, was established on the land. Despite the loss of the house, the gardens survive and are among the best examples of Lutyens' work in Ireland.

The formal gardens contrast with breathtaking views of the landscape. A walk lined with pollarded lime trees leads to a formal terrace overlooking the surrounding countryside. Another terrace overlooks one of the lakes dug by Trench in the eighteenth century, where it is possible to spot moorhens, kingfishers and other waterbirds.

In the sunken garden, circular terraces descend to an elliptical pool, where small statues of turtles gaze inquisitively at the grand fountain. On the top level, a loggia, roofed with red tiles, includes an inscription taken from the writings of Alexander Pope. In the wall surrounding the garden, each circular window frames a spectacular view of the landscape so carefully constructed by Frederick Trench.

Heywood's sunken garden

Heywood is a lovely place for a summer stroll and is a short drive from the village of Ballinakill.

HEYWOOD GARDENS

Coordinates: Lat: 52.888316, Long: -7.308956

Grid reference: S 47030 81739

Opening times: Open all year round

Entry fee: Free

Facilities: None

Car parking: Large car park at the site

Directions: To find Heywood Gardens, exit at Junction 17 on the M7 (signed Portlaoise, Durrow, Abbeyleix), then take the N77 to Abbeyleix. In Abbeyleix, turn left onto the Ballinakill Road (R430). At the Y-junction continue onto the R432 and drive for around 3km until you reach the large gates of the estate. Turn left and the entrance to the gardens will be on the right.

Nearest town: Ballinakill, 1.4km to the south, and Abbeyleix, approx. 7km to the north

34 | TIMAHOE ROUND TOWER
COUNTY LAOIS

The imposing round tower at Timahoe in County Laois has to be one of the finest in Ireland. It stands on the site of a monastery, said to have been founded by St Mochua in the seventh century. The dwelling where the saint lived, *Teach Mochua,* gives its name to Timahoe. St Mochua was a warrior who converted to Christianity and became a hermit. One of the stories of Mochua tells that he had no worldly possessions apart from his psalter, a rooster, a mouse and a fly. The rooster kept the hour of matins for him so he never missed prayers, the mouse made sure he never slept more than three hours a night by licking his ears if he fell asleep while praying, and the fly would mark his position in the psalter so he never lost his place. When his three animal friends died, Mochua wrote of his sadness to his friend St Colmcille. Colmcille, somewhat bleakly, replied: 'My brother, marvel not that thy flock should have died, for misfortune ever waits upon wealth.'

The site is most famous for the round tower, which is thought to date from the early part of the twelfth century. It has the most ornate, Romanesque-style doorway of any round tower in Ireland, and on a bright morning, the wonderfully intricate carvings of interlacing chevrons and representations of human heads can be discerned. This doorway is positioned approximately 5 metres (16 ft) up from the ground level, with the tower itself standing almost 30 metres (98 ft) tall.

There are also the remains of a fifteenth-century Franciscan friary church. After the Dissolution of the Monasteries in the 1540s, the

Left: The nineteenth-century church and round tower at Timahoe

Facing page: Timahoe round tower

church and friary were converted into a defensive castle, though little of that survives today. The nineteenth-century Church of Ireland church next to the round tower is now the Timahoe Heritage Centre.

This is a wonderfully peaceful site to visit and is very easy to access. If visiting Timahoe, why not try the Rock of Dunamase (Site 35), which is located nearby to the north?

TIMAHOE ROUND TOWER SITE MAP 4

Coordinates: Lat: 52.960425, Long: -7.203308

Grid reference: S 53515 90247

Opening times: Open all year round. There is a heritage centre in the former Church of Ireland church on site, which is open from 11 a.m. to 2 p.m. weekdays and from noon to 3 p.m. at weekends.

Entry fee: Free entry to the site and heritage centre

Facilities: Toilets, coffee shop and exhibition in heritage centre

Car parking: Car park at the site

Directions: To get to Timahoe from Portlaoise, travel south on the R426 for about 5km. At the T-Junction, turn right onto the R425 and stay left to rejoin the R426. Continue on this road for about 4km to arrive at Timahoe.

Nearest town: Portlaoise, about 12km to the north

---

35 | THE ROCK OF DUNAMASE
COUNTY LAOIS

The once mighty fortress of the Rock of Dunamase is dramatically perched on top of a steep limestone outcrop that towers above the low-lying plains of Laois. The position of this site was first marked on a map by the Greek astronomer, mathematician and geographer Claudius Ptolemy in the second century AD. He labelled the site as Dunum, but no archaeological evidence dating to this early period has been discovered on the Rock. However, its extremely strategic position was always likely to have been a desirable location as there

The Rock of Dunamase

are commanding views across the landscape, and the steep slopes of the Rock would have been formidable natural defences.

The earliest evidence of a fort at the Rock of Dunamase dates to the early medieval period, and the remains of a drystone wall thought to date to this time can be found just north of the gatehouse on the site. During this early stage the site was known as *Dún Masc* and it is recorded in the Annals of Ireland that Vikings raided the site in 844. They managed to fight their way past the defences and murdered the abbot of Terryglass, who was seeking shelter inside the fort.

The site was refortified after the Norman invasions of Ireland that had begun in 1169. Dunamase was part of the dowry paid by the King of Leinster, Diarmait MacMurchada, when his daughter Aoife married Richard de Clare (Strongbow), the leader of the Norman invasions. He appointed Meiler FitzHenry to hold the castle, which was on the dangerous and unsettled borderland with powerful Gaelic Irish tribes. The famous chronicler Giraldus Cambrensis, who was a first-hand witness to the early days of the Norman invasion, described FitzHenry as 'a dark man with black, stern eyes and keen face … he was very strong, with a square chest … was high-spirited, proud, and brave to rashness.'

FitzHenry became highly disgruntled when Dunamase was given to William Marshal as part of the dowry Marshal received upon marrying de Clare's daughter, Isabella. Marshal continued the work begun by FitzHenry, and transformed Dunamase into a truly formidable fortress.

The view through the window of the Great Hall

The sun beginning to set on the Rock of Dunamase

The castle had a series of strong defensive features that made use of the unusual natural topography. The remains of the Outer Barbican appear as a large ditch that surrounds the base of the hill. It was originally roughly triangular in plan, and would have featured a strong wooden palisade and earthworks behind the ditches to form an impressive first line of defence. A barbican gate now stands isolated on the path, just above the remnants of a deep ditch. The gate has a number of defensive features, such as murder holes and a slot for a portcullis. It gave access into the Inner Barbican, where attackers would have to overcome steep ditches and tall stone walls.

The walls feature fighting platforms and wall-walks, from where archers could have rained arrows down upon the enemy. The twin-towered gatehouse gave access into the Lower Ward. This area had a number of buildings, including accommodation for the troops and essential facilities such as forges and blacksmiths' workshops to ensure the weapons and armour were well maintained. The Upper Ward was once separated from the Lower by a stone wall, which has since been demolished. The Upper Ward was the heart of the fortress, and housed the most important structure on the site: the Great Hall. From this vantage point you can enjoy stunning views over the rolling countryside of County Laois.

In the early fourteenth century Norman control in the midlands began to weaken and crumble under the relentless pressure of the local O'Mordha clan. The castle at the Rock of Dunamase was recorded as being burned in 1323, which must have severely weakened the defences. The O'Mordhas finally managed to seize Dunamase in 1330, but left the site unoccupied. The castle fell into disrepair and then much of the fortress was deliberately destroyed. This destruction is often attributed to Colonel Hewson, one of Oliver Cromwell's officers during his invasion of Ireland in the mid seventeenth century, although no records of this survive in Cromwell's accounts and the damage may have occurred much later.

The Rock of Dunamase was acquired in the eighteenth century by John Parnell (great-grandfather of the famous Charles Stewart Parnell). It had become fashionable during the eighteenth century to refurbish old romantic ruins to serve as picturesque settings for glamorous soirées and dinner parties. John Parnell took many features, such as the stone-lintelled doorway and the window mouldings, from other later medieval sites in the area and brought them up to decorate his hall at Dunamase. Originally the hall itself was a single-storey structure, with a two-storey solar added later. The work was never completed by Parnell and after his death the site continued to fall into disrepair.

Today the Rock of Dunamase is owned and maintained by the OPW, which has carried out excavations and conservation work to ensure the site's safety for the future. The Rock of Dunamase is one of the most atmospheric sites to visit in Ireland, with superb views across the landscape.

36 | EMO COURT
COUNTY LAOIS

Emo Court is a country villa designed by architect James Gandon (1743–1823), one of most celebrated architects to have worked in Ireland. He is best known for his great public buildings, including the Custom House and Four Courts in Dublin. With a demesne of over 4,500 hectares, Emo Court was the second-largest enclosed estate in Ireland after the Phoenix Park in Dublin. It recalls an era when the Anglo-Irish Ascendancy was at its height and the so-called Big House dominated the Irish rural landscape.

The house itself is a stunning example of the Neoclassical style, inspired by the architecture of ancient Greece and Rome, with its Ionic columns and large dome. Gandon designed Emo Court in 1790 for John Dawson, the first Earl of Portarlington. The Earl died during the 1798 Rebellion when he caught pneumonia while guarding French prisoners in County Mayo. As a result, the house

Emo Court, County Laois

remained incomplete. He was succeeded by his son, the second Earl, who carried out some work in the 1830s. During this phase the garden was completed and work commenced on the interior, but the Earl's financial difficulties prevented further progress. Starting in 1860, the third Earl oversaw building of the copper dome on the rotunda, as well as work on the interior and construction of a bachelor wing. Emo Court became the setting for many lavish social events during the second half of the nineteenth century.

When the Portarlingtons left Emo Court in 1920, the estate was sold to the Irish Land Commission and the house fell into decline. The Jesuit Order purchased the house in 1930 and used it as a seminary, ensuring that it did not fall into decay like similar houses around Ireland. The noted Jesuit photographer Fr Frank Browne, who took thousands of photos documenting Irish life, lived here from 1930 to 1957.

In 1969, the Order sold Emo Court to Major Cholmley-Harrison. He was a stockbroker who had served as a Royal Marine during the Second World War. He had previously owned Woodstown House in County Waterford but when he rented that house to Jacqueline Kennedy in 1967 it became the focus of unwanted media attention and he decided to look for a new residence. It is said that he stopped off to view Emo Court on his way to the Irish Derby at the Curragh and decided to purchase the house from the Jesuits for £40,000. He began the laborious process of restoring the house and its grounds, reinstating many of the important architectural features

Emo Court viewed from the grounds

of Emo Court, some of which had been put in storage by the Jesuits. He even found pieces of marble columns that had been dismantled by the Jesuits and scattered throughout the gardens. In 1994, Major Cholmley-Harrison donated the house and estate to the Irish people. He continued to live at Emo Court until his death in 2008. A cherry blossom has been planted in the grounds in his memory.

Today, Emo Court is managed by the OPW, and you can enjoy a guided tour of the building. At any time of year, Emo Court is a delightful place for a walk.

EMO COURT SITE MAP 4

Coordinates: Lat: 53.107817, Long: -7.198708

Grid reference: N 53668 06658

Opening times: The parklands are open all year round. The house is open from April to end September and access is by guided tour only.

Entry fee: Please visit www.heritageireland.ie/en/midlands-eastcoast/emocourt/

Facilities: Toilets, tea rooms (which are open every day from February to October and only at weekends from November to February), parklands and guided tours of the house.

Car parking: Large car park at site

Directions: Emo Court is located close to Portlaoise off the M7. Exit at junction 15 and follow signs for Emo Court.

Nearest town: Portlaoise, about 14km to the south-west

The twelfth-century church at Killeshin, County Laois

Killeshin was originally founded in the sixth century by St Dermot, but it was St Comhdan who became the patron of the site. Killeshin had a turbulent history with many accounts of raids by warring Irish tribes, particularly in the eleventh century. It was plundered and demolished in 1041, and it is recorded that Diarmuid, son of Mael na mBó, was responsible. He was lord of the tribe known as the Uí Chennselaigh, who were mortal enemies of the Uí Bairrche tribe that held the lands around Killeshin. It is reputed that Diarmuid tore down or 'broke' the oratory on the site, killed over 100 people and took hundreds more as slaves. More desecration was recorded in 1077, when the monastery was again raided and several yew trees were burned. This was a clear act of aggression and desecration as yew trees were often planted by monks to mark the sacred boundaries of monasteries.

The church that can be seen today is on the site of the broken oratory. It was built in the twelfth century in the Romanesque style. Killeshin is one of Ireland's finest examples of this style of architecture, which features rounded arches and highly decorated doorways. At Killeshin, the doorway is simply magnificent. There are four arches around the doorway, featuring carvings of chevrons, zigzags, animals and foliage designs. The capitals of the arches have human faces carved on them with different expressions and some even have beards. It has been suggested that use of shallow carvings and different-coloured stone indicates that this doorway was probably painted. There are also two inscriptions carved into the doorway. One is for Cellachan, who may have been the master stonemason or artist on the site; the other refers to Diarmait MacMurchada, the King of Leinster from around 1126 to 1171, who is credited with inviting the Normans into Ireland. It has been suggested that the boundary between the two warring tribes, the Uí Bairrche and Uí Chennselaigh, was incorporated into a new diocese in 1152, and this may have prompted Diarmait as king of the entire province to commission this masterpiece of Irish craftsmanship and continental design.

The chancel of the church, where the altar would have stood, was probably built years after the nave and doorway. The windows that

The Romanesque heads of the doorway at Killeshin

can be seen in the wall of the chancel are ogee-headed and this style was used around the fifteenth and sixteenth centuries. A round tower once stood to the north-west of the church, constructed probably in the tenth or eleventh century. The round tower was unfortunately pulled down in 1703 by the local landowner, Captain Wolseley. It is said that a local farmer was afraid masonry from the tower might fall on his cattle. The stone from the round tower was used to build houses in the locality. A medieval baptismal font can still be seen outside the wonderful doorway.

When the Anglo-Norman mercenaries came to Ireland to help Diarmait MacMurchada defeat his enemies, tracts of land throughout Leinster came into Anglo-Norman ownership. When Diarmait died shortly after the initial wave of Normans landed on the eastern shores of Ireland, their leader, Richard de Clare, became the Lord of Leinster and he granted the lands around Killeshin to a loyal knight named de Clahull. He constructed a motte and bailey, and later a castle, in a field across the road from the monastery at Killeshin. Today there is no visible trace of that castle, but a flat mound can still be made out in the field where it would have once stood. The monastery at Killeshin became a parish church after the Norman Conquest and it survived the Reformation, continuing in use up until the nineteenth century.

KILLESHIN SITE MAP 5

Coordinates: Lat: 52.847276, Long: -7.001748

Grid reference: S 67286 77825

Opening times: Open all year round

Entry fee: Free

Facilities: None

Car parking: Limited parking at the side of the site

Directions: Killeshin Church is located south of the R430. From Carlow take the R430 (known as the Castlecomer Road). Continue on this road for about 4km. At Killeshin village turn left, then take the next right and continue past the modern Roman Catholic church. The site will be on the right.

Nearest town: Carlow, about 5km to the south-east

Situated alongside the River Liffey within easy reach of Dublin, Castletown House in Celbridge, County Kildare, is one of Ireland's most spectacular landed estates. It was the palatial residence of William Conolly. Originally from Ballyshannon in County Donegal, Conolly was the son of a publican, but had a stratospheric rise through the ranks of Irish society to become one of the wealthiest and most powerful men in Ireland and Britain. He achieved this in the aftermath of the Williamite Wars that had ravaged Ireland in the late seventeenth century. In the wake of King William's victory, many Irish Catholic landowners were dispossessed of their lands and estates, which were then granted to King

William's Protestant supporters. This period became known as the Protestant Ascendancy. William Conolly had trained as a lawyer, and specialised in land transfers. Many who had been granted land immediately sought to sell it in order to make a fast profit. Conolly's shrewdness and legal expertise helped him acquire large tracts of land across Ireland, often at knock-down prices. He also improved his fortunes with his marriage in 1694 to Katherine Conyngham, the daughter of a prominent Williamite general, which brought with it a substantial dowry of £2,300. Conolly soon owned land in eight Irish counties along with estates in Wales. His properties brought him an annual rental income of £25,000, a massive sum at the time, equivalent to many millions in today's terms.

A view across the 'Long Lake' to Castletown House

Supported by his new wealth and his wife Katherine, William Conolly embarked on a political career, and was duly elected to the Irish Parliament for Donegal in 1692. He became a famous parliamentarian, and achieved the rank of Speaker in the Irish Parliament from 1715 to 1729, a role that became so synonymous with him that he was known as William 'Speaker' Conolly.

In 1707 William Conolly purchased his lands at Castletown. Construction of the mansion began in 1722 and the main part of the construction was completed by 1729, although the grand staircase was not installed until 1759–60. Its design was influenced

Castletown House

by the renowned Italian architect Alessandro Galilei, who met Conolly while visiting Ireland. The work was directed by the noted Irish architect Edward Lovett Pearce.

Unfortunately William Conolly did not have time to enjoy his beautiful house, as he died in 1729. His widow Katherine continued to live in the house and commissioned a number of spectacular follies (like the nearby Wonderful Barn and Conolly Folly) to keep local people employed during periods of hardship. Following Katherine's death in 1752, Conolly's nephew (also called William) inherited the estate. He died two years later and his son Thomas and his wife Lady Louisa came to inherit Castletown. Lady Louisa in particular left her mark and made a number of improvements to the house and gardens. Thomas Conolly was a member of Parliament and became an important figure in late eighteenth-century Irish politics.

A guided tour of the house is the best way to get a full appreciation of the architectural marvel that is Castletown. Notable features

The Conolly Folly, commissioned by Katherine Conolly

include the Long Gallery, a 24-metre (80-ft) room on the first floor that was used to entertain guests. Intricate decorative stucco plasterwork by the Lafranchini brothers adorns the house, while the staircase with its brass balustrades is another eye-catching feature. Castletown contains 100 rooms and 229 windows, and is set in 120 acres of beautiful landscaped grounds stretching down to the River Liffey. Its scale alone, quite apart from its design, makes it hugely impressive. As one eighteenth-century commentator remarked: 'This I believe to be the only house in Ireland to which the term "palace" can be applied.'

The house remained in the Conolly family until the 1960s, but when it was sold to property developers its future appeared uncertain. Fortunately, it was purchased by Desmond Guinness, of the famed brewing family, who led a project of restoration with the support of the Irish Georgian Society. The Castletown Foundation was established in 1979 and it was one of the key organisations (along with the Irish Georgian Society and OPW) that brought the

The avenue that leads to Celbridge

house back to its former glory. The house was transferred to the Irish state in 1994 and has since been maintained and conserved by the OPW. It is open to the public and there are daily guided tours from early March to the end of October.

Castletown is connected to the town of Celbridge by a long, tree-lined avenue. Celbridge is also packed with fascinating historical features and stories. It has strong connections with famous historical figures like the Conollys, Jonathan Swift, Henry Grattan and Arthur Guinness. The name Celbridge derives from the Irish *Cill Droichid*, meaning 'the Church of the Bridge', and there are references to this name in documents from the thirteenth century. As the name indicates, Celbridge originated as an ecclesiastical settlement. St Mochua is said to have founded a religious community here in the early seventh century. His church was probably located within the atmospheric historical graveyard of Tea Lane, just off Main Street.

Celbridge developed alongside Castletown House. The Conollys ensured that the buildings along the Main Street were constructed to the highest standards to give the town a pleasing aspect, and they sponsored many educational institutions in the town.

Celbridge became known as the Home of Georgian Ireland, but the history of the area spans the centuries and a visit to Castletown and Celbridge makes for a wonderful day out.

Coordinates: Lat: 53.349029, Long: -6.530481

Grid reference: N 99185 35428

Opening times: The parklands are open all year round and are free to access. Access to the house is by guided tour only and the house is open seasonally, usually from March to end of October. Please see www.castletown.ie for more information about opening times.

Entry fee: Please visit www.castletown.ie

Facilities: Toilets, cafe (similar opening times to the house)

Car parking: Large car park located just off the M4 motorway

Directions: To find Castletown House from Dublin, head west on the M4. Exit at Junction 6 (Celbridge West/Leixlip West/R449), signposted for Castletown House. Stay in the left-hand lane when exiting the motorway and bear left on the slip road. This will bring you to the new entrance to Castletown House (on the right) and to the car park. Alternatively, go to Celbridge and the original entrance to Castletown House is at the top of the Main Street. There is only pedestrian access through this entrance.

Nearest town: Castletown House is located at the edge of Celbridge and is 20km from Dublin

39 | MAYNOOTH CASTLE
COUNTY KILDARE

For over fifty years in the late fifteenth to the middle of the sixteenth century, Ireland was not ruled from Dublin but from Kildare, by the powerful Fitzgerald dynasty, based in their castle in Maynooth.

After the Norman invasions of Ireland, the land around Maynooth in Kildare that had formerly belonged to the O'Byrne family was granted by Richard de Clare (also known as Strongbow), the leader of the Norman forces, to Gerald Fitzmaurice Fitzgerald in 1176. Fitzgerald chose Maynooth to be his base. There are a number

The keep of Maynooth Castle

of architectural similarities between the keep (or donjon) of Maynooth and that of Trim Castle (Site 20). It is possible that there was sharing of knowledge, architects and builders between the two powerful medieval magnates, de Lacy and Fitzgerald.

By the end of the thirteenth century, the Fitzgeralds were one of the leading Anglo-Norman families in Ireland. Their profile was boosted considerably in 1316 when King Edward II raised John Fitzthomas Fitzgerald to the Earldom of Kildare for his services during Edward the Bruce's invasion of Ireland. However, it was in the late fifteenth century that the Fitzgeralds reached their apogee. Gerald Fitzgerald was trusted by King Henry VII to rule Ireland in his name. This brought huge wealth to Fitzgerald and it was noted that Maynooth Castle was richly decorated. His son (also called Gerald but known as Gearóid Óg) was Lord Deputy of Ireland for King Henry VIII three times (1513–34, 1524–28 and 1532–34).

He had unprecedented power in Ireland and jealously guarded his family's interests. Fitzgerald was summoned to London in 1534 by King Henry VIII, and left his son Thomas as deputy governor in his absence. Thomas was a flamboyant young hothead, known as Silken Thomas for the silk his men wove into their helmets. A false rumour spread that the Earl had been executed by the king, which enraged

Through the gateway of Maynooth Castle

The ruins of the Boyle Manor House

Silken Thomas. He charged into St Mary's Abbey, where the King's Council in Ireland were meeting, and threw down the sword of state in an act of defiance. He immediately began a campaign against the King's forces in Ireland. He had his men cut off the water supply to Dublin and laid siege to the city. The campaign was going well, until the Crown forces realised that Silken Thomas had neglected to defend his own stronghold of Maynooth. The English army under William Skeffington managed to negotiate their way into Maynooth Castle, but once inside they slaughtered many of the inhabitants. Silken Thomas heard of the bloodshed and marched to try and save his family home, but he was ambushed and captured on the way. He was brought in chains to London, where he heard that his father had actually died of natural causes and had not been executed. Thomas and his five uncles were brought to the place of execution in London, Tyburn, and executed by being hanged, drawn and quartered. The castle was thought to have been betrayed by Thomas's foster brother, Christopher Paris. The morning after Skeffington took the castle he offered his thanks to Christopher Paris and paid him for his services, but then ordered Paris to be beheaded, presumably because he had shown himself to be a duplicitous character who could not be trusted.

The execution of Silken Thomas and his uncles marked the effective end of the Fitzgerald ascendancy, and by the early seventeenth century Maynooth Castle had started to fall into disrepair. Richard Boyle, father of the famous scientist Robert Boyle, became the guardian of the young George Fitzgerald and became his father-in-law when George married Boyle's daughter, Joan. He spent large sums renovating Maynooth Castle and constructed a fashionable manor house on the site. As part of his works many of the original medieval domestic buildings were demolished. The castle suffered a number of sieges and attacks during the Catholic Confederacy Wars of the 1640s and was largely ruined. Squatters took over the castle and extorted money from travellers by charging a toll for using the path that runs through the castle, which was once the main Dublin-to-Galway road. The Fitzgeralds left their ancient family seat and eventually made the nearby Carton House their home.

Today, the castle is an OPW heritage site and you can still enjoy the lovely grounds and a trip around the imposing medieval keep. The lower levels have a number of panels that interpret the story of the castle and guided tours of the keep are available on request from May to the end of September.

MAYNOOTH CASTLE   SITE MAP 5

Coordinates: Lat: 53.380922, Long: -6.594493

Grid reference: N 93517 37669

Opening times: Open seasonally from mid May to end September. During those months the castle is open Wednesday to Sunday (and bank holidays)

Entry fee: Please visit www.heritageireland.ie/en/midlands-eastcoast/maynoothcastle/

Facilities: Toilets, exhibitions, guided tour of castle

Car parking: Car parking available in Maynooth

Directions: Maynooth Castle is located in the centre of Maynooth on Main Street

Nearest town: Kilcock, about 6km to the west

St Brigid's Cathedral, Kildare

Kildare is a town steeped in history, with origins that stretch into the distant past. Overlooking the Curragh to the south-east stands Dún Áilinne, the ceremonial home for a series of ancient Leinster kings. To the north-east lies the Hill of Allen – home to the legendary warriors of ancient Ireland, the Fianna. Through this countryside ran the *Slí Dála* – one of five roads that led to the Hill of Tara, which are said to have magically sprung up on the night of the birth of Conn of the Hundred Battles. However, it was with the arrival of a devout woman called Brigid that this area became famous throughout Ireland and the Christian world. Kildare's name derives from the Irish *Cill Dara,* meaning 'Church of the Oak' – specifically, the church founded here under an oak tree by St Brigid in *c.* 480 AD.

KILDARE

The high cross and round tower in Kildare

Over time, Kildare developed into a great monastery, a place where visitors and pilgrims were welcome and plentiful, and a place famed across Europe. All of this wealth did not go unnoticed, and the Vikings raided Kildare fifteen times from 835. Kildare was also attacked and raided at least thirty-eight times by Irish war bands.

In 1223 the Norman Bishop of Kildare, Ralph de Bristol, constructed a stone cathedral on the site of the original church of Brigid. By the mid seventeenth century, it was almost entirely in ruins, and was replaced in the nineteenth century by the grand neo-Gothic structure that we can visit today. Inside the cathedral there is an exhibition on the history of Brigid and Kildare, along with a number of medieval stone sculptures and tombs, such as that of Walter Wellesley, Bishop of Kildare, who died in 1539.

The cathedral has an impressive vaulted ceiling and beautiful stained glass. In the grounds are a twelfth-century high cross and one of the tallest round towers in Ireland. It is one of only two round towers in Ireland that visitors can climb to the top of to experience the views (the other is at St Canice's Cathedral in Kilkenny, Site 58). It dates to the early twelfth century and stands an impressive

33 metres (108 ft) tall, despite it missing its original conical roof. One of the other more unusual things to see in the cathedral grounds are the reconstructed foundations of St Brigid's Fire-House, where a sacred fire was kept burning until the mid thirteenth century.

The town was also an attractive base of operations for the Normans during their conquest of Ireland. Their leader, Richard de Clare, built an earth-and-timber fortification here. William Marshal transformed this into a great four-towered stone fortress, though unfortunately only one tower survives today.

Kildare also became famous through its associations with the mighty Fitzgerald dynasty, who were the de facto rulers of Ireland for almost a century in the fourteenth and fifteenth centuries. They enabled the three abbeys of Kildare to flourish. These abbeys were named after the colour of the habits worn by their monks or nuns. The Grey Abbey was a thirteenth-century Franciscan foundation, and the burial place of at least four Earls of Kildare. The White Abbey was a foundation of Carmelite nuns, established in 1290 by William de Vesci, and the Black Abbey was named after the black tunic emblazoned with a white cross worn by the soldier monks known as the Knights Hospitallers. The remains of their abbey can be seen at Tully, where you can also find St Brigid's Well and the Irish National Stud and Gardens. On the Market Square is Kildare town's Heritage Centre, housed within the old nineteenth-century Market House. The centre is full of information and a visit is highly recommended.

KILDARE   SITE MAP 5

Coordinates: Lat: 53.157161, Long: -6.910484

Grid reference: N 72779 12507

Opening times: Open all year round

Entry fee: Free

Facilities: Tourist information point at Kildare Town Heritage Centre

Car parking: Car parking throughout Kildare town

Directions: Kildare is located just off the M7 Cork–Dublin motorway. All sites in the town are within easy walking distance.

Nearest town: Newbridge, about 8km to the north

41 | OLD KILCULLEN
COUNTY KILDARE

The ruins of the round tower at Old Kilcullen

Old Kilcullen is, as its name implies, the original site of the settlement of Kilcullen. The hilltop was the site of an early medieval monastery believed to have been founded in the sixth century; however, hagiographic legend relates that the monastery was originally founded by St Patrick himself, who gave it to a bishop called Mac Táil. Mac Táil was one of Patrick's smiths or craftsmen, and indeed his name translates as 'Son of the Adze', an adze being an axe-like woodworking tool used by craftsmen of the time. He is depicted on the shaft of an early medieval high cross on the site happily using his adze to decapitate an enemy. Along with Mac Táil, it also depicts more conventional biblical scenes, like the Flight into Egypt and the Twelve Apostles.

A second cross, to the east, is taller, though unfortunately the shaft is too worn to make out any depictions. The base of a third high cross lies to the south of an eleventh-century round tower, which would have served as the bell tower for the monastery and a repository for valuable items. Its round-headed Romanesque doorway faces to the north. Although now in ruins and standing

13 metres (43 ft) high, it was in a good state of preservation until it was badly damaged during the 1798 Rebellion. It was here at Old Kilcullen that the rebels scored a notable victory in one of the early engagements of the uprising. Some 300 rebels assembled here on 24 May and used the walls of the graveyard to defend themselves when they were charged by a force of British cavalry. It seems the round tower suffered extensive damage during this skirmish; a sketch from the 1780s shows that it was in a much better state prior to the battle. The rebels were defeated in a subsequent battle and surrendered just a few days later.

A carving on the shaft of the high cross shows Mac Táil cheerfully decapitating his enemy

Just to the north-west of the graveyard, a round hill is visible, under a kilometre away. This is Dún Áilinne, one of Ireland's ancient royal sites (though sadly there is no access to the site today). This was a place of large assemblies, and is believed to have housed a palace and a fortress, with royal roads leading to it from different directions. Archaeological excavations during the 1960s and 1970s revealed evidence of palisade enclosures dating back to the Iron Age. At the centre of the site, archaeologists discovered a circular podium, which may have been a ceremonial inauguration place. It is perhaps no coincidence that the monastery at Old Kilcullen was located within sight of this ancient royal seat.

OLD KILCULLEN   SITE MAP 5

Coordinates: Lat: 53.107886, Long: -6.760830

Grid reference: N 82972 07075

Opening times: Open all year round

Entry fee: Free

Facilities: None

Car parking: Car parking at the site

Directions: From Kilcullen, travel south on the R418 for about 1km. At the crossroads turn left. The site is at the end of this road.

Nearest town: Kilcullen, about 3km to the north

Moone High Cross, County Kildare

In the small village of Moone in County Kildare you can find one of Ireland's historic treasures: the Moone High Cross. This remarkable piece of early medieval artistic craftsmanship is believed to date from around the eighth or early ninth century. It is sculpted from granite, and it is carved in a unique style. At over 5 metres (16 ft) tall, it is the second-tallest high cross in Ireland after the West Cross of Monasterboice (Site 5).

High crosses were built as symbols of ecclesiastical prestige but were also monastic boundary markers. Additionally, their detailed carvings were used for religious instruction with the symbols serving as visual aids and prompts to convey biblical stories to the largely illiterate population of the time. The top of the cross is ringed in a typical Irish style. It has a long square shaft and a large rectangular base with a truncated pyramid on top. The numerous figures that decorate this high cross are a marvel to study. The decoration consists of panels with scriptural scenes carved in false relief, such as the Crucifixion, Daniel in the Lion's Den, the Sacrifice of Isaac and the Flight into Egypt, as well as fantastical monsters like the one pictured below, which possibly depicts the Beast from the Book of Revelation.

In the sixth century, the monastery was dedicated to St Colmcille (also known as Columba). He is associated with numerous sites across Ireland and Scotland. Together with Patrick and Brigid, he is one of Ireland's most renowned saints. In the Martyrology of Donegal and the Book of Lismore, the monastic settlement here was called *Maoin Colum Cille* ('the Property of Colmcille'). It is from this

This strange creature may represent the Beast from the Book of Revelation

A depiction of a rather stoic Daniel in the Lion's Den on the Moone High Cross

that the name Moone is derived.

It is said that Christianity was originally brought to Moone by the Roman bishop Palladius, who arrived in Ireland before St Patrick. Later legends state that when Patrick set out to visit the Moone area, the local Laoighis tribe planned to ambush him because they considered him a heretic as his teachings differed from those of Palladius. Patrick was warned by a woman called Brígh and changed his route to avoid the attack. As he passed, he blessed Brígh and her brother Fionán and cursed Moone, saying no one born there would ever assume the rank of king or bishop.

The remarkable state of preservation of the cross, despite it being at least 1,200 years old, is due to the fact that it remained buried for several centuries. It was discovered in 1835 near the south-eastern wall of the abbey church. In fact, only the base and top of the cross were uncovered initially and it was re-erected in 1850 with the support of the Duke of Leinster. The shaft was unearthed later and the entire structure was reassembled in 1895. In the 1990s, it was placed inside the medieval church to provide protection from the elements.

Apart from the remarkable high cross, Moone contains portions of three other high crosses. Fragments of the head of a holed stone cross have been reassembled within the medieval church. The upper part of the shaft, the lower portion of the head and one arm of this cross can be viewed, and it is also possible to decipher carvings of some animals, including serpents, on the fragments. There are also interpretative drawings showing what this unique cross would have looked like in its original state. Within the graveyard, there are the bases of two more high crosses, one to the south of the church, the second to the east. Taken as a whole, the presence of these remarkable features points to the significance of Moone as an ecclesiastical centre over many centuries.

MOONE HIGH CROSS　　　　　　　　　　　　　SITE MAP 5

Coordinates: Lat: 52.979346, Long: -6.826105

Grid reference: S 78847 92678

Opening times: Open all year round

Entry fee: Free

Facilities: None

Car parking: Limited car parking at the site

Directions: Moone village is situated on the R448 road, which was formerly the main route between Dublin and Kilkenny. As you enter the village from the direction of Castledermot, turn left in the village centre and follow the signs to the High Cross. It is on a bad bend and it is easy to miss as the entrance is through a small stile (next to a green gate) in a high stone wall.

Nearest town: Athy, about 11km to the west

---

43 | CASTLEDERMOT
COUNTY KILDARE

Despite its relatively small size, Castledermot contains a wealth of history and heritage. It takes its name from St Dermot (also known as Diarmuid), who founded a monastery here in 812. The monastery was known as *Díseart Diarmada* or 'Dermot's Hermitage' and it has been suggested it was founded on the site of an even earlier hermitage dating back to around 600. Dermot was of royal lineage and descended from the kings of east Ulster. He was associated with the Culdee or *Céile Dé* movement that emerged in Ireland in the eighth century. These were hermitic monks who sought out isolated places to live and worship. Dermot died in 825 and his feast day is celebrated on 21 June. He was described as the 'teacher of religion for all Ireland'.

The annals record that Vikings raided the monastery at least twice in the century after its foundation and that it was burned in 1106. In spite of this turbulent history, evidence of this early monastic settlement can still be seen. The most prominent feature is the tenth-century round tower. Standing at 20 metres (65 ft) high and constructed of granite, it is unusual in a number of respects: its doorway is just slightly above ground level, unlike other round towers, which have doorways elevated well above the ground; the original conical cap was replaced by battlements in the eighteenth century; and it was built to the north of the monastic church rather than the west, as was the norm. St James's Church of Ireland church, to which the tower is now attached, was built at a much later date, though there are elements of the earlier church preserved in its structure.

As you enter the site, the base of an early medieval high cross can be seen on the right. Just beyond, the Romanesque arched doorway that formed part of the early church still stands. The Viking influence on Castledermot is indicated by the presence of a hogback stone. This is a carved grave marker or 'house of the dead' of Scandinavian origin, and Castledermot's is the only hogback grave in Ireland, though similar monuments are found in north Yorkshire and Northumbria. The unusual hogback shape is thought to represent the shape of a Viking longhouse. Although there is some decoration on the stone, it is not known whom the hogback commemorates.

Left: The hogback grave at Castledermot

Facing page: Castledermot's southern high cross

Close to the hogback is the southern high cross, which stands over 2 metres (6 ft) tall and dates from the ninth century. The carvings depict various scenes from the Bible. Moving along the south side of the church, there is a probable early Christian cross slab with a hole in it. It is known locally as the 'Swearing Stone' as people traditionally made agreements by shaking hands through the hole. The northern high cross is also thought to date from the late ninth or early tenth century and is carved from granite. Various Biblical scenes can be seen. The monastic site is located on the site of what is now St James's Church of Ireland on Church Lane, in the town.

To the south-west of the former monastic site are the ruins of the Franciscan friary on Abbey Street, which marks the next phase in the ecclesiastical development of the town. Castledermot came under the influence of the Normans following their invasion in 1169, when it was known as Tristeldermot. Walter de Riddlesford, a close ally of the Norman leader Strongbow, was granted the Manor of Castledermot and Kilkea following the Norman conquest. His descendants were influential in bringing the Franciscan Order to the town in the mid thirteenth century. In 1247, John Fitz Geoffrey, the Justiciar of Ireland, granted a sum for the construction of the nave-and-chancel church. This is the first part of the building you enter and it is the oldest part of the friary. It was constructed in the Gothic style, which was prevalent at the time.

In 1317, the friary was destroyed in a raid by the Scottish armies of Edward Bruce, who had invaded Ireland to open a second front during the wars between England and Scotland. It was rebuilt during the following decade and the transept, aisle and tower, which are to the north of the nave and chancel, were added by Thomas, second Earl of Kildare. The Gothic arched windows are the most impressive feature of this part of the building. A unique cadaver-style tomb, with a carved figure of Death on top, can be seen within the church, the only one of its type in County Kildare.

Castledermot was a significant walled settlement during this period and was situated on the main route from Dublin to Kilkenny. It was a market town, which explains why the walls were built (they protected and controlled access to the marketplace). Part of the wall is still visible and accessible on Carlowgate Street. It was also a centre of administration and law enforcement, and the earliest known Irish Parliament met in Castledermot on 18 June 1264.

CASTLEDERMOT SITE MAP 5

Coordinates: Lat: 52.910341, Long: -6.834959

Grid reference: S 78373 85019

Opening times: Open all year round. See notice on the friary gate for information about obtaining the key.

Entry fee: Free

Facilities: None

Car parking: Parking in town

Directions: Castledermot is located off Junction 4 on the M9 Dublin–Waterford motorway. After exiting the M9, follow the R448 north and turn left at the village. The abbey is on the left and the church and round tower is off the main street on your right.

Nearest town: Athy, 15km to the north-west

Russborough House, County Wicklow

44 | RUSSBOROUGH HOUSE
COUNTY WICKLOW

Russborough House is a superb example of Palladian architecture, and it has remained relatively unaltered since it was built in the middle of the eighteenth century. It was originally constructed for Joseph Leeson, who had inherited a substantial sum of money from his father, as well as a successful brewing business. He commissioned the eminent architect Richard Castle to design one of the finest mansions in Ireland. Castle had gained fame through his work on Powerscourt (Site 46), Carton House and Leinster House in Dublin.

As well as being beautiful externally, the interior of Russborough is also striking. It was the first house of this kind to use West Indian mahogany (which was usually ballast in ships and was sold off cheaply in Dublin but acted as a great replacement for the more expensive and rarer native woods). Leeson also had marble imported from Sicily, and commissioned marvellously detailed stucco work from the Lafranchini family, which took fifteen years to complete.

As work began on the construction, Leeson went on a 'Grand Tour' to find the finest art and treasures to fill his house. However, the ship bearing his treasures was captured by the French and never made it to Ireland. Undeterred, Joseph set sail again with his son and nephew to gather more fine works of art, statues and furniture.

Joseph became Earl of Milltown in 1763, and his descendants continued to collect fine art, until 1902 when Geraldine Evelyn Stanhope, wife of the sixth Lord Milltown, donated the contents of the house to the National Gallery in Dublin, where much of it is on display today in the Milltown Wing.

In 1931, Russborough House was sold to Captain Denis Daly, who sold it twenty years later to Sir Alfred Beit, who, like Joseph Leeson, was an avid collector of art. Sir Alfred and his wife, Lady Clementine, were immensely wealthy. The Beit family had earned their fortune through mining in Africa, and Sir Alfred's uncle had co-founded the famous De Beers Diamond Mining Company. The Beits' love of art began when Alfred's grandfather began collecting. He left the collection to his son Otto, who in turn left it, and the passion for art, to his son Alfred. He lined the walls of Russborough with works by masters such as Goya, Velázquez, Vermeer and Rubens. Unfortunately for the Beits, their collection had become internationally famous. Paintings were stolen from the house in 1974 and 1986; most were recovered, but in 1986 some were damaged beyond repair. In 1988 the Beits donated the majority of their collection to the National Gallery (on display in the Beit Wing). Russborough was broken into on two further occasions, but the paintings were recovered both times.

The Beits established the Alfred Beit Foundation that has managed the house since 1976. Sir Alfred died in Dublin in 1994 and Lady Beit continued to live on at Russborough until her death in 2005. Today Russborough is an enchanting place to visit. Along with the beautiful house and art you can also enjoy the gardens and parkland. The parkland surrounding Russborough was laid out in an eighteenth-century style and original demesne features still exist, such as a walled garden, ice house, lime kiln and grand entrance arch, as well as field obelisks and terracing.

RUSSBOROUGH HOUSE

SITE MAP 5

Coordinates: Lat: 53.141458, Long: -6.569238

Grid reference: N 95739 11034

Opening times: Russborough House is open March–December (10 a.m. – 5 p.m.). Tour times for the house vary during the winter months.

Entry fee: Please visit www.russborough.ie

Facilities: Guided tours of the house and gardens, maze, fairy trail, sheepdog demonstrations, 3D exhibition, tea rooms, gift shop, toilets

Car parking: Large car park at Russborough House

Directions: To find Russborough House from Dublin, take the N81 (Junction 11 off the M50), and continue heading south through Blessington. Continue to follow the N81 south for about 4km. Russborough will be on the right.

Nearest town: Blessington, about 4km to the north

45 | SEEFIN PASSAGE TOMB
COUNTY WICKLOW

The Neolithic passage tomb of Seefin stands on top of a 650-metre (2,133-ft) mountain in north Wicklow. This large stone cairn measures around 25 metres (82 ft) in diameter and 3 metres (10 ft) in height. A number of large kerbstones around the base of the tomb define its outer edge. The tomb has a passageway about 10 metres (33 ft) long and opens into a chamber with five compartments. There are two decorated stones at the entrance, though they can be extremely difficult to make out in less-than-perfect light.

The cairn of Seefin, County Wicklow

The tomb dates to the Neolithic period, making it approximately 5,000 years old. It is part of an upland cemetery of passage tombs that dot the mountaintops of Dublin and Wicklow. The peaks of these hills are all around 650–750 metres (2,133–2,460 ft) above sea level, making the construction of the tombs a difficult undertaking in the Neolithic period, despite the abundant supply of stone at the hilltops. Why would they have built these large and elaborate stone tombs up here? When you arrive at Seefin it immediately becomes apparent: the views are simply spectacular. The whole of south County Dublin and Wicklow opens up around

you, rolling hills, well-ordered fields and shining lakes all stitched together like a neat quilt. It is as if those who constructed the graves wanted to claim ownership of all they could see, and that by placing their ancestors far above the low-lying lands of the living, the shades of their forebears could watch over them from their tombs.

But who was buried at Seefin? The tomb was excavated by R. A. Macalister in 1931. He reported finding no artefacts and, stranger still, no human remains in the tomb. Perhaps the remains were removed

The entrance into Seefin tomb

in antiquity, by the descendants of the tribe (if they had migrated from the area they may have wanted their ancestors with them). Or perhaps in some remote period the grave was desecrated and all traces of those interred removed and destroyed. Or perhaps no one was buried at Seefin in the first place, and the tomb was merely a symbolic marker in the landscape. Perhaps more likely, the remains were there and Macalister missed them. In the future, an investigation of the unexcavated tomb of nearby Seefingan might provide the answer. It is possible to walk to Seefingan, a sister peak also crowned with a Neolithic passage tomb. It appears as a simple large cairn and is well worth the walk for even more spectacular views as Seefingan is about 100 metres higher above sea level. Simply follow the rough path to the north-east through the bog for 20 minutes or so to arrive at the tomb.

SEEFIN PASSAGE TOMB   SITE MAP 5

Coordinates: Lat: 53.186371, Long: -6.394968

Grid reference: O 07296 16294

Opening times: Open all year round

Entry fee: Free

Facilities: None

Car parking: Limited car parking at the side of the road

Directions: Seefin is in County Wicklow, roughly halfway between the Sally Gap and Manor Kilbride on the R759. From Dublin, take the N7 and exit onto the N81 at Citywest. Turn left onto the R759 and continue along this road. The turn-off for Seefin – a small lane – is on the left, immediately before the large entrance to the Kippure Estate and Kippure Bridge (turn here if you have missed the turn-off). Drive for a few minutes up this steep track. If you come to the fences and warning signs for the Army Rifle Range, you have gone too far; simply turn back and park in a handy lay-by. Be sure to approach Seefin from the south (as the Army range is to the north but is well marked by a fence and signs). Follow the track through the fir plantation. At a fallen fence where the path seems to disappear, cross to the left side of the fence and keep following the fence up. The total climb to the tomb on the summit is approx. 30 to 45 minutes. The views are wonderful. Good boots and appropriate waterproof clothing are essential.

Nearest town: Seefin is about 35km south of Dublin city centre

Powerscourt House viewed from Triton Lake

Powerscourt has a long and fascinating history. A medieval castle once stood on the site, owned by the Norman de Paor family, from whom the estate takes its name ('Paor's Court' became Powerscourt). The castle's strategic location commanded the nearby Dargle, Glencree and Glencullen Rivers. By the end of the fourteenth century, the powerful Gaelic-Irish O'Toole family were in possession of Powerscourt. The Wicklow Mountains had become a highly dangerous region for the English communities, and powerful families like the O'Tooles asserted their dominance and demanded protection money and tribute along the southern border of the Pale. In 1540, after centuries of conflict between the English forces and the O'Tooles, Turlough O'Toole was finally persuaded to make peace with the Crown. In exchange for recognition of the lands he had won, he pledged to obey the King's law, speak English, keep Powerscourt Castle in a good state, and clear ways through the forested mountains. Turlough was to encourage more farming by keeping arable lands in tillage and building houses for farmers. He was also to encourage his followers to adopt English and English dress, and not to harbour enemies of the Crown. However, just decades later, the O'Tooles were to have Powerscourt and their lands confiscated, following the disastrous Battle of Kinsale, where the O'Tooles once again took arms against the Crown.

Powerscourt and its lands were granted to Richard Wingfield, a favourite of Queen Elizabeth I. In 1618, when he was sixty-eight, Wingfield became the first Viscount of Powerscourt but the title died with him as he and his wife had no children, though the estate passed to his cousin Edward. When Cromwell invaded Ireland in the middle of the seventeenth century, Powerscourt was burned and partially levelled to prevent Cromwell's forces from using it as a base. Despite this, the Wingfields retained control of their lands. Their fortunes were uplifted when Folliot Wingfield married Elizabeth, eldest daughter of the wealthy Robert Boyle. Folliot went on to become Viscount Powerscourt of the second creation. Folliot and his wife Elizabeth rebuilt parts of the castle during their fifty-year marriage. They had no children so the title died once again, and the estate passed to a cousin who died shortly after inheritance. The estate then passed to his son, Richard Wingfield. It was this Richard who was responsible for the reconstruction of the house in the eighteenth century. He appointed the famous architect Richard Castle, who designed Leinster House and Russborough House (Site 44) and redesigned Carton House. The stately Palladian-style edifice was completed in 1741, with sixty-eight rooms.

Powerscourt was passed through the Wingfield family until 1961 when it was sold to the Slazenger family, who had become wealthy through sports and leisure products. They began a large programme of restoration and renovation but a large fire destroyed the house and most of its contents in 1974. The house remained roofless until 1996, when another large programme of works was begun to transform Powerscourt into the fine visitor attraction it is today.

The 'Pepperpot' Tower

The historic gardens of Powerscourt are world renowned, and have been voted third best in the world by *National Geographic* magazine. There were two main phases of development: the first began in the eighteenth century, at the same time that the house was being redesigned. The second phase of landscaping was carried out in the nineteenth century under the direction of architect Daniel Robertson. He was highly renowned and his work shows influence from Italianate garden design, in a number of beautiful terraces and the fountain in the lake, which is based on the famous fountain of Piazza Barberini in Rome. Robertson was said to be quite a character. He apparently suffered badly from gout, so he commanded the works from a wheelbarrow while clutching a bottle of sherry to fortify him. Works on the gardens of Powerscourt continued throughout the nineteenth century, with some of the iconic features, such as the Pepperpot Tower and Japanese Gardens being added.

Powerscourt is also home to Ireland's highest waterfall, which is 121 metres (nearly 400 ft) high. Powerscourt truly is an enchanting and captivating place.

POWERSCOURT HOUSE AND GARDENS SITE MAP 5

Coordinates: Lat: 53.18472, Long: -6.18694

Grid reference: O 21126 16416

Opening times: Powerscourt Gardens are open daily from 9.30 a.m. – 5.30 p.m. (the gardens close at dusk in winter)

Entry fee: Please visit www.powerscourt.com

Facilities: Gardens, waterfall, toilets, gift shops, tea rooms

Car parking: Large car park at the site

Directions: If travelling from Dublin city, take the N11 southbound (Wexford). After about 19km, exit at Junction 7 (signposted Bray south/Enniskerry/Powerscourt Gardens). Turn left at the roundabout and rejoin the N11 heading north. Take the first left for Enniskerry Village (Exit 6a). Continue to Enniskerry Village. Bear left at the clock tower in the village square and continue up the steep hill for about 600 metres. Powerscourt entrance is on the right-hand side, opposite the church entrance.

Nearest town: Dublin, approx. 20km to the north

Glendalough, County Wicklow

The name Glendalough comes from the Irish *Gleann Dá Loch*, or 'Valley of the Two Lakes'. The monastery was founded by St Kevin some time in the later part of the sixth century. St Kevin, or *Cóemhghein*, meaning 'fair begotten' or 'gentle one', is believed to have been the descendant of one of the ruling families in Leinster, the Dál Messin Corb. He wanted to worship God by living the harsh life of an ascetic hermit, and legend has it that on one occasion he prayed for so long while standing in the freezing waters of the Upper Lake at Glendalough, birds built nests in his outstretched hands and laid eggs there. Although the site Kevin chose to found his community at Glendalough appears wild and solitary, it is actually close to the Wicklow Gap, then a major trading route through the hills. This gave the growing Christian community a good balance between monastic isolation and easy access to the pilgrims who would have increased the wealth and significance of the site.

Above: St Kevin's Church at Glendalough
Facing page: Glendalough's round tower

The original churches and monastic buildings were constructed of timber so nothing survives of those above ground. Most of the structures you see now at Glendalough date to around the tenth to twelfth centuries. The most famous here are clustered near to the Lower Lake, only a very short stroll from the car park.

St Kevin's Church (also known as St Kevin's Kitchen because the belfry on the stone roof has the appearance of a chimney on an old-fashioned stove) is one of the most recognisable of Glendalough's buildings. It is thought to date to the middle part of the twelfth century. It is one of a very few stone vaulted and roofed churches in Ireland. Also in this area you can see the stone foundations of St Ciarán's Church and the large Cathedral. The Cathedral was constructed in several phases from the tenth to the thirteenth century. On entering the doorway, look at the remains of the chancel arch decorated with the chevrons and zigzags that are typical of Romanesque architecture and much-used in Irish churches of the twelfth century. Another good example of Romanesque decoration is the small chapel known as the Priest's House, just to the south of the Cathedral. Passing through the graveyard towards the round tower, you can see a number of gravestones dating from the eighteenth to the twentieth centuries in this beautifully scenic final resting place.

The round tower itself is one of the finest examples in Ireland. It stands over 30 metres (98 ft) tall, and is thought to have been

The Lower Lake at Glendalough

constructed *c*. 950. The conical cap forming the roof of the round tower was rebuilt in 1879 by a team including William Wilde, father of the famous Oscar Wilde. William was a noted antiquarian and was responsible for much of the renovation and restoration of Glendalough as well as a number of other ancient Irish sites. Nearby is the original medieval gateway to the site. Originally the monastic site was surrounded by an enclosing wall. One of the stones just inside the gateway is incised with a large cross: this marked the boundary of sanctuary. Sanctuary meant immunity from prosecution; by passing or touching the stone in the gatehouse any criminal or hunted person could gain a respite from his pursuers (unless, of course, the pursuers were Vikings, who didn't follow such niceties).

From here, go back the way you came, past the round tower and St Kevin's Kitchen, back over the wooden bridge and onto the Green Road. Follow this along, taking in the beautiful scenery and be sure to stop for a moment at the Lower Lake. The Lower Lake and Upper Lake were once a single large body of water that was fed by the Lugduff Brook. Over time sediments brought down by the brook from the surrounding hills built up and separated the two lakes. Continue along the Green Road and come to a small grove of trees

Reefert Church at Glendalough

where there is another small stone church, known as Reefert Church and which dates to the early twelfth century. The name comes from the Irish *Rig Fearta*, which translates as 'the Burial Place of Kings'.

A cave in the rock face above the Upper Lake is known as St Kevin's Bed, where, according to tradition, Kevin spent many days in prayerful isolation. The cave is thought to have been partially man-made sometime in the prehistoric period, perhaps as a Bronze Age tomb or an early mine. In the past no pilgrimage to Glendalough was complete without a visit to this cave, and even into the eighteenth century expectant mothers would make the arduous climb into the cave to seek protection during their pregnancy and childbirth.

Temple-na-Skellig (meaning 'Church of the Rock') is located nearby. This church dates from the twelfth century, and is likely to have been constructed on the site of an earlier wooden church. Archaeological excavations nearby revealed evidence of huts made from hazel wattle, suggesting that there could have been an early settlement here; it was perhaps the location for the earliest phase of the monastery. Unfortunately, there is currently no access to St Kevin's Bed or Temple-na-Skellig.

About a 10- to 15-minute walk along the R756, south-east of the main complex of Glendalough, is Trinity Church, another nave-and-chancel church that dates to the early twelfth century. This once had a small round tower until it was destroyed by a storm in 1818.

Further still is St Saviour's Church. This is thought to be the latest of the churches at Glendalough, and dates from the second half of the twelfth century. It has very Romanesque influences, such as the richly decorated chancel arch and east window, and was probably constructed under the direction of St Laurence O'Toole, Abbot of Glendalough and later the Archbishop of Dublin. The chancel arch consists of three sets of pillars with arches, all magnificently decorated with chevrons, heads and Hiberno-Romanesque designs, and represents some of the finest stone carvings at Glendalough. The adjoining building was possibly domestic quarters for the priors. To access St Saviour's Church from the visitor centre, cross the bridge to the Green Road, turn left and follow the path until you get to a signpost for the church to the left, pointing down towards the river. It is about a 15-minute walk from the visitor centre.

One of the hidden treasures of Glendalough is the field known as 'Seven Fonts'. There is a remarkable collection of bullaun stones

Bullaun stones at Seven Fonts, Glendalough

dotted throughout the field and a number are visible in the adjacent river. 'Bullaun' comes from the Irish word for 'bowl'. These hollowed stones are found at a number of sites around Ireland, often (though not always) in association with early medieval church sites. They are thought to have possibly served a number of roles, from being fonts of holy water, to a more practical role such as a large mortar for crushing herbs or cereals or even for crushing iron ore in metallurgy. Bullauns often have legends or folklore attached to them. It was believed that women who bathed their faces in water from the hollow of a bullaun stone would keep their looks forever, or that the water in the hollow had curative properties. To find Seven Fonts, head right when you exit the car park of the visitor centre and turn left onto the R756 (essentially doubling back on your tracks). Tucked in just behind the large road sign you can see an early medieval cross slab. Continue past this on the R756 heading north-west. After a 5-minute walk you will see a recessed gate into a field on the left-hand side of the road. This is the entry point to Seven Fonts. Please be aware this is private land so be sure to close all gates behind you and do not enter if livestock are present.

GLENDALOUGH SITE MAP 5

Coordinates: Lat: 53.010392, Long: -6.322632

Grid reference: T 12323 96911

Opening times: Open all year. Please see: www.heritageireland.ie/en/midlands-eastcoast/glendaloughvisitorcentre for specific opening hours

Entry fee: Please visit www.heritageireland.ie/en/midlands-eastcoast/glendaloughvisitorcentre/

Facilities: At the visitor centre there are toilets, an audiovisual exhibition and guided tours of the site

Car parking: Large car parks at the site

Directions: To get to Glendalough from Dublin, follow the M11 south and take the R755 exit towards Roundwood/Glendalough. Continue on the R755 for about 24km. As you enter Laragh, take a slight right onto the R756 and continue for about 1.7km. Bear left at the fork on the road to join the R757 and in approximately 200 metres the site will be on the left.

Nearest town: Dublin, approximately 51km to the north

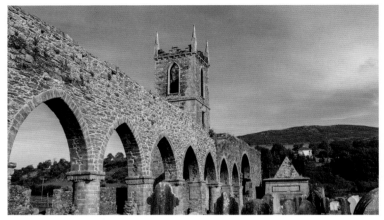

Baltinglass Abbey, County Wicklow

Baltinglass Abbey is located on the outskirts of the modern town of Baltinglass, near to the River Slaney in a valley in the Wicklow Mountains. This valley was a strategic point on an important route between north and south Leinster. This region has a long history, and there is evidence of high-status occupation at the hillfort of Rathcoran on nearby Baltinglass Hill.

The abbey was founded by the King of Leinster, Diarmait MacMurchada. Diarmait was an ambitious king and he endowed a number of abbeys and monastic foundations across Leinster, such as Killeshin in County Laois (Site 37), All Hallows Priory in Dublin, and St Mary's Abbey in Ferns, County Wexford. Diarmait is most remembered for inviting the Normans to Ireland to assist him in his wars against rival kings. Baltinglass Abbey was founded in 1148 for the Cistercian order, as a daughter house to Mellifont (Site 4).

The abbey would have once had a large range of domestic buildings where the large community of Cistercian monks lived, worked and worshipped, though little remains of the original monastery apart from the church. If you look closely at the capitals of some of the columns you can see fine Romanesque decoration. The tall crossing tower was originally inserted in the later medieval period, though it was reconstructed in the neo-Gothic style in 1815. Baltinglass Abbey was suppressed in 1536 during the Dissolution of the Monasteries under King Henry VIII. The eastern end of the church continued to be used as a Church of Ireland place of worship until 1883, when it was replaced by the church beside it.

One of the most interesting features of the abbey is the large, intricately decorated tomb slab. Translated, the Latin inscription reads: 'Here lies that noble and illustrious man, James Grace, formerly of Killerige, an inhabitant of Rathvilly, who, when living in the world, was both courageous in war and distinguished in hospitality; but now, being taken from among the living, he craves, of your charity, the support of your prayers. He died truly full of days, in the year of Our Lord's Incarnation 1605 on the 23rd day of February, in the 68th year of his age. May he rest in peace.'

The tomb of James Grace (d. 1605) in Baltinglass Abbey

BALTINGLASS ABBEY SITE MAP 5

Coordinates: Lat: 52.943677, Long: -6.710249

Grid reference: S 86690 88873

Opening times: Open all year round

Entry fee: Free

Facilities: None

Car parking: Small car park in front of the abbey

Directions: The abbey is located in Baltinglass. If travelling south on the N81, turn left after the bridge over the River Slaney and continue up Church Lane (a cul-de-sac). The abbey is at the end of the lane.

Nearest town: The abbey is located on the outskirts of Baltinglass

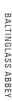

The rampart of the inner enclosure of Rathgall Hillfort, County Wicklow

The inner enclosure of Rathgall Hillfort

Rathgall Hillfort was a hilltop settlement that was enclosed and protected by four concentric ramparts made of stone and earth. The site overlooks the beautiful landscape of counties Wicklow and Carlow. The name Rathgall derives from *An Ráth Geal,* meaning 'The Bright Fort'.

The site has a very long history. Archaeological excavations carried out at Rathgall by Prof. Barry Raftery in the 1970s revealed that the site had its origins in the Bronze Age, as a small settlement was discovered on the southern slopes of the hill. Later in the Bronze Age, activity at Rathgall increased, and it appears to have become an important place of settlement, industry, ritual and ceremony.

A significant number of artefacts dating to this period were recovered during the excavation. These included bits of pottery, glass beads, bracelets made from lignite, and moulds for casting bronze weapons such as swords, spearheads, axe heads and possibly even a sickle. The most spectacular finds included a copper ring recovered from a pit that contained human remains, a bronze ring covered with gold foil, a biconical gold bead, and a bronze disc featuring mercury gilding. This is a skill thought not to be present in Ireland for nearly another thousand years, evidence that Rathgall was a significant workshop where exceptional craftspeople worked, producing large numbers of weapons and prestigious items.

The excavations revealed several cremated burials on site. A circular ditch enclosed a number of these cremations, dating to the Late Bronze Age. The three outer ramparts are thought to date from this period, around 1000 BC. The ramparts were constructed of earth and stone and enclosed a total area of approximately 18 acres. The innermost enclosure is a drystone construction and dates to the medieval period, showing that the site was a place of importance for millennia.

The presence of such high-status artefacts, weaponry production, habitation debris and cremations along with the position of the hillfort in a prominent location with great views around the surrounding landscape all imply that Rathgall was once a highly important site in the later Bronze Age, over 3,000 years ago.

RATHGALL HILLFORT SITE MAP 6

Coordinates: Lat: 52.802227, Long: -6.663133

Grid reference: S 90158 73191

Opening times: Open all year round

Entry fee: Free

Facilities: None

Car parking: Limited car parking available at the site

Directions: To get to Rathgall, travel east from Tullow on the R725. After about 2.8km, bear left at the fork in the road and continue on for another 2.5km. Rathgall will be on the right.

Nearest town: Tullow, 5.5km to the west

Carlow has a number of fascinating historical features to discover, and the excellent Carlow County Museum (located on College Street in the town) provides great insights into life in Carlow from its earliest phase to the twentieth century.

The once mighty Carlow Castle was established by William Marshal in the thirteenth century, on the site of an earlier Norman fort. The town of Carlow grew up in the shadow of the castle, and many of the streets reflect the medieval street pattern laid out by Marshal. The castle stood intact right up until 1814, when it was leased to a physician, Dr Phillip Parry Middleton, who intended to convert it into a mental asylum. He attempted to create more space

Carlow Castle

Browneshill Dolmen, County Carlow

by opening out the vaulted interior. Unfortunately, he used blasting powder to speed up the process and in doing so blew half the castle to smithereens, leaving the castle in its present precarious condition. Today you can walk around the base of the castle for free (access from Mill Lane off Castle Hill).

The early origins of Carlow can be seen in the incredible Browneshill Dolmen, located just a 10-minute drive east of Carlow on the R726. Browneshill is around 5,000 years old. It is Ireland's largest example of a portal tomb, and the massive capstone is thought to weigh well in excess of 100 tonnes. Originally the tomb would have been set in an earthen mound or stone cairn, with the burial chamber sheltered under the enormous capstone. The huge size and weight of the capstone must have required the cooperation of a large number of people to put it in position. They may have used the partially constructed earthen or stone mound as a ramp to heave the stone up, using log rollers to perch it on the stone supports. Browneshill is a marvel and a great place to consider the ingenuity of our Neolithic ancestors who created monuments like this over five millennia ago.

CARLOW   SITE MAP 6

Coordinates: Lat: 52.836261, Long: -6.936066

Grid reference: S 71668 76664

Opening times: Open all year round. See: www.carlowtourism.com for details about events and festivals that may be taking place in the town.

Entry fee: Free

Facilities: Toilets, tourist information point, county museum

Car parking: Parking in town

Directions: Carlow is in the south-east of Ireland and is located off Junction 5 on the M9 motorway from Dublin to Waterford.

Nearest town: Dublin, about 85km to the north-east, and Kilkenny, about 37km to the south-west

51 | DUCKETT'S GROVE
COUNTY CARLOW

Duckett's Grove, County Carlow

Duckett's Grove in County Carlow is an absolutely stunning example of Gothic Revival architecture. The building dates back to the eighteenth century, and it was the home of the Duckett family. They owned over 12,000 acres of land in County Carlow, and were one of the wealthiest and most pre-eminent families in the region.

Constructed in a flamboyant style as an expression of their wealth and taste, the building was expanded and altered regularly throughout the eighteenth, nineteenth and early twentieth centuries. The Ducketts were popular and enjoyed a long-standing reputation for generosity towards their estate workers.

Mrs Maria Duckett was the last inhabitant of Duckett's Grove. She abandoned the property around 1916. The vast estates surrounding the house were broken up by the Land Acts and distributed to a number of farmers. The building changed hands several times before it was destroyed in a fire in 1933. Today the site is a picturesque spot to visit and well worth a trip. Some of the gardens have been restored, and you can enjoy a tour of the site.

DUCKETT'S GROVE   SITE MAP 6

Coordinates: Lat: 52.857318, Long: -6.812443

Grid reference: S 79958 79163

Opening times: Open all year during daylight hours

Entry fee: Free

Facilities: Toilets and tea rooms (opens on selected days throughout the year)

Car parking: Large car park at site

Directions: Travelling from Carlow, take the R726 Hacketstown Road for about 10km to Killerig Crossroads. Turn left at this junction onto the R418 for 2.5km, then turn left again at the signed junction.

Nearest town: Carlow, about 12km to the west

---

52 | HAROLDSTOWN DOLMEN
COUNTY CARLOW

Haroldstown Dolmen in County Carlow is a stunning example of a portal tomb. Also known as dolmens, portal tombs generally date to the Neolithic period (4200–2400 BC, the time of the first farmers in Ireland). Typically they have huge capstones supported by a series of large upright stones set on end to create a chamber. They are most commonly found in lowland settings, such as near rivers or streams, and though the majority of portal tombs are located in the northern half of Ireland, there is a notable amount in the south-east and in

Haroldstown Dolmen, County Carlow

the west in counties Clare and Galway. Carlow has two particularly fine examples with Browneshill Dolmen (see p. 167) and this beautiful example at Haroldstown.

The portal tomb at Haroldstown consists of two massive and slightly tilted capstones, supported by ten vertical stones. There are suggestions that this tomb was used as a family home during the nineteenth century, as the gaps between the supporting stones were once plugged with turf and mud.

HAROLDSTOWN DOLMEN   SITE MAP 6

Coordinates: Lat: 52.845097, Long: -6.663922

Grid reference: S 89989 77890

Opening times: Open all year. Site is on private land – a working farm – so please be careful crossing the field and close all gates behind you.

Entry fee: Free

Facilities: None

Car parking: Very limited parking on the side of the road. Please do not block gates

Directions: From the M9, exit at Junction 4 (signed for Castledermot, Tullow, Carlow North) and take the R448 for 500m to the T-junction, where you turn right and head south on the R418. After 8km turn left onto the R726, and after 1.5km follow the road around the bend and continue onto the R727. At the junction with the N81, turn right and then immediately left back onto the R727. Continue on this road for nearly 4km and the site will be on your right after the bridge.

Nearest town: Carlow, about 20km to the west, and Tullow, about 8km to the south-west

Huntington Castle, County Carlow

Just off the main street of the charming Carlow village of Clonegal, you can discover Huntington Castle, still the home of the family whose ancestors constructed the castle centuries before.

Huntington Castle was first constructed by Sir Laurence Esmonde in 1625. Sir Laurence was an experienced soldier in the service of Elizabeth I, and later became major general of King James I's forces in Ireland, and governor of Duncannon Fort. He was rewarded for his loyal service with a peerage, becoming Lord Esmonde. He caused quite a family scandal when he married Ailish O'Flaherty, a devout Catholic and granddaughter of the pirate queen Gráinne Mhaol (Grace O'Malley, or Granuaile).

The dining room of Huntington Castle

Huntington Castle has continually changed and adapted over the centuries. In the 1680s the grandson of the original builder, also Sir Laurence, began to make the castle a more comfortable and fashionable family home, establishing the beautiful formal gardens. The gardens are a wonderfully tranquil place, from the striking formality of the lime-tree-lined avenue that leads to the castle, to the haunting line of English yews that drape their branches to create an atmospheric natural tunnel.

The castle was extensively altered in the 1860s by Alexander Durdin, whose uncle had married the Esmonde heiress. His daughter Helen inherited Huntington Castle in turn, and she married Herbert Robertson, giving the current name of the family: Durdin-Robertson. They further altered the castle, and their son, Manning Durdin-Robertson, an architect, also put his stamp on the building, leaving Huntington with a wonderful mixture of architectural styles and influences.

Inside the castle you can enjoy an engaging tour by one of the Durdin-Robertsons. The most unusual feature of the castle is undoubtedly the Temple of Isis in the basement. This eclectic spiritual centre, established in 1976, celebrates the role of the female aspect of divinity. It has become an established world religion, with thousands of devotees all around the world, making Huntington its Jerusalem.

HUNTINGTON CASTLE   SITE MAP 6

Coordinates: Lat: 52.690605, Long: -6.648866

Grid reference: S 91249 60769

Opening times: The house is open every day in June, July and August and at weekends in May and September. The gardens are open daily from 10 a.m. to 6 p.m. from May to September.

Entry fee: Please visit www.huntingtoncastle.com

Facilities: Toilets, gift shop, tea rooms, guided tours of castle, gardens

Car parking: Large car park at site

Directions: Travelling from Dublin/Kildare/Carlow, take the M7 south and exit at Junction 11 for the M9/Waterford. At Junction 5 take the N80 south and 5km after the village of Ballon, Huntington Castle is signposted to the left. Continue to Clonegal. Turn right and the entrance gates to the castle will be at the bottom of the village on the right.

Nearest town: Huntington Castle is located in the village of Clonegal and is 9km north of Bunclody

54 | BALLYMOON CASTLE
COUNTY CARLOW

Ballymoon is arguably the most mysterious castle in Ireland. It consists of a square-walled enclosure with all the rooms arranged around a central courtyard. The outer wall is well preserved and survives largely intact; however, the inner wall is much more fragmentary and only appears as isolated chunks of masonry. A series of garderobe towers survive in the outer wall, as do a number of defensive cruciform arrow loops, which would have been used to provide flanking fire along portions of the walls, though the castle lacks many of the defensive features usually found in a fortress of

Ballymoon Castle, County Carlow

The interior of Ballymoon Castle

this period. A large fireplace in the western wall shows the probable location of the great hall of the castle, and it is likely that the private chambers of the lord conjoined with the hall. What makes the castle so intriguing and unique is that not only does it have an extremely unusual design not seen elsewhere in Ireland or Britain, but that it appears to have been left unfinished.

Unfortunately there is no record of who built Ballymoon Castle or when, but it is thought to have been constructed in the late thirteenth or early fourteenth century, possibly by the Fifth Earl of

Norfolk, Roger Bigod. He died without an heir in 1306 and it is plausible that in the confusion of sorting out the succession to his estates all work ceased on the castle, never to be resumed. His lands in Carlow eventually passed to John Carew. Perhaps Carew decided the huge sums of money to complete the castle at Ballymoon were not economical or strategically worthwhile.

It is also likely that the changing political climate of the region played a key role in the abandonment of Ballymoon. The early fourteenth century was an extremely turbulent time for the Norman colonists. A series of devastating famines coincided with an upsurge in violence as the Gaelic Irish fought to recapture lands. Carlow and neighbouring Wicklow became something of a lawless frontier, and were subjected to raids and counter-raids throughout the early decades of the fourteenth century. The invasion of the Anglo-Norman colonies in Ireland by Edward Bruce in 1315 also caused devastation across the land. Perhaps in light of this hostile environment, the decision was made to abandon the costly and time-consuming work at Ballymoon.

BALLYMOON CASTLE SITE MAP 6

Coordinates: Lat: 52.700390, Long: -6.906835

Grid reference: S 73900 61565

Opening times: Open all year round. Please seek landowner's permission before entering fields. Be aware of livestock and please close fences and gates behind you.

Entry fee: None

Facilities: None

Car parking: There is a small area to park on the opposite side of the road from the castle. Please be aware that this is a busy road with traffic travelling at speed, so exercise caution.

Directions: From the M9, exit at Junction 6 (signed Carlow, Bagenalstown and Leighlinbridge). At the roundabout take the R448 and follow the signs for Bagenalstown (*Muine Bheag*), continuing on this road for 3km. In Leighlinbridge, turn left onto the Carlow road (R705) and continue on this road for over 5km to reach Bagenalstown (*Muine Bheag*). From here, travel east on the R724 for about 3km. Ballymoon Castle will be on the left.

Nearest town: Bagenalstown is about 3km west

55 | BALLYLOUGHAN CASTLE
COUNTY CARLOW

Ballyloughan Castle, County Carlow

Though today only the twin-towered gatehouse and a small stone hall are still visible, Ballyloughan Castle would have originally had a large walled rectangular courtyard, with the gatehouse in the centre of the southern wall. Though relatively small in size, the gatehouse of Ballyloughan Castle is considered to be one of the finest of its type in Ireland. The two towers offered protection, while the upper parts of the gatehouse served as accommodation. Archaeological excavations in the 1950s revealed that the castle was further protected by a moat, perhaps filled with water from a nearby lake, which gives the area its name: *Baile an Locháin*, or the 'townland of the little lake'.

Little is known of the castle's early history, though from its architectural design it is thought to have been constructed by an

Anglo-Norman lord some time around the thirteenth or early fourteenth century. By the end of the fourteenth century, Ballyloughan Castle, along with much of County Carlow, was under the control of the Gaelic-Irish Kavanagh family. The gatehouse appears to have been modified and converted in its later history to be more like the tower houses of the period. The Kavanaghs occupied the castle until the middle of the seventeenth century. Following the Cromwellian conquest, the lands around Ballyloughan were granted to John Beauchamp, who built the fine stone house on the hill north of the castle.

BALLYLOUGHAN CASTLE SITE MAP 6

Coordinates: Lat: 52.673950, Long: -6.896583

Grid reference: S 74520 58567

Opening times: Open all year round. Please seek landowner's permission before entering fields. Be aware of livestock and please close fences and gates behind you.

Entry fee: None

Facilities: None

Car parking: None, though a space near the gate is large enough to park in. Please try not to block the gate.

Directions: From the M9, exit at Junction 6 (signed Carlow, Bagenalstown and Leighlinbridge). At the roundabout take the R448 and follow the signs for Bagenalstown (*Muine Bheag*), continuing on this road for 3km. In Leighlinbridge, turn left onto the Carlow Road (R705) and continue on this road for over 5km where you will reach Bagenalstown (*Muine Bheag*). From here, travel east on the R724. At the fork in the road, keep right and continue on this road for a further 2km. Take the third right off this road and continue straight for a couple of kilometres. Ballyloughan is in a field to the right. You will see a number of signposts for the castle along the route.

Nearest town: Bagenalstown, 7km to the north-west

The oratory of St Mullin's

Overlooking the Barrow Valley in County Carlow, the small village of St Mullin's has a wonderful array of medieval monuments: the foundations of a round tower, a high cross, a number of churches, a holy well and a mill, along with a fine example of a Norman motte and bailey.

The name St Mullin's comes from the Irish *Teach Moling*, meaning 'the Church of Moling'. St Moling founded the original monastery here in the seventh century, and is thought to be buried on the site. The monastery gained a reputation as a place of learning, and the eighth-century Book of Moling (now housed in Trinity College Dublin) was compiled here. The story of Moling is entwined with that of his monastery. He is credited with establishing one of Ireland's first mills at the monastery, and according to legend he dug the deep mill race with his own hands. He is also credited with the introduction of rye to Ireland. He also carried out baptisms at the holy well nearby (visible in a field to the north). The well became an important place for pilgrimage. According to the *Bethada Náem nÉrenn* (Lives of the Saints), 'in September and October, 1348, many

The large motte just outside the monastic site

thousands assembled at St Mullin's to wade in the water from fear of the plague that had begun to affect Ireland.' The well is the focus of pilgrimage to this day with the annual Pattern day usually held the Sunday before 25 July.

From its foundation the site quickly grew in importance and status, and became closely associated with the other great monasteries of Glendalough and Ferns. In the twelfth century the monastery was wholly under the control of the Augustinian abbey at Ferns. Many kings of Leinster were buried in the graveyard, and a nineteenth-century mausoleum of the MacMurrough Kavanaghs indicates that the family continued to be buried in the same hallowed ground as their royal ancestors.

At the start of the thirteenth century, following the Norman invasion of Ireland, the lands of St Mullin's were granted to William de Carew, who built the large motte and bailey adjacent to the monastery. He chose the site as St Mullin's was in a strategic location overlooking the Barrow Valley. There is more information about St Mullin's in the Church of Ireland church, which now serves as a heritage centre.

57 | ST MARY'S CHURCH
COUNTY KILKENNY

St Mary's Church (officially named the Church of the Assumption of the Blessed Virgin) is home to one of Ireland's finest collections of medieval sculpture. It stands in the town of Gowran in County Kilkenny. Gowran takes its name from *Bealach Gabhráin*, the ancient routeway into the kingdom of Ossory. The town of Gowran was founded after 1185, when Theobald Walter, patriarch of the powerful Butler family, was granted the land by Prince John. The Butlers would go on to become the pre-eminent power in County Kilkenny and the south-east of Ireland, and were the key patrons of

St Mary's Church in Gowran, County Kilkenny

St Mary's. In 1312, Edmund Butler founded a college of four priests to serve in the church.

St Mary's became the family's main place of burial, and even after the Butlers moved into Kilkenny Castle in 1391 they continued to be laid to rest here up until the sixteenth century. Several members of the Butler family are interred within the church in beautifully ornate tombs. The chancel of the church also houses a wonderful collection of grave slabs, effigies and other sepulchral sculpture. These tombs give insights into medieval fashion as well as ritual belief. One of the oldest effigies is that of Radoulfus, a rector of Gowran who died in 1253. He is depicted in priestly vestments. Other notable effigies include that of James Butler (first Earl of Ormond) and his wife, and the early fifteenth-century tomb of Sadhbh Mac Murrough Kavanagh who was the wife of James MacEdmond MacRichard Butler. She is dressed in the finery of a medieval noblewoman, with a horned headdress, a long pleated gown with a girdle, and a pendant decorated with flowers and the letter 'S'.

These sixteenth-century Butler tombs may have been commissioned by her son, Piers Rua Butler, the eighth Earl of Ormond. Theirs was a minor branch of the Butler family but by thus commemorating his mother, father and two older brothers (who predeceased him), Piers Rua strengthened his claim to the overlordship.

One of the interesting wall plaques from the seventeenth century was erected by James Kelly, and it commemorates him and his two wives. It dates to 1646 and has the following inscription: 'Both wives alive at once he could not have, Both to enjoy at once he made this grave.' Many other memorials can be seen inside the chancel, like the fine eighteenth-century tombs dedicated to the Agar family, and the poignant stained-glass window that commemorates Aubrey Cecil White, who died at the Battle of the Somme in 1916.

Sculpture of a human head, thought to be the work of the 'Gowran Master'

Outside in the nave is an impressive array of carved human heads located on capitals and stops for hood mouldings. It is thought that these heads or masks were the work of a highly skilled mason known as the 'Gowran Master' who also worked on St Canice's and Thomastown Church.

During the fourteenth and fifteenth centuries Gowran became increasingly vulnerable as it was located in the border territories between Anglo-Norman and Gaelic Irish controlled areas. It was raided a number of times, and in the 1420s restoration works were carried out to repair the church, with the Pope offering indulgences to anyone who assisted the fundraising to carry out the repairs. Despite this unsettled period the Butlers remained in control of Gowran until the Cromwellian confiscations. The church passed through a number of owners until it was purchased by James Agar in the early eighteenth century. The medieval chancel remained in use until 1826, but was then demolished and rebuilt to the design of architect William Robertson. The ruined nave was in state care for many years. When the chancel was deconsecrated in the 1970s it too was acquired by the state and has since been restored. Today St Mary's is an OPW visitor centre, an ideal place to discover the craftsmanship of medieval Ireland.

ST MARY'S CHURCH SITE MAP 6

Coordinates: Lat: 52.629056, Long: -7.065168

Grid reference: S 63305 53477

Opening times: Open from end May to the start of September daily (10.30 a.m. – 5 p.m.). Last admission 45 minutes before closing.

Entry fee: Free

Facilities: Toilets

Car parking: Car parking on street in front of the church

Directions: St Mary's Church is located in the centre of Gowran. The town is located on the R448 between Paulstown (to the north) and Thomastown (to the south). If travelling from Dublin on the M9, exit at Junction 7 (signed Thomastown, Gowran, Paulstown), and then head south on the R448.

Nearest town: Kilkenny, 13km to the west, and Thomastown, 13km to the south

58 | KILKENNY
COUNTY KILKENNY

Kilkenny takes its name from *Cill Cainnigh*, meaning the 'Church of Cainnech'. St Canice (Cainnech) was a sixth-century monk who came from County Derry. The sites most associated with him were Aghaboe Abbey in County Laois (Site 32) and the monastic site here in Kilkenny. The earliest visible trace of an early medieval monastic foundation can be seen at St Canice's Cathedral in the well-preserved round tower. Despite being built on precariously shallow foundations, the tower stands approximately 30 metres (99 ft) tall and is over 1,000 years old. Along with the tower at St Brigid's Cathedral, Kildare (Site 40), this is one of only two round towers in Ireland that can still be climbed. The cathedral we see today largely

A true Kilkenny Cat leads the way inside St Canice's Cathedral

dates to the thirteenth century, although it was extensively renovated throughout its history. Construction of the cathedral began *c.* 1202, under the patronage of the powerful Ango-Norman magnate William Marshal (who was also responsible for the construction of Kilkenny Castle and the Black Abbey in Kilkenny, amongst many other towns, castles, cathedrals and churches).

Throughout the medieval period the cathedral was expanded, altered and redeveloped. Inside the cathedral you can experience one of Ireland's most evocative and atmospheric medieval buildings. St Canice's is home to a fascinating collection of medieval tombs and effigies. These tombs house the remains of powerful and wealthy members of high society in Kilkenny. Many of the men are depicted in full armour, and have dogs lying at their feet, symbolising their loyalty and fidelity. The tombs also provide

Tomb effigy of Honorina Grace (d. 1596)

glimpses into late medieval fashion, as many of the women are depicted with elaborate headdresses and gowns. One the more prominent tombs in the cathedral is that of Bishop Ledrede. He was infamous for his part in the trial of Dame Alice Kyteler, a wealthy and well-educated woman in Kilkenny society. She married four times, with each husband dying somewhat conveniently, and each death increasing her wealth. An accusation of witchcraft was made against her, along with her maid Petronilla and her son William Outlaw. Bishop Ledrede presided over the trial. Dame Alice managed to escape to England but Petronilla was burned at the stake. William Outlaw was sentenced to do penance of attending three masses per day for a year, feeding paupers and re-covering the cathedral roof with lead. Four years after William had completed work on the roof, it mysteriously collapsed. There is also the grave slab of Alice Kyteler's father. It was found in 1894,under the pavement outside Dame Alice's former home (now Kyteler's Inn on St Kieran Street).

The Black Abbey is located close to St Canice's. It is believed to have been founded for the Dominican Order by William Marshal in c. 1235. The Black Abbey takes its name from the black habits worn by the Dominican monks. The abbey is still used as a parish church by the local community, and retains many of its medieval features, along with beautiful stained-glass windows.

Further down Parliament Street is the handsome Rothe House, a superb example of a wealthy merchant's town house. It was built between 1594 and 1610 by the influential merchant John Rothe Fitz-Piers. Rothe actually built three houses one behind the other to

Rothe House in Kilkenny

provide increased space and luxury for his growing family, with the oldest at the front facing onto the street and the most recent (built in 1610) at the back. The charming gardens of the house faithfully reconstruct a typical seventeenth-century garden, with vegetables, herbs and plants that would have been familiar to the original occupants. Today Rothe House is owned by the Kilkenny Archaeological Society and houses their extensive collection of artefacts. It is an excellent place to visit to get a sense of everyday life in medieval Kilkenny.

Across the road from Rothe House is the Smithwick's Experience, which tells the story behind one of Ireland's oldest and best ales. The brewery was founded by John Smithwick in 1710. The ale is now brewed in St James's Gate in Dublin, while the old brewery in Kilkenny has been turned into an entertaining visitor attraction. The ruins of a medieval Franciscan abbey founded by Richard Marshal (son of William) stand in the grounds of the old brewery. The monks were the first to brew ale on the site during the medieval period. One of the friars of this abbey was John Clyn. He documented the harrowing and almost apocalyptic days of the outbreak of the Black Death in Kilkenny in the mid fourteenth century. His final entry in 1349 reads:

Kilkenny Castle

So that notable deeds should not perish with time, and be lost from the memory of future generations, I, seeing these many ills, and that the whole world encompassed by evil, waiting among the dead for death to come, have committed to writing what I have truly heard and examined; and so that the writing does not perish with the writer, or the work fail with the workman, I leave parchment for continuing the work, in case anyone should still be alive in the future and any son of Adam can escape this pestilence and continue the work thus begun.

At this point the narrative ends with a note written in a different hand: 'here it seems the author died.'

Further along, Parliament Street splits into St Kieran Street and High Street, and it is possible to gain a sense of the development of the medieval streetscape, especially from the small alleys that join the two streets together (known as 'slips'). Continue onto the Parade, where the edifice of Kilkenny Castle comes into full view. Kilkenny Castle was built by William Marshal in the early thirteenth century on the site of an earlier Norman fortification. The castle was originally designed as a large trapezoidal block with four large corner towers; one tower and a wing of the castle have long since been demolished. In 1391, the castle became the main seat of the Butler family and it remained in the family until it was sold to the state in 1967 for the nominal fee of £50. During its long history the castle was steadily transformed from a medieval fortress into an elegant baronial-style mansion. The splendid castle gateway that now forms the main entrance was constructed in the early 1680s. The design was influenced by the architecture of the classical triumphal arch. The castle was modified and refashioned in the late seventeenth to nineteenth centuries. Today the interior reflects the tastes and fashions of the late nineteenth and early twentieth centuries. The castle is a fascinating place to visit with beautiful grounds. Directly across the Parade from Kilkenny Castle is the Kilkenny Design Centre and the Butler House and Garden.

Kilkenny is one of Ireland's most charming heritage towns, with many more medieval and historic buildings to discover. Other notable places include St Mary's Cathedral on James's Street. This grand cathedral was built by 1857. Its beautiful apse has recently been restored and it is a breathtaking sight. St Mary's Church and St John's Priory give more insights into Christianity in medieval Kilkenny, and the fragmentary remains of the town walls can still be seen. You can find out more about Kilkenny from the tourist information office, located inside the Shee Almshouse that was built in 1582.

KILKENNY SITE MAP 6

Coordinates: Lat: 52.650700, Long: -7.251823

Grid reference: S 50799 55682

Opening times: Open all year. Kilkenny Castle, St Canice's and Rothe House are open daily – see:
www.heritageireland.ie/en/kilkennycastle
www.stcanicescathedral.ie and www.rothehouse.com for more information about specific opening hours.

Entry fee: Entry fees are charged at Kilkenny Castle, St Canice's Cathedral and Rothe House

Facilities: Tourist information point, coffee shops, toilets located throughout Kilkenny

Car parking: Paid parking available at various locations in the city

Directions: Kilkenny is located just off the M9 Dublin–Waterford motorway. All sites in the city are within walking distance.

Nearest town: Carlow, about 40km to the north

Dunmore Cave is approximately 11km north of Kilkenny city, near the town of Castlecomer. The cave contains around 300 metres (984 ft) of known passages and caverns. In terms of geology, it is a rare example of a cave formed directly by glacial meltwaters. Although not a particularly large cave system, Dunmore has a number of great examples of calcite formations, such as stalagmites and stalactites. However, the cave's interest comes not just from its geology but its dark history.

Located in the north of County Kilkenny, in the ancient Irish kingdom of Ossory, Dunmore Cave was situated right in the middle of a disputed territory between the Viking powerbases of Dublin, Waterford and Limerick. The Vikings of Ireland were not one people with a united ambition and government, but were instead rival powers who regularly came into conflict with each other. The cave at Dunmore has a chilling story to tell. The Annals of the Four Masters record that over 1,000 people were massacred here in 928 AD. Vikings from Dublin were en route to attack rival Vikings at Waterford. They raided the surrounding land and discovered a large number of people (mainly women and children) hiding in the cave at Dunmore. In an attempt to drive them from the cave, they lit large fires, hoping to smoke out those in hiding in order to capture them and sell them in the slave markets. However, the fires were too large and burned all the oxygen in the deep cave, so many suffocated to death. Antiquarians in the eighteenth and nineteenth centuries collected large quantities of human remains from within the cave, presumably those of the people massacred in that raid.

It appears that some Vikings returned to the site later to conceal their wealth. In 1999, a small hoard of treasure was discovered in a cleft deep in the cave. The hoard was dated to 970 and consisted of silver ingots and conical buttons woven from fine silver. These precious objects were found with a luxurious silk garment. The dye that coloured the garment purple was reserved for the highest-ranking members of society, and it was derived from the purple murex snail that can only be found on the north coast of Africa, evidence of the

Inside Dunmore Cave

vast trading network of the Vikings. Perhaps the owner of the hoard concealed it here, hoping that the cave's dark reputation would keep it from prying eyes, but they were never able to return to retrieve it. It is also possible that they left it as an offering to chthonic (subterranean) gods or spirits.

Today Dunmore Cave is a rewarding place to visit, with a fine visitor centre.

DUNMORE CAVE   SITE MAP 6

Coordinates: Lat: 52.734092, Long: -7.247489

Grid reference: S 50869 65024

Opening times: The caves are open all year. Please see: www.heritageireland.ie/en/south-east/dunmorecave for specific opening hours.

Entry fee: Please visit www.heritageireland.ie/en/south-east/dunmorecave/

Facilities: Toilets, audiovisual presentation and exhibition area

Car parking: Available

Directions: To get to the caves, travel towards Castlecomer on the N77 and continue onto the N78. Turn right at the signpost for the caves and turn right again after about 900 metres. The site will be directly in front.

Nearest town: Kilkenny, about 10km to the south

The steps down to the entrance of the Dunmore Cave

The winter solstice sun begins to set over the hills opposite the ancient tomb of Knockroe

60 | KNOCKROE PASSAGE TOMB
COUNTY KILKENNY

Knockroe Passage Tomb is located in a picturesque setting on the slopes above the Lingaun River and old slate quarries, which were abandoned in the early twentieth century. The site dates to around 3000 BC and has many similarities with the far more famous examples at Newgrange and Knowth in the Brú na Bóinne complex in County Meath (Site 25).

Originally Knockroe would have been a similar tomb to Newgrange, albeit on a considerably smaller scale, and would have had an earthen mound surrounded by large kerbstones. Knockroe has two burial chambers, located at the eastern and western sides of the feature. These tombs are exposed, having long ago lost their earthen cover. Many of the stones lining the passageways of these tombs are highly decorated with megalithic art such as spirals, hollowed 'cup marks' and zigzags. You can still find them in their original locations, and it is impossible not to wonder about the meaning of the art: was it purely decorative or did it have a deeper symbolism, and what messages does it convey? You can also still see the quartz stones, which possibly would have formed a wall around the entrance to the passageways.

Also like Newgrange, Knockroe is aligned with the winter solstice. Every year around 21 December, people gather at Knockroe to witness the sun setting in perfect alignment with the length of the western tomb.

Knockroe is one of a group of tombs located in this region, all of which are aligned with the large mound on the summit of Slievenamon in County Tipperary. Knockroe is one of those intriguing sites that remains in the mind long after your visit. Without its earthen mound, Knockroe is like the stony skeleton of a Neolithic passage tomb.

A beam of light begins to illuminate the passage during the winter solstice

KNOCKROE PASSAGE TOMB SITE MAP 7

Coordinates: Lat: 52.431731, Long: -7.399879

Grid reference: S 40819 31299

Opening times: Open all year round

Entry fee: Free

Facilities: None

Car parking: No car park – it is possible to park at the top of the lane and walk down to the site.

Directions: To get to Knockroe from Carrick-on-Suir, take the R697 going north. Take the left-hand turn for the R698 and continue down this road, until reaching a crossroads. Go left here and continue straight on, through another, smaller crossroads, after which, take the next left and drive carefully down this lane to the site. The lanes are narrow and you might be better to park at the top of the lane. The site is fenced off and situated on relatively dry ground but boots or reasonably sturdy footwear are still advised.

Nearest town: Carrick-on-Suir, about 14km to the south

Kilree is located just 2km from Kells Priory (Site 62). Though much smaller and less immediately visually imposing than Kells Priory, Kilree is still an evocative and rewarding site to visit. The trees that surround the graveyard block the wind, and provide an atmospheric hush.

Visiting the two sites in one day serves as a fine contrast between the Irish monasteries of the early medieval period, and those larger, more formal and orderly establishments of the continental orders that came centuries later.

Kilree is said to have been founded by St Brigid, though no remains dating from her time during the sixth century have been discovered at the site. The ruin of the medieval church has architectural features known as antae, which are projections of the sidewalls past the exterior end walls, a typically pre-Romanesque architectural style. The church was modified and expanded in later medieval periods and inside are some tombs of late medieval date.

The fine round tower stands on the boundary wall of the old churchyard. Apart from missing its original conical roof, the round tower is in good condition. It stands nearly 27 metres (88 ft) tall, and is about 5 metres (16 ft) in diameter. The tower is constructed from irregularly coursed limestone, and has sandstone dressing around the doorway, which faces the door of the early medieval part of the church, a typical orientation of many round towers. What makes Kilree almost unique is that the tower stands on a rectangular stone pad foundation; this is replicated on only one other round tower, that of Aghaviller, also in County Kilkenny, located nearby to the south-east. This may mean that the same architect was involved in the construction of both towers, perhaps giving insights into the skilled craftsmen, like architects, stonemasons, millwrights and engineers, who travelled around Ireland in the early medieval period, helping to establish the flourishing monasteries that sprang up around the country.

Near the round tower is a small stile that you can cross to leave the churchyard to access the field where the high cross stands. The delicate geometric design of the cross is similar to other examples in the western part of the ancient kingdom of Ossory, particularly

Facing page: The ruins of the medieval church at Kilree, County Kilkenny

The high cross and round tower at Kilree

those of Ahenny, located nearby to the south. The fine geometric design might be following the tradition of decorative metalwork of the eighth century, with the large stud-like features representing enamel studs on the metal crosses.

KILREE MONASTIC SITE   SITE MAP 6

Coordinates: Lat: 52.518200, Long: -7.268531

Grid reference: S 49668 40994

Opening times: Open all year round

Entry fee: Free

Facilities: None. The site is on private land. Please seek landowner's permission before crossing fields and always close gates behind you.

Car parking: No car park – just park at the side of the road, taking care not to block any gates or the road.

Directions: To get to Kilree, simply follow the signpost up from Kells Priory (Site 62), it is just a short drive away. There is little parking, so just pull your car off the road and cross the field to the churchyard (taking careful note of the 'beware of the bull' sign!).

Nearest town: Kells, less than 2km to the north

62 | KELLS PRIORY
COUNTY KILKENNY

Kells Priory, County Kilkenny

This enormous site has the appearance of a large castle with high walls and strong towers, but despite its military appearance, it was a monastic foundation, founded by the Norman knight Geoffrey FitzRobert *c.* 1193 for the Augustinian canons.

As the priory flourished, the wealth of the site did not go unnoticed. Kells Priory was attacked a number of times in the thirteenth and fourteenth centuries. In 1252, William de Bermingham attacked Kells, then around 1317 it was the turn of the armies of Edward Bruce (brother of the Scottish king Robert the Bruce), who had launched an invasion of Ireland to try to break England's colonies there and to open a second front in the Scottish wars with England. Later, the Irish friar and chronicler John Clyn recorded that Kells was burned and the surrounding area devastated in the course of a baronial war led by another William de Bermingham in 1327.

The troubles continued into the fifteenth century, as various factions battled for supremacy in the region. The walls and towers were constructed as a defence and refuge for the people and livestock of the area as well as for the priors. As you pass around the outside of the towers you can see evidence of the defensive features, like

Kells Priory

machicolations and murder holes, from where the defenders could pour down boiling fat, bad language, large stones and even the contents of the latrine to make life nasty for any attackers.

These strong walls enclose an area of nearly 3 acres, and the enormous scale makes this one of the most remarkable heritage sites to explore in Ireland. Inside the walls are the remains of the churches, the cloister area and the domestic buildings of the priors, such as kitchens and dormitories. After visiting the site, you can enjoy a pleasant walk alongside the King's River. The priors operated a series of mills and fisheries along the river to help make the priory economically viable, and the remains of these can just about be discerned from the stonework in the river. The abbey prospered later in the fourteenth and fifteenth centuries. A kitchen list has survived from 1382 and includes items like olive oil, pepper (which would have been imported from south-east Asia), saffron (from Spain, France or Italy) and figs.

Kells Priory is simply enormous and well worth taking a couple of hours to explore. If you have time and are in the mood to visit more monastic ruins, follow the signpost to Kilree monastic site (Site 61), located just 2km up the road.

The path to one of the towers of Kells Priory

63 | NEWTOWN JERPOINT
COUNTY KILKENNY

The now deserted Newtown Jerpoint was once a medieval town of major importance. The town was founded *c.* 1200, at a crossing point of the River Nore. It is located very close to the more famous Jerpoint Abbey (Site 64). The town was probably founded by a tenant of William Marshal named Griffin FitzWilliam, brother of the Norman warlord Raymond le Gros. It was a thriving and vibrant settlement constructed around two intersecting roads (one running north–south, the other east–west). The town was divided into around twenty-two burgage plots. These plots would have had houses at least partly constructed by stone, and the remains of a number of these survive today as piles of stone inside the earthen banks of the burgage plots.

The town also had at least two watermills and is said to have had a marketplace, a brewery, taverns, a courthouse and a tannery. Near

St Nicholas' Church surrounded by the lost medieval village of Newtown Jerpoint that slumbers under Kilkenny pastures

the centre of the town you can see the remains of an urban tower house, probably the home of a wealthy merchant, which would have offered a defensive position for the town during raids.

Perhaps most significant are the remains of St Nicholas' Church. Constructed around the time that the town was founded *c.* 1200, the church still survives well today, the most visible and tangible remains on the site. There is evidence of a number of alterations over the centuries, of which the most notable are the construction of a very unusual rood screen and a fifteenth-century domestic tower where the priest would have lived. Historical records show the church still in use in 1622, but it probably fell into disuse and disrepair in the late seventeenth century.

The church is surrounded by a graveyard, with a number of graves dating from medieval times to the nineteenth century. The most significant by far is the grave of St Nicholas of Myra: yes, Father Christmas is buried at Newtown Jerpoint in County Kilkenny (don't tell the kids). Legend has it that his remains were brought back from Bari in Italy by two knights returning from a crusade. They are said to have reburied him in this fine tomb at St Nicholas' Church. Look closely at the tomb: you can see depicted the heads of the two knights who brought his remains to Newtown Jerpoint. Having the tomb of such an important saint would have brought great wealth

Above: Medieval grave slab at Newtown Jerpoint

Left: The medieval tomb effigy thought to depict St Nicholas of Myra. The heads of two Norman-type knights are visible flanking his head.

and prestige to the town, as pilgrims would have travelled huge distances to pray at the site of the mortal remains of St Nicholas.

The graveyard alone is worth exploring: the large number of gravestones, both medieval and post-medieval, are interesting for the craftsmanship and symbolism. Near the churchyard is the burial plot of the Hunt family in a small enclosure, with tombs dating from 1771–1975, some of which are beautifully carved, showing the high level of skill and craftsmanship of the stonemason.

The town developed around the bridge that crossed the River Nore at the junction with the smaller River Arrigle. Very little remains to be seen of the bridge today, but its original position can be made out where a large number of stones in the river force the waters to churn and break.

The town was deserted probably in the later part of the seventeenth century. It seems that the bridge either fell into disrepair, or a newer bridge was constructed elsewhere on the Nore, which meant that the main road no longer passed through Newtown Jerpoint, causing a great loss in revenue for the town and perhaps starting its decline. The town was eventually abandoned, and the lands came into the possession of the Hunt family, who leased this area to the Earl of Belmore. He constructed the handsome Belmore

House *c.* 1780 as a hunting lodge. This fine house is now the family home of the site owners, Joe and Maeve O'Connell. Today Jerpoint Park is open to the public for guided tours on request.

NEWTOWN JERPOINT   SITE MAP 6

Coordinates: Lat: 52.512732, Long: -7.166966

Grid reference: S 56764 40422

Opening times: Jerpoint Park is open daily from end April to the start of October. Please see: www.jerpointpark.com for specific opening hours and tour times.

Entry fee: Please visit www.jerpointpark.com

Facilities: Toilets, tea rooms, guided tours of the site and sheepdog demonstrations

Car parking: Car parking at the site

Directions: If travelling from Dublin on M9, exit at Junction 7 (signed Thomastown, Gowran, Paulstown) and follow the R448 to Thomastown. From Thomastown, travel south on the R448. Turn right after Jerpoint Abbey (Site 64) and Newtown Jerpoint will be on your right.

Nearest town: Thomastown, about 4km to the north

64 | JERPOINT ABBEY
COUNTY KILKENNY

Jerpoint Abbey near Thomastown in County Kilkenny has one of Ireland's best collections of medieval sculpture and architecture. The abbey is believed to have been founded by a donation from the King of Ossory, Dónal Mac Gilla Pátraic, *c.* 1160. It was perhaps originally a Benedictine foundation but it was taken over by the Cistercian order by the late twelfth century.

The abbey is laid out in the traditional Cistercian way, with a cruciform church with cloisters to the south. The abbey was adapted and changed throughout its history, particularly in the fifteenth

Medieval sculpture at Jerpoint Abbey, County Kilkenny

century, when a papal indulgence was granted to raise funds for the renovation and repair of many of the buildings.

The Cistercians first came to Ireland *c.* 1142, and established their first foundation at Mellifont in County Louth (Site 4). By this time, the Cistercians were one of the most powerful religious orders in Europe. The life of a Cistercian monk was strictly apportioned between religious study and manual labour, with all tasks scheduled to fit around regular communal prayers. Every night the monks arose for Matins at about 2 a.m., Lauds at 5 a.m. and Prime at 6 a.m., then Terce at 9 a.m., Sext at noon, Nones at 3 p.m., Vespers around 5 p.m. and finally Compline at 6 p.m. It was a life of almost unvarying routine and absolute discipline. Monks performed their tasks in silence, their meals were plain and largely vegetarian, and their habits were made of coarse, undyed wool. A Cistercian monk in England, Ailred of Rievaulx, described the daily experience: 'Our food is scanty, our garments rough; our drink is from the stream and our sleep often upon our book. Under our tired limbs there is but a hard mat; when sleep is sweetest, we must rise at bell's bidding. Self-will has no place; there is no moment for idleness or dissipation.'

Jerpoint Abbey

This austere life contrasts quite sharply with some of the elaborate, charming and sometimes humorous sculptures and depictions around the abbey. Inside the church is a wealth of medieval tombs, some with 'weepers' (i.e. sculptures of the apostles and saints surrounding the base of the tomb). Many of these were created by the medieval master-sculptor Rory O'Tunney, who was based nearby at Callan. The saints are recognisable as many hold a symbol to identify them, like St Peter who is often depicted holding the keys of heaven. Others hold symbols of their martyrdom; for example, St Thomas holds a lance, St Simon a saw, St Andrew an X-shaped cross, St Bartholomew his skin (he was flayed alive), and St Paul a sword.

A number of other fascinating tomb effigies can also be seen, the earliest of which is that of Abbot O'Dulany who died in 1202. Perhaps most intriguing is the effigy of two Norman knights known as 'The Brethren', depicted in their armour side by side. It is suggested that they may represent two of the sons of William Marshal.

The cloister contains an almost unparalleled wealth of sculpture, where saints, religious figures, courtly ladies, knights and fantastical

beasts like dragons and manticores can all be seen, some carved with a sense of humour that one might not expect in an austere Cistercian abbey.

Exploring Jerpoint is always a rewarding day out, and each time I visit I notice some other great sculpture or detail I had overlooked before. Jerpoint is under the auspices of the OPW. It has an informative visitor centre and there are guided tours.

A view through the cloisters of Jerpoint Abbey

JERPOINT ABBEY SITE MAP 6

Coordinates: Lat: 52.511699, Long: -7.157453

Grid reference: S 57185 40271

Opening times: Open daily from March to end November. From December to March, the abbey is only opened for pre-booked tours. See: www.heritageireland.ie/en/en/south-east/jerpointabbey/ for more information on opening hours.

Entry fee: Please visit www.heritageireland.ie/en/south-east/jerpointabbey/

Facilities: Toilets, guided tours of the abbey, visitor centre

Car parking: Large car park at site

Directions: If travelling from Dublin on M9, exit at Junction 7 (signed Thomastown, Gowran, Paulstown) and follow the R448 to Thomastown. Jerpoint Abbey is located on the R448. Travelling south from Thomastown on the R448, the abbey will be on the left after about 2.5km. It is well signposted.

Nearest town: Thomastown, about 2.5km to the north-east

The interior of the ruined medieval church at Kilfane, County Kilkenny

Just a short drive from Jerpoint Abbey (Site 64) and Thomastown are the ruins of the medieval parish church of Kilfane. Inside the church, propped against the wall, is something truly special: the Cantwell Fada (also known as The Long Man of Kilfane), probably the most impressive medieval effigy of a knight found anywhere in either Ireland or Britain.

This incredible knight stands over 8 ft tall, and is the largest of its type, described by Prof. Roger Stalley of Trinity College Dublin as 'a colossus among medieval effigies'. It depicts a knight wearing a metal skullcap covered by a coif, with a chainmail hauberk protecting his torso as far as his knees. The chainmail is under a cloth surcoat with deep folds, and he wears a sword belt. He has prominent spurs on his feet, showing that he fought from horseback. His shield bears

The Cantwell Fada

the arms of the Cantwell family, a prominent family of Norman nobles who accompanied Theobold Walter during the Norman arrival in the late twelfth century. For their distinguished service, the Cantwells became lords of Kilfane. It is not certain what member of the Cantwell family is represented by the effigy, though some scholars believe it to be Thomas Cantwell, who died *c.* 1320.

Apart from this truly incredible effigy, Kilfane Church itself is well worth exploring. It is a long, rectangular church that probably dates to the thirteenth century. Inside are a number of features like the sedile (the priest's seat) and a very fine tower. It is a lovely atmospheric site, made really special by a stunning piece of medieval sculpture.

KILFANE CHURCH   SITE MAP 6

Coordinates: Lat: 52.555151, Long: -7.119077

Grid reference: S 59807 45110

Opening times: Open all year round

Entry fee: Free

Facilities: None

Car parking: Limited car parking opposite the modern Church of Ireland church

Directions: If travelling from Dublin on M9, exit at Junction 7 (signed Thomastown, Gowran, Paulstown) and follow the R448 to Thomastown. Follow the R448 through Thomastown heading north towards the village of Dungarvan (not to be confused with Dungarvan in County Waterford). There is a sign for Kilfane Church (and Kilfane Waterfall and Historic Garden) on the right after around 4.5km. Drive up the narrow road and park opposite the late nineteenth-century Church of Ireland church. Pass through the small black gate opposite the modern church and follow the little path under the trees to the medieval ruins.

Nearest town: Thomastown, about 6km to the south-west

Woodstock House, County Kilkenny

Woodstock House was first built *c.* 1745 for Sir William Fownes by the renowned architect Francis Bindon. Fownes' daughter Sarah married William Tighe, though he died just four years later and the estate passed to their son. When he in turn died in 1816, his son William Frederick Fownes Tighe inherited Woodstock. He married Lady Louisa Lennox. The beautiful gardens of Woodstock are largely down to the efforts of Lady Louisa and her head gardeners Pierce Butler and Charles MacDonald. They had tree specimens brought in from Asia and South America. By the late nineteenth century, Woodstock was considered to have one of the finest gardens in Ireland. Recent conservation work by Kilkenny County Council has begun to restore the gardens to their original splendour. The lovely woodland walks, box hedging, walled garden, rose garden and reconstructed Turner Conservatory all help to create a beautiful and tranquil place.

After the death of Lady Louisa in 1900, the house was left unoccupied as the rest of the family lived in London. The notorious Black and Tans based themselves in the empty house; later it was

Woodstock Gardens

occupied by troops of the Free State Army. When they were withdrawn in July 1922, the IRA burned down the house. Today all that remains of Woodstock House is an empty shell, surrounded by its beautiful gardens.

One of the most romantic and intriguing stories surrounding Woodstock is that of Sarah Ponsonby, a relative of the Fownes Tighes, who stayed at Woodstock in the 1770s. Young and pretty, Sarah was in receipt of much unwanted attention from Sir William, whose wife, Betty, was in ailing health. Sarah felt trapped in an unbearable situation, until she met Eleanor Butler, daughter of the Earl of Ormond, who lived in Kilkenny Castle. Clever, witty and bookish, Eleanor was still unwed at thirty-nine and determined to resist any forced marriage or being sent to live in a nunnery. Sarah and Eleanor became very close, and the two ran away together. Dressed as men and carrying a pistol, and accompanied by Sarah's dog Frisk, they rode for Waterford to catch a ship. Unfortunately it did not sail and they were caught. However, due to their determination never to be separated, eventually the families relented.

They set up home in Wales, on a hillside above Llangollen, in a five-room cottage that they renamed Plas Newydd. Their love for art and history came to the fore, and the cottage became a remarkable wonderland of intricately carved and decorated timbers and furniture, with a well-stocked library and antiques. Though the 'Ladies of Llangollen', as they became known, wished for a quiet life, the fashionable world soon took them into their hearts. Their visitors included the highest ranks of society, with the Duke of Wellington, Prince Paul Esterhazy, the Duke of Gloucester, Wordsworth, Shelley and Lord Byron all calling to pay their respects. They lived a long and happy life at Llangollen spending more than fifty years together, along with their indefatigable housekeeper Mary Carryll who had accompanied them from Kilkenny. When Mary died, they erected an elaborate stone monument in their gardens, under which they later joined her.

WOODSTOCK HOUSE AND GARDEN   SITE MAP 6

Coordinates: Lat: 52.475511, Long: -7.057464

Grid reference: S 63870 36370

Opening times: Open all year round

Entry fee: Please visit www.woodstock.ie

Facilities: Guided tours of the gardens can be booked in advance. There are toilets, along with a playground, picnic area and coffee kiosk at the gardens.

Car parking: Large car park at the site

Directions: Woodstock Gardens are located close to the village of Inistioge in County Kilkenny. Travelling into Inistioge from Kilkenny, turn right at the square and continue up the steep hill through the village. Continue on this road for about 1km until reaching the large stone gates to Woodstock. There is a large car park at the end of the avenue.

Nearest town: Inistioge, about 2km to the north-east

67 | DUISKE ABBEY
COUNTY KILKENNY

Duiske Abbey is one of the finest, and largest, Cistercian buildings in Ireland, and the extensive cloister garth was only equalled by that of Dunbrody Abbey (Site 84). The abbey was founded in 1204 by William Marshal. The First Earl of Pembroke, William Marshal (1146–1219), was undoubtedly one of the most influential figures in Irish history. He was a prolific builder of castles (including Kilkenny), towns and abbeys across his vast territories in Ireland, Wales, England and Normandy. He founded Duiske as a 'daughter house' to the Cistercian monastery of Stanley in Wiltshire, England. The community that settled at Duiske found it to be the perfect place for a life of contemplation and religious service, located in a picturesque setting in the shadow of Brandon Hill close to the

The interior of Duiske Abbey

Duiske River. It was the abbey that gave the nearby town its name, Graiguenamanagh, as it derives from the Irish *Gráig na Manach*, meaning 'hamlet (or village) of the monks'.

The Cistercians raised revenue through the wool trade, but by the end of the thirteenth century the abbey was recorded as being in serious debt, owing substantial sums to Italian bankers. However, the abbey endured and continued to flourish. The last abbot, Charles Kavanagh, was a generous benefactor, and donated much wealth to the abbey, including precious vestments and a silver gilt cross. He travelled on pilgrimage to Santiago de Compostela in 1530, though the abbey's days were soon to end. Duiske Abbey was dissolved in 1536, and it passed into the ownership of the Earls of Ormond. By the eighteenth century, the abbey was suffering badly from neglect, and the tower collapsed into the nave in 1744. In 1813, the roof of the ruined chancel, transepts and part of the nave was restored and repaired. Due to centuries of accumulated burials, the level of the floor was raised 1.5 metres (5 ft) above its original height.

Medieval decorative sculpture in Duiske Abbey

The abbey was further restored in 1886. A programme of restoration and archaeological investigation in the 1970s revealed a thirteenth-century tiled floor (still visible to the right of the main entrance). There is also a fine tomb effigy of an unidentified knight inside the church, as well as a number of other medieval features. The churchyard is home to the Aghakiltawn and Ballyogen Crosses, both probably dating from the eighth century. A medieval cross slab is built into the wall of the abbey, and there is also the base of a third cross in the abbey grounds.

The church became a place of worship for the Church of Ireland community, but it was returned to the Catholic faith in 1812. Though it appears quite simple from the outside, the interior of Duiske Abbey is one of the most atmospheric and fascinating places to visit in Ireland. It still plays a key role in the daily lives of the inhabitants of the charming town of Graiguenamanagh in south Kilkenny.

DUISKE ABBEY   SITE MAP 6

Coordinates: Lat: 52.541184, Long: -6.954925

Grid reference: S 70862 43804

Opening times: Open all year round

Entry fee: Free

Facilities: None

Car parking: Car parking available

Directions: Located in the town of Graiguenamanagh on the R705

Nearest town: Duiske is in the town of Graiguenamanagh, about 30km south-east of Kilkenny

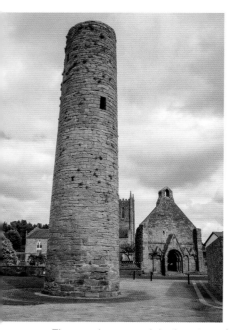

The round tower and the façade of the twelfth-century Church of St Cronán in Roscrea

Roscrea was originally founded as an early medieval monastery by St Cronán in the seventh century. It was positioned on the important routeway, the *Slí Dála*, that brought travellers, pilgrims and tradesmen. The monastery grew in importance, and produced many great treasures, including the eighth-century Book of Dimma (now housed in Trinity College Dublin) and the beautiful Roscrea Brooch that is on display in the National Museum of Ireland. The monastery is thought to have been originally located where the round tower and church façade stand today. The round tower of Roscrea was mentioned in the annals of 1135 when it was struck by lightning. Constructed of sandstone, the upper portion of this round tower was demolished after 1798 as it had been used by rebel snipers shooting at Roscrea Castle (see facing page). The doorway of the round tower stands over 2 metres (nearly 7 ft) off the ground and faces towards the doorway of the twelfth-century Romanesque-style church. This façade is all that remains of the church, which once would have been beautiful and ornate. From this surviving section it appears to have been influenced perhaps by Cormac's Chapel at the Rock of Cashel. The rest of the church was demolished in 1812 to make way for the Church of Ireland church that is still in use. There is also a replica of the high cross that once stood on the site. The original cross is carved from sandstone and dates to the twelfth century. Unfortunately, the cross is quite heavily eroded and

Roscrea Castle

weathered so it is very difficult to discern the carvings, though it appears to show typical biblical scenes.

Roscrea Castle is located nearby in the town on Castle Street. The first castle on this site is thought to have been constructed *c*. 1213 as an earth-and-timber fortification known as a motte and bailey. When large amounts of silver were discovered nearby at the Silvermines at the end of the thirteenth century, a Norman noble, John de Lydiard, was ordered to reconstruct the timber fort in stone, and the castle of Roscrea as we see it today is largely the result of his work *c*. 1280. The castle was well defended, with a moat surrounding it and a gatehouse that still houses a drawbridge and a portcullis. The castle and town were granted to the powerful Butler family in 1315. However, during the turbulent years of the fifteenth century, Roscrea appears to have been in the hands of the Gaelic-Irish O'Carroll family. A note in a manuscript held in Lambeth Palace records that John O'Carroll was occupying Roscrea Castle in 1477, and in 1490 the O'Carrolls were rebuilding the Franciscan friary that had been established on the southern side of the town decades earlier. Little remains of the friary today, apart from the belfry tower, the east and northern walls of the chancel and part of the nave. The O'Carrolls had taken advantage of the Butlers' involvement in English affairs and the fact that they had absented themselves from

The eighteenth-century Damer House

Ireland to support the Lancastrian side in the War of the Roses. However, by the sixteenth century the Butlers had returned to exert their authority in Ireland. Black Tom Butler (who became a close friend of Queen Elizabeth I) managed to recapture all the Butler lands in Tipperary. In the turmoil of the mid seventeenth century, the castle was captured in 1646 by Owen Roe O'Neill, who stormed it with 1,200 men and killed everyone within, with the exception of Mary Butler, the daughter of the eleventh Earl.

O'Neill attacked again in 1649, and a year later the beleaguered castle surrendered to Cromwell. The castle was nearly completely destroyed after the Williamite Wars at the end of the seventeenth century, when King William ordered that it be demolished to prevent it ever falling into enemy hands again, but his orders were ignored because the castle provided valuable shelter for the livestock of the townspeople. The Butlers sold the castle in 1703 to Robert Curtis, who sold it in turn to John Damer in 1722. He began work to construct what became one of Ireland's best examples of an early eighteenth-century townhouse. The house became a military barracks at the end of the eighteenth century, and then was used for various purposes, including as a sanatorium and a school. The house is a wonderful (and rare) example of pre-Palladian architecture in

Ireland and was lovingly restored by the Old Roscrea Society and the Irish Georgian Society in the 1960s.

ROSCREA   SITE MAP 4

Coordinates: Lat: 52.955195, Long: -7.797981

Grid reference: S 13575 89369

Opening times: Roscrea Castle and Damer House are open from the start of April to end September, 10 a.m. – 6 p.m. Last admission is 45 minutes before closing.
   The high cross and church site is open all year round.

Entry fee: Please visit www.heritageireland.ie/en/midlands-eastcoast/roscreaheritagecentre-roscreacastleanddamer/

Facilities: Toilets and gardens, guided tours of the castle and Damer House

Car parking: Car parking in Roscrea town

Directions: Roscrea Castle, Damer House, the monastic site and the friary are all located in Roscrea town centre and are within walking distance of one another.

Nearest town: Nenagh, about 30km to the south-west

69 | MONAINCHA ABBEY
COUNTY TIPPERARY

St Elair is said to have founded a monastic site at Monaincha in the seventh century, but most of the visible remains on the site date to the Augustinians, who established a small monastery here dedicated to St Mary between the twelfth and fifteenth centuries.

   The name Monaincha comes from *Mainistir Inse na mBeo* meaning 'the Monastery of the Island of the Living'. Originally the monastery was on a small island in a lake, but agricultural drainage works in the eighteenth and nineteenth centuries drained the water and left the monastery perched conspicuously on top of a mound in a low, boggy field.

Monaincha Abbey, County Tipperary

The strange powers of the island were recorded by the twelfth-century Norman clergyman and chronicler Gerald of Wales. He described the island on which the monastery stands. In this excerpt, Monaincha is the smaller island (the location of the larger island is unknown):

> There is a lake in the north of Munster which contains two islands, one rather large and the other rather small. The larger has a church venerated from the earliest times. The smaller [Monaincha] has a chapel cared for most devotedly by a few celibates called 'heaven-worshippers'.
>
> In the smaller island no one has ever died or could die a natural death. Accordingly it is called the Island of the Living. Nevertheless the inhabitants sometimes suffer mortal sicknesses and endure the agony almost to their last gasp.
>
> When there is no hope left; when they feel that they have not a spark of life left; when as the strength decreases they are eventually so distressed that they prefer to die in death than drag out a life of death, they get themselves finally transported in a boat to the larger island, and, as soon as they touch ground there, they give up the ghost.

The high cross at Monaincha is a composite of two different crosses. The base appears to be decorated but it is very weathered and difficult to make out. It is believed to date to around the ninth century. The long thin shaft with a depiction of Christ at the apex is later, dating to the twelfth century. The church has a Romanesque-style doorway resplendent with designs of chevrons, zigzags and

foliage carved into the sandstone. The church itself is quite a simple nave-and-chancel church, with the chancel arch again in the Romanesque style. However, evidence of the later activity on site can be seen in the architecture of some of the windows. A small addition to the church was made in probably the fifteenth century, a vaulted chamber that may have been a sacristy and a set of steps leading to an upper chamber, little of which survives. The construction of this addition seems a little coarser than the original parts of the church.

The composite high cross at Monaincha

Monaincha is along a very narrow bumpy track, which even in good weather is a bit of a hair-raising experience and there is very little room to turn at the end of the track. I would recommend leaving the car safely pulled in before the track and walking the 400 metres or so down to the site. The site is in a field full of livestock so be sure to wear adequate footwear and please close any gates behind you.

MONAINCHA ABBEY   SITE MAP 4

Coordinates: Lat: 52.946340, Long: -7.747952

Grid reference: S 16939 88408

Opening times: Open all year round

Entry fee: Free

Facilities: None

Car parking: Car parking at side of the road. Please take care to avoid blocking gates, always seek the landowner's permission before crossing private farmland and always close all gates behind you.

Directions: To find Monaincha from Roscrea, drive north-east along the old Dublin Road (R445) until you come to a roundabout. Take the third exit (signposted for Monaincha Abbey). Then take the first left (again signed for Monaincha Abbey) and follow this road until you come to a left turn with a black-and-white sign for Monaincha Abbey. I recommend parking here, pulled in close to the sign so as not to impede other cars, then walking down the track on foot to the site.

Nearest town: Roscrea, about 5km west

Kilcooley Abbey is located in the scenic Sliabh Ardagh region of Tipperary, within the walls of the Kilcooley Estate, an impressive Georgian house with over 1,000 acres of land.

Kilcooley Abbey was founded in 1182 after a grant of land to the Cistercians by Donal Mór O'Briain, King of Munster. It was the daughter house of Jerpoint Abbey in County Kilkenny (Site 64). Kilcooley is without a doubt one of Ireland's finest Cistercian abbeys and is a wonderful example of the Gothic architectural style.

The abbey is recorded as being attacked and burned in 1418 and again it was almost completely levelled by an armed force in 1444. After this attack, the Ormond Butlers instigated a programme of reconstruction, removing the nave aisles and adding a new north transept and tower. Most of the stunning sculpture around the abbey dates to this reconstruction. The works were carried out under the eye of the abbot, Philip O'Molwanayn, and his grave slab dating to 1463 shows him holding his bishop's crozier and book of prayer. Translated, the Latin epitaph on his tomb reads, 'Here lies Philip O'Molwanayn, formerly abbot of this house, together with his parents, who performed many good works both spiritual and temporal; on whose souls God have mercy'.

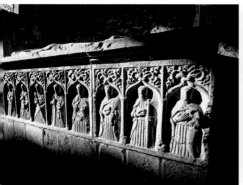

Above: Apostles depicted on the tomb of Pierce Fitz Óg Butler, Kilcooley Abbey

Right: The crossing tower of Kilcooley Abbey

Facing page: Kilcooley Abbey, County Tipperary

The Butlers were rewarded for their patronage by having their tombs placed inside the sacred areas of Kilcooley. The most stunning of these is the impressive tomb of Pierce Fitz Óg Butler, which probably dates to 1526, and depicts him in his armour. At his feet a small dog represents his faithfulness and loyalty, and ten of the twelve apostles are depicted below (from left to right): St Peter holding the keys to Heaven, St Andrew, St James (major), St John, St Thomas, St James (minor), St Philip, St Bartholomew, St Simon and St Matthew. Unusually, we know who actually created the tomb, as the name of the sculptor, Rory O'Tunney (Roricus O'Tuyne), is clearly marked.

The ornate Gothic east window is delicately carved, with the stone formed to look almost like flames or foliage. The 'abbot's chair' (or sedile) is also stunning, and is matched on the other side by another, slightly plainer example, perhaps for a prior. The screen wall separating the southern transept from the sacristy is elaborately decorated with a number of scenes including St Christopher crossing a river with the infant Jesus, the Crucifixion with Mary and St John on either side, a pelican feeding its young within a chalice, a mermaid with a comb and mirror, and the Butler coat of arms.

The cloisters of Kilcooley Abbey

Beyond this area is the cloister. Very little remains of any covered walkway at Kilcooley, and it appears that perhaps the cloister was converted to a courtyard in its later history. There are domestic quarters at Kilcooley, though some are kept locked and inaccessible to the public for health and safety reasons. Outside of the abbey is a small circular tower: a dovecote where the monks kept pigeons. The pigeons were a useful source of protein and their droppings also made good fertiliser (very little was wasted in a medieval monastery!). In its heyday, the abbey would have also had other agricultural buildings like mills and a large lay population to work the land.

Kilcooley Abbey was surrendered during the Dissolution of the Monasteries in 1540. However, the lands were granted directly to the Butlers, who allowed monks to remain at Kilcooley until they sold it to Sir Jerome Alexander in 1636. After the Catholic Confederacy rebellion in 1641, Cistercian monks returned to Kilcooley, until they were finally removed from the site by Cromwell's forces in 1650. Ten years later the Alexander family regained the abbey and, when Elizabeth Alexander married Sir William Barker of Essex in 1676, the abbey was converted into a domestic house.

In 1790 the grand Kilcooley House was built and replaced the abbey as the main residence. Today the abbey is a National

Monument, and under the care of the OPW. The site is gated, but the gate is often left unlocked during the day to allow visitors to enjoy one of the finest heritage sites in the country.

KILCOOLEY ABBEY SITE MAP 7

Coordinates: Lat: 52.670877, Long: -7.571071

Grid reference: S 29370 57958

Opening times: Open all year round

Entry fee: Free

Facilities: None

Car parking: Small car park at the Church of Ireland church

Directions: To get to Kilcooley Abbey from Dublin/Cork, exit the M8 motorway at Junction 4 and follow the signs for Urlingford. In Urlingford, turn left onto Togher Road (R689) and follow this road for about 2.7km. Turn left onto the R690 and continue for 2.5km. The entrance to the abbey and Kilcooley estate will be on the left. Continue up the avenue and park at the Church of Ireland church. A path from the church leads past the graveyard and pyramid monument to the Barker family. The abbey is located in the field at the end of the path.

Nearest town: Urlingford, about 6km to the north

71 | HOLY CROSS ABBEY
COUNTY TIPPERARY

Holy Cross Abbey in County Tipperary is one of the true ecclesiastical jewels in all of Ireland. It was founded by the Cistercians after a donation by Domhnall Mór O'Brien, King of Thomond in 1182, and the charter he granted to the Cistercians survives to this day. The O'Brien dynasty were strong supporters of church reform during the twelfth century, and their loyalty to Rome was rewarded when Pope Paschal II presented a fragment of the True Cross to Muirchertach O'Brien in 1110. This was a powerful relic, believed to be a splinter of the very cross on which Jesus was crucified and its

Holy Cross Abbey, County Tipperary

presence in the abbey would have attracted thousands of pilgrims, making Holy Cross an extremely wealthy institution. At one point in history, Holy Cross Abbey housed at least two, if not three, relics of the True Cross.

The nave of the church is the oldest surviving part of the abbey and reflects the simple architectural style of the Cistercian order. Under the patronage of the Butlers of Ormond, the abbey underwent a major restoration in the fifteenth century and its most outstanding architectural features date from this period.

The ribbed stone vaulting over the transept and chancel is a marvel of stonework and bears numerous marks of the masons who carved it. The elaborate sedilia, seating places for the abbot and his deacons, have been referred to as the most outstanding piece of medieval church furniture in Ireland. On the west wall of the north transept there is a mural depicting a hunting scene, an unusually secular scene within a church. Other architectural highlights of this spectacular site include 'the waking monk's bier', the east window, rose window, night stairs (which connected the monks' dormitory to the church), chapterhouse door and cloister.

The last Cistercian monk in Holy Cross died in the 1730s and the abbey, already in a state of disrepair, fell into ruin. In the late 1960s

a major initiative to bring Holy Cross back to life as a place of worship began. Led by local priest Willie Hayes, and with the support of Archbishop Thomas Morris and the OPW, careful restoration and conservation work began in 1970, taking over five years to complete.

On the traditional parish feast day of Michaelmas, 25 September 1975, the abbey was consecrated and Mass was celebrated at Holy Cross once more.

The night stairs in Holy Cross Abbey

HOLY CROSS ABBEY   SITE MAP 7

Coordinates: Lat: 52.639291, Long: -7.868287

Grid reference: S 08894 54235

Opening times: Open all year round

Entry fee: Free

Facilities: Toilets and gift shop

Car parking: Large car park at site

Directions: Holy Cross Abbey is easy to locate in the village of Holycross. Travelling from Dublin/Cork, leave the M8 motorway at Junction 6 and follow the N62 to Thurles. After 1km, turn left onto the R660 and follow this road for 4km. At the T-junction, turn right onto the R659 and continue to Holycross. The abbey is just after the bridge.

Nearest town: Thurles, about 7km to the north

The medieval bridge to Athassel Abbey

72 | ATHASSEL ABBEY
COUNTY TIPPERARY

Athassel Abbey is located close to the village of Golden in County Tipperary, and is a fine example of an Augustianian priory. The abbey was once an important urban centre in medieval Ireland. Today, however, the ruin slumbers beside the meandering River Suir, with no visible traces of the vibrant settlement, said to have numbered 2,000 people, that once surrounded it.

This abbey site was founded *c.* 1200, by a prominent Anglo-Norman named William Fitz Aldhelm de Burgo. He was granted extensive land in Tipperary and decided to donate to the church a portion on which to create a bastion of Anglo-Norman worship. It is likely that William de Burgo himself lived quite close by: the remains of a motte stand across the river from the abbey. Mottes

The remains of the cloisters of Athassel

were built by Norman lords in the years after their arrival in Ireland as defensive sites to gain control of strategic areas. Today the motte at Athassel is very overgrown but it is an interesting indication of a strong Anglo-Norman military presence in the area.

Augustinian canons came to Athassel on de Burgo's request and initially built half a church, followed by a cloister area, then a chapter house and dormitories with a refectory or eating area, before turning their attention back to the church to complete the nave. The priory was dedicated to St Edmund. The support from a wealthy family like the de Burgos and the location of the abbey on the banks of the navigable River Suir insured that it would become a prominent economic hub, and settlement quickly grew around it. The burgeoning town was granted the valuable privilege of the right to hold an annual fair for seven days, attracting people from miles around. To put this in context, at this time Dublin was granted an annual fair of fifteen days.

However, by the 1480s the abbey was in decline. It had suffered during the fourteenth century from raids, burnings and plague, and by the fifteenth century Ireland had become more lawless as the power of the Anglo-Norman lords dwindled. In 1512, the strong connection with the de Burgo family was broken, and another family took precedence, the Butlers of Ormond, who had landholdings in south Tipperary and Kilkenny. The break with the de Burgos was the beginning of the end for Athassel. Shortly afterwards, King Henry VIII ordered the Dissolution of the Monasteries. Athassel was spared until 1552, when King Edward VI ordered its abandonment. It was burned one final time in 1581 by a member of the Fitzgerald family, who destroyed the monastery in search of 'spoils and booty'.

Athassel stands today as a testament to the different fortunes of the Anglo-Norman families who came to Ireland in search of opportunities and land. One of the largest medieval priories to be found in Ireland, it is incredibly well preserved and highlights the strong connections between the Norman lords and the Church, and the value of strong patronage. The complex stretches across 4 acres of land and features one of Ireland's only medieval gate-and-bridge complexes, a truly wonderful site to explore.

ATHASSEL ABBEY   SITE MAP 7

Coordinates: Lat: 52.479532, Long: -7.982877

Grid reference: S 01141 36397

Opening times: Open all year round

Entry fee: Free

Facilities: None

Car parking: No car park. Limited parking on side of road.

Directions: To get to Athassel, make your way to the village of Golden, Co. Tipperary, via the N74. Drive through the village and over the bridge. Directly after the bridge turn left (the site is signposted) and continue down this small lane. The site will be on your left.

Nearest town: Golden, about 2.5km to the north, and Cashel, 9km to the north-east

73 | THE ROCK OF CASHEL
COUNTY TIPPERARY

The Rock of Cashel, seen from the R639

Undoubtedly one of Ireland's most iconic heritage sites, the Rock of Cashel perches majestically on a high stony outcrop overlooking the lush green plains of South Tipperary. The Rock was originally home to the Eóganacht, once Kings of Munster. After a series of wars, they lost the lands in the late tenth century to their great rivals the Dál Cais, who became the pre-eminent dynasty of Munster. One of their number was Brian Boru. He became King of Cashel in 978, and went on to become the most famous of the High Kings of Ireland, until his death in the aftermath of the Battle of Clontarf in 1014. Brian's great-grandson, Muircheartach Ua Briain, changed the destiny of the Rock of Cashel forever when he granted it to the Church in 1101. Rather than being solely an act of spiritual generosity, it was also a shrewd political move, as it ensured the Eóganacht could never reclaim their ancient seat. Ua Briain also gained favour with the Church. However, it was not long before the Eóganacht influence returned to the Rock of Cashel. Cormac Mac Cárthaigh (a member of the Eóganacht and King of Munster) became the patron of the most spectacular building on the site, Cormac's Chapel. Along with the round tower and the high cross, Cormac's Chapel is one of the oldest visible monuments on the Rock of Cashel. It was

The interior of Cormac's Chapel

commissioned in 1127 and completed by 1134. It is one of Ireland's most important, and finest, examples of the Romanesque style of architecture, which had recently arrived on these shores. Typical Romanesque features on Cormac's Chapel include blind arcading on the exterior, rounded doorways and a chancel arch featuring sculpted human heads. On the ceiling and walls of the chapel there are still traces of the beautiful painted frescoes, dating back to the twelfth century. From the fragments of colour it is possible to imagine that this was once a bright and vivid place of worship. Within the chapel is a large, highly decorated sarcophagus. This tomb features Urnes decoration, a Scandinavian style that became popular in Ireland in the eleventh and twelfth centuries. The design features two interlinking serpents in a figure of eight, and may represent infinity, as the serpents have no beginning and end. It is thought that this was the tomb of Cormac's predecessor as it was not originally located within the chapel. In the nave, above a doorway (which leads to a small space behind the cathedral) is a carving that depicts a large lion being shot at by a small centaur. The centaur is using a bow and arrow and wears a Norman-style helmet. To the left of this doorway on the exterior is a tomb thought to be perhaps be that of Cormac himself.

The doorway into the cathedral

The original high cross of the Rock is now located within the undercroft of the Vicars Choral to protect it against weathering. A replica stands in its place. It is believed that this unusual high cross was commissioned to mark the handing-over of the Rock of Cashel to the Church. Known as St Patrick's Cross, it features a depiction of Christ on one side and a bishop on the reverse, with Urnes-style decoration on the base. Folklore tells that if you can put your arms around the widest part of the cross and touch your fingers, you will never suffer a toothache again.

The Cathedral is the largest building on the Rock and dates to around the thirteenth century. It is almost unique, as the nave is considerably shorter than the chancel; a bishop's tower built onto the end of the nave shortens it even further. The cathedral contains a myriad of medieval sculptures; a number of carved heads can be seen high on the capitals, and grave slabs and tomb niches can also be seen throughout. One of the most famous graves is that of Miler Magrath (d. 1622). He was Archbishop of Cashel and was notorious for controversy and corruption. Throughout his life he made many enemies, and so he became concerned that, after his death, enemies would exhume his body and remove it from the sacred ground of the Rock of Cashel. To confuse his enemies, his tomb epitaph contains the following cryptic lines: 'Here where I'm placed I'm not; and thus the Case is, I'm not in both, yet am in both the Places.' The tower at the end of the nave dates to the fifteenth century. It served as a home for the Archbishop of Cashel. From the tower the Archbishop could access the intramural passageways that extend throughout the upper floors of the cathedral.

A fine example of a round tower stands outside the cathedral. It is likely to have been one of the first stone buildings on the Rock, and was probably built some time between the ninth and eleventh centuries. At approximately 28 metres (92 ft) tall, the round tower would have soared above the other church buildings and acted as a potent symbol of the Christian community at the Rock of Cashel.

The Hall of the Vicars Choral was the last building to be constructed on the Rock. It housed the choir that served the cathedral. Restored and renovated in the 1980s, its undercroft houses a number of artefacts from the Rock and its locality, including St Patrick's Cross. High on the south-eastern exterior wall of the Vicars Choral is a Sheela-na-gig.

The Rock of Cashel was notoriously attacked in 1647, when Murrough O'Brien (known as Lord Inchiquin) marched into Cashel on behalf of the English Parliament. It is said that the townspeople fled to the cathedral of the Rock for protection, but Inchiquin and his men stormed the place, slaughtering hundreds (some estimate 3,000) of townspeople and clergy. Soon after, the site became Protestant. The Archbishop continued to live on site until the time of Archbishop Arthur Price in the mid eighteenth century. When St John's Cathedral and a new residence for the Archbishop were constructed in the town, the Rock was finally abandoned. It began to fall into decay until it was taken into state care in the 1870s.

In a neighbouring field at the foot of the Rock are the ruins of Hore Abbey. This was the last Cistercian abbey to have been founded in Ireland. A daughter house of Mellifont (Site 19), it was founded in 1272 by David Mac Cearbhaill. The name Hore (Hoar) Abbey comes from the grey-coloured tunics the monks wore. Originally Benedictine monks had been invited to the site but they were expelled by the Archbishop, allegedly after he had a dream that they would cut his throat. It is thought that the same masons who worked on the cathedral of the Rock of Cashel may also have worked on this construction.

Nearby in Cashel there is a host of other fascinating medieval buildings. The town itself was founded in the thirteenth century and was granted a charter by King Charles I in 1639. The Dominican friary is located on a small street that links the town with the Rock. All that can be seen today are the ruins of the church that belonged to the friary. It was established in 1243 by Archbishop David Ó Gilla Pátraic. Other historical buildings include St John's Church of

Hore Abbey

Ireland, which became the cathedral when the Rock was abandoned. It stands on the site of a medieval parish church, and a number of interesting effigies and tombs can be seen leaning against the old town wall at the back of the graveyard.

SITE MAP 7

ROCK OF CASHEL

Coordinates: Lat: 52.520092, Long: -7.890574

Grid reference: S 07463 40952

Opening times: Open all year round

Entry fee: Please visit www.heritageireland.ie/en/south-east/rockofcashel/

Facilities: Toilets are located at the foot of the Rock. Guided tours are available. There is an audiovisual presentation and a small museum in the undercroft of the Vicars Choral building.

Car parking: Large car park at the foot of the Rock

Directions: The Rock of Cashel is about 500 metres from the centre of Cashel off the Dublin Road.

Nearest town: Located in the town of Cashel

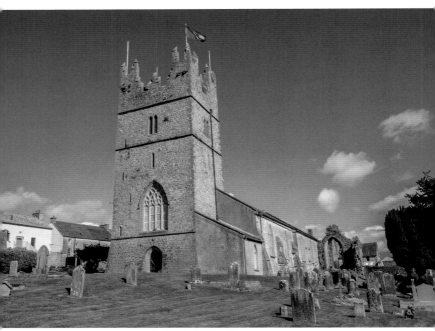

Holy Trinity Church, Fethard, County Tipperary

74 | FETHARD
COUNTY TIPPERARY

Hidden away in a valley of the Clashawley River is the lovely historic town of Fethard. It is a superb example of a medieval walled town with a wealth of fascinating medieval features in its streets. The town originated *c.* 1200, when William de Braose became the chief tenant of vast tracts of land in County Tipperary. He was a Norman knight from South Wales. Known as the 'Ogre of Abergavenny', De Braose had a reputation for violence and malice. One story recounts how, in 1175, he invited three Welsh princes and their supporters to a Christmas feast at his castle at Abergavenny in a gesture of peace. All were murdered. De Braose eventually fell foul of the English Crown, and lost his lands *c.* 1208 following a dispute with King John. The lands were granted to the Archbishop of Cashel in 1215.

Fethard's town walls

The early thirteenth century was a time of great prosperity for Fethard, though by the end of the century the increasing lawlessness of the land led to the construction of town walls. There are records of grants of money to the townspeople to build and maintain the walls in the late thirteenth, fourteenth and fifteenth centuries. The latter grant for reconstruction is likely to have been necessitated by an attack on the town by the Earl of Desmond in 1468.

The town continued to develop throughout the fifteenth century, and in 1523 Fethard was granted a charter. This allowed the townspeople to form a corporation for the management of Fethard, and as a result they ceased to pay rents to the Archbishop of Cashel, effectively ending his influence over the town's affairs. The corporation was successful and was granted a second charter in 1608. At this time the pre-eminent figure in Fethard was Sir John Everard, who helped to accelerate the development of the town. He had two almshouses built, and reconstructed the dilapidated south side of the main street. He also had a large house constructed for his family. Fethard largely managed to escape the depredations of Lord

Inchiquin and Cromwell, who both threatened the town. In both cases the town quickly surrendered and so was left in peace. According to local folklore, when Cromwell entered the town, he fell from his horse in Barrack Street and cursed the ground. To this day it is said that no funeral will pass the cursed spot.

By the eighteenth century Fethard had begun to fall into decay. Many of the medieval buildings were demolished and the town slipped from prominence. The once powerful Everard family who had done so much to develop the town now fell into obscurity, and through mismanagement of finances, eventually sold all their land and properties in Fethard.

Today Fethard is a wonderful place to gain a sense of a medieval Irish town. The town walls survive almost in their entirety. They enclose an area of 7.5 acres, and in places still stand over 7 metres (23 ft) high. Within the walls, the layout of the streets has changed little since medieval times and there are still many buildings dating back to that time.

The Holy Trinity Church is one of the best examples in Ireland of a medieval parish church. It was originally dedicated to St John the Baptist, but had become known as Holy Trinity by the sixteenth century. The church was largely renovated and restored in the late eighteenth and early nineteenth centuries; however, it retains much of its original medieval fabric and character. In recent years conservation architects discovered oak timbers dating to 1489 that still survive underneath the nineteenth-century roof. Inside the church are replicas of remarkable painted oak statues that date to the late fifteenth century. They are almost life-sized and represent God the Father, Christ on Calvary and St John the Baptist. They had been hidden in Fethard during the Reformation and kept safe for over 500 years. They are amongst the tiny number of these precious artefacts to have survived in Ireland. The originals are on display in the National Museum of Ireland, on Kildare Street, Dublin.

The North Gate is the only surviving gate into the town and dates to the fifteenth century. Originally the town had five gates that controlled access into the town. The Tholsel stands on Main Street. It was constructed in the seventeenth century and it has had a number of roles over the centuries. It originally served as an alms-house, and the Everard coat of arms can still be seen on the façade.

Sheela-na-gig at the Augustinian abbey in Fethard

Subsequently it was used as a town hall, and a place of punishment (records document the erection of stocks or a pillory outside the building in the nineteenth century). It has also served as a fire station, a library and a centre for country markets. It is currently being developed into a heritage centre that will help to tell the story of the town.

On Watergate Street you can see an urban tower house, often known as Court Castle. Local legend states that it was built by the Knights Templar, but it was constructed in the fifteenth century, over two centuries after the Templars had been suppressed. It was, in fact, constructed by the Knights Hospitaller, who share many similarities with the Templars, as both orders originated in the Holy Land during the Crusades. The last prior of the order was Sir Thomas Everard. He established a court in the building, leading to the name of 'Court Castle'. It was substantially altered in the late sixteenth century, around the time that the building known as Watergate Castle was adjoined to the south wall of Court Castle. Close to Watergate Castle stands Edmond's Castle, a three-storey urban tower house. Historical records suggest the owner may have been Redmond Everard, who is recorded as having two castles in Fethard in 1585.

The Augustinian abbey has its origins in 1306. The Augustinians built their monastic foundations on a claustral plan (church and other buildings arranged around a cloister). The parish church that stands on the site today is the original fourteenth-century building with numerous modifications. The Augustinian monks remained in Fethard until the dissolution of the monastery in the sixteenth century. After Catholic Emancipation, the monks were allowed to return and immediately set about rebuilding their church. They demolished the dilapidated tower that stood on the site, and rebuilt the façade of the church. Within the chapel you can discover many masons' marks that date to the fifteenth century. The eastern range of the monastery still survives. Originally, this would have accommodated the dormitory and chapter house. Unfortunately, the southern and western ranges no longer survive, and the area where the cloister once stood is now under a car park. However, within the graveyard are a number of fascinating medieval grave slabs, medieval sculptures and a fine example of a Sheela-na-gig.

FETHARD SITE MAP 7

Coordinates: Lat: 52.466164, Long: -7.695441

Grid reference: S 20688 34990

Opening times: Open all year round

Entry fee: Free

Facilities: There is a coffee shop in the village. The new Fethard Horse Country Experience housed in the old Tholsel is certainly well worth a visit (entry fees apply).

Car parking: Car parking throughout the town

Directions: Fethard is located in County Tipperary close to Cashel and Clonmel. To get to Fethard, exit the M8 motorway at Junction 8 and take the R692. This leads to Fethard.

Nearest town: Clonmel, 14km to the south, and Cashel, 16km to the north-west

75 | ORMOND CASTLE
COUNTY TIPPERARY

Ormond Castle, County Tipperary

Ormond Castle in the town of Carrick-on-Suir originally dates to the fourteenth century. It is named after the Butler family, a highly influential and powerful Norman dynasty who became Earls of Ormond.

In 1315 Edmund FitzWalter (sixth Chief Butler) was granted the Lordship and Manor of Carrick by King Edward II, and his son James made an advantageous marriage to Eleanor de Bohun, a granddaughter of the King. By the middle of the fourteenth century, the Butlers were Earls of Ormond and had cemented their position as one of the wealthiest and most powerful dynasties in Ireland.

The castle at Carrick-on-Suir is thought to have an early origin, but the remains visible today largely date to later than the fourteenth century. In the grounds are the ruins of a medieval bawn (a fortified walled enclosure), with two tall fourteenth- or fifteenth-century towers. One of the towers is in ruins, while the other tower (thought to be the earliest of the two) is still well preserved. Other buildings in the area exist only at foundation level, though it is possible to see the remains of the large bricked-up Water Gate in the exterior wall.

The ruins of the medieval bawn of Ormond Castle

In the medieval period, the River Suir flowed at the base of the castle walls, and the River Gate allowed goods and people to be transported easily up and down the river to the other major centres nearby at Cahir, Clonmel and Waterford.

The Tudor period was a turbulent time in Irish history. An uprising by the Butlers' long-time rivals, the Fitzgeralds, had just been defeated, and King Henry VIII had become the first English monarch to declare himself King of Ireland. He began a process of plantations and conquest that was continued after his death, during the reigns of Mary and then Elizabeth. During this chaotic period, Thomas Butler, Earl of Ossory and tenth Earl of Ormond, succeeded to his lands and titles in 1546 when he was just fifteen years old. Thomas had grown up at the English Court, and was seen as a faithful friend to the Crown. He was a personal friend to the young Elizabeth (and some suggest perhaps their friendship was more romantic than platonic) and he shared a tutor with the future King Edward VI. Following King Henry VIII's death, Thomas Butler was present at the coronation of the young King Edward and he was proclaimed a Knight of the Order of Bath, a very high honour. Following Edward's death at a young age, Thomas remained at court during Mary's reign and rose to high favour and prominence when Elizabeth became queen. She named him Lord Treasurer of Ireland, a position that brought great wealth and prestige.

He returned to Ireland, where he was thought of favourably, though he was considered to be 'wholly English' by the locals. He fought a number of bloody campaigns against the rebellious O'Moores of County Laois. However, despite occasionally earning the displeasure of the English court due to ongoing feuding with the Fitzgeralds, Thomas (or Black Tom as he became known) maintained the good favour of the Crown. He was awarded a number of titles: President of Munster, Lord High Marshal of Ireland and Commander in Chief of Her Majesty's Forces in Ireland.

It is said that he had the handsome Manor House of Ormond Castle constructed in preparation for a planned visit by Queen Elizabeth I. However, she never journeyed to Ireland.

Guided tours of Ormond Castle are available and visitors may enter a number of the rooms, most impressively the Long Gallery, which features musket-loops, showing a formidable defensive, as well as fashionable, design. It has a number of pieces of period furniture, though none are original to the building. They give a good sense of the style and furniture of the period. Perhaps most impressive of all is the rare plaster stucco friezes that depict the coat of arms of the Butler family as well as griffins, falcons and portrait busts of Elizabeth I. You can also see impressive grand fireplaces in this stately room that once would have been filled with portraits and tapestries, leaving contemporary visitors to Ormond Castle in no doubt about the wealth and taste of the Earl of Ormond.

ORMOND CASTLE   SITE MAP 7

Coordinates: Lat: 52.345500, Long: -7.407371

Grid reference: S 40406 21664

Opening times: The castle is usually open from May to September

Entry fee: Please visit www.heritageireland.ie/en/south-east/ormondcastle/

Facilities: Toilets and guided tour of the site

Car parking: Car parking close to the site

Directions: Ormond Castle is in the town of Carrick-on-Suir, on the banks of the River Suir, off Castle Street.

Nearest town: Clonmel, about 20km to the west

St Patrick's Well, County Tipperary

St Patrick's Well is situated in a tranquil valley to the west of Clonmel, close to the village of Marlfield in County Tipperary. It is a picturesque setting for this holy site, which has been revered for centuries. There are over 3,000 holy wells in Ireland and St Patrick's Well is thought to be one of the largest. Holy wells are sacred places where natural springs or man-made hollows that collect water are thought to have a religious significance because of their association with a saint. Many are thought to have originally been places of pre-Christian worship and tradition that were co-opted as Christian sites following the conversion of the local population.

Legend has it that St Patrick stopped off at this valley on his journey through Waterford and South Tipperary where he reputedly converted the King of Munster to Christianity at the Rock of Cashel. St Patrick was said to have stopped here to bathe and baptise local people. Unfortunately, however, it is unlikely that Patrick was ever in this part of Ireland, as he does not mention travelling to the south of the country in his writings, *Confessio* and *Epistola*. In fact, the story of Patrick's journey in Munster comes from a source written nearly 500 years after Patrick's death, the tenth-century Life of St Declan, but despite this, St Patrick's association with the well lives on.

Like many holy wells around the country, St Patrick's Well is said to have many curative properties in local belief and folklore. It is said that by drinking the water from the well or even washing in it, ailments like sore lips, sore eyes and many other chronic diseases can be cured. Indeed, it is thought that this well has miraculous properties as the water that flows through it never freezes. This is more likely owing to the well being sited over natural springs that maintain a constant temperature.

The well has been enclosed by a circular wall. The natural water that bubbles up is channeled through two narrow stone-cut openings that an archaeologist has identified as possible flumes from an early medieval mill. The water descends into a large, shallow pool, from where it flows into a narrow stream, a tributary of the River Suir, which flows nearby to the south of the site.

The water chutes at St Patrick's Well, possibly salvaged from an early medieval watermill

Standing on a small island in the pool is a small sandstone cross, one of the oldest archaeological monuments at St Patrick's Well. This cross is thought to date to the eighth century. It was originally positioned close to the church on marshy ground, but a programme of renovation and reconstruction was carried out at this site in the 1960s and the cross was moved to its current position.

The stone church to the south appears to date to the fifteenth or sixteenth century. There is a historical record of the Abbot of Inislounaght being buried at the church in 1617. Inislounaght was once a thriving Cistercian abbey but there are no traces left of it today. However, some architectural fragments may have been brought from the abbey to St Patrick's Well and incorporated into the parish church. Within the now roofless parish church there is an altar tomb dating from 1622, dedicated to the White family.

St Patrick's Well is a great example of this type of archaeological monument that transcends the boundaries between paganism and Christianity. If you visit this spiritual and tranquil spot it is easy to see why it was chosen hundreds or even thousands of years ago as a place of worship as there is a clear connection between the natural and sacred world at this site.

ST PATRICK'S WELL　　　　　　　　　　　　　　SITE MAP 7

Coordinates: Lat: 52.357662, Long: -7.752550

Grid reference: S 16853 22913

Opening times: All year round

Entry fee: Free

Facilities: None

Car parking: Limited car parking at the site

Directions: The easiest way to get to St Patrick's Well from Clonmel is to take the left-hand turn after the Poppyfields Shopping Centre on the Cahir Road (signposted for St Patrick's Well). Follow this narrow road until reaching a crossroads. Turn right and continue on this road. There will be parking spaces on the left. The well is accessed through a painted gate and is signposted.

Nearest town: Clonmel, about 6km to the east

77 | CAHIR CASTLE
COUNTY TIPPERARY

Cahir Castle, County Tipperary

Cahir Castle was constructed in the thirteenth century, on the site of an earlier Irish stone fort known as *Cathair Dún Iascaigh* ('the Stone Fort of the Fortress of the Fishery'). According to the seventeenth-century historian Geoffrey Keating, the stone fort of Dún Iascaigh was one of the ancient royal residences of the kings of Munster before the arrival of Christianity. It is from the word *Cathair* that the modern name of the town is derived.

The castle that we can see today dates from many different periods. It is possible that it was originally built by Philip de Worcester in the middle of the thirteenth century, though for much of its history it has been in the possession of the Butler family. The structure, layout and appearance of the castle altered over the years

CAHIR CASTLE

The interior of the Great Hall in Cahir Castle

as the defensive features sometimes outweighed comfort and fashion owing to political stress and upheaval. Further works were completed on the castle in the fifteenth and sixteenth centuries and the last remodelling of the castle was carried out in the nineteenth century, which is why it is one of the finest preserved castles in Ireland today.

If you look carefully at the stone wall surrounding the castle, you may notice an iron cannonball, a legacy of the first serious siege of the castle, which occurred in 1599 when it was attacked by Crown forces under the command of Robert Deveraux, Earl of Essex.

As the nature of warfare changed with the arrival of the cannon, the old stone fortresses had become vulnerable (as so clearly demonstrated in 1599). As their strategic and military worth lessened, they began to take on more of a domestic role as high-status grand houses. Despite this, the castle was still seen as an obstacle to Oliver Cromwell during his campaign in 1650. His letter to the garrison still survives:

Sir – having brought the army and my cannon near this place, according to my usual manner in summoning places, I thought fit to offer you terms honourable to soldiers: that you may march away, with your baggage, arms and colours, free from injuries or violence. But if I be, notwithstanding, necessitated to bend my cannon upon you, you must expect the extremity usual in such cases. To avoid blood, this is offered to you, by Your Servant – Oliver Cromwell.

By this time Cromwell's ruthless reputation was known across Ireland, and the garrison at Cahir decided to take him up on his offer and marched away without loss of life.

Much of the castle that we see today is a result of extensive renovations in the nineteenth century. It is still an imposing and atmospheric place, and served as a setting for Stanley Kubrick's 1975 classic *Barry Lyndon*. Visitors today can enjoy a tour through the castle and see many of the features that made it such a formidable fortress in the medieval period.

If you have the time I highly recommend taking the 2-km riverside walk (or 5-minute drive) to the Swiss Cottage. This beautiful *cottage orné* was built in 1810 by Richard Butler, first Earl of Glengall, to a design by the Regency architect John Nash. Richard Butler himself had a quite remarkable story of rags to riches. When James Butler died in 1786, his wealth, titles and estates passed to his brother Piers, who died just two years later in Paris. It passed again to an impoverished and distant cousin, who in turn died in the East Indies in 1788 without ever having learned of his sudden new-found wealth and position. The title passed to his son Richard, who was only twelve years old at the time and living in abject poverty with his mother and sister in Cahir.

While still unaware of their new status, the children were transported to France by avaricious relatives who hoped to contest the inheritance. They were rescued by Mrs Jeffereys of Blarney Castle who returned Richard, his sister and their mother to their magnificent inheritance. The Swiss Cottage was primarily used as a place to get away from it all. It features two rooms downstairs and two bedrooms (though it is believed the Butlers never spent a night), and is lavishly decorated with themes of nature – an enchanting place to visit.

The Swiss Cottage fell into disrepair in the 1970s and 1980s, but a careful conservation and restoration plan was undertaken by Cahir

Swiss Cottage, at Cahir, County Tipperary

Community Council, the OPW, the Irish Georgian Society, Fás and Sally Aall, a generous American benefactor.

Cahir is a charming town that is absolutely packed with other historical features like a medieval Augustinian priory, and the historic Church of St Paul's.

CAHIR CASTLE   SITE MAP 7

Coordinates: Lat: 52.374642, Long: -7.927122

Grid reference: S 05013 24760

Opening times: Open all year round.
See: www.heritageireland.ie/en/south-east/cahircastle
for specific opening hours

Entry fee: Please visit www.heritageireland.ie/en/south-east/cahircastle/

Facilities: Toilets, guided tours, audiovisual exhibition

Car parking: Paid parking beside castle

Directions: Cahir Castle is located in the centre of Cahir town and is well signposted

Nearest town: Clonmel, about 20km to the east

Lough Gur, with Knockadoon Hill as a backdrop

Lough Gur in County Limerick is one of the most important and remarkable archaeological landscapes in Ireland. This small, horseshoe-shaped lake has been a focal point for settlement and activity for millennia, beginning in the Neolithic period. This was a time of Ireland's first farmers, people who began the backbreaking labour of clearing the vast forests that covered Ireland.

Lough Gur's Neolithic settlement consists of several houses, forming a small village on the south-facing slopes of the Knockadoon peninsula, which extends out into the lake. During excavations, both rectangular and circular houses were discovered. Our Neolithic ancestors built the houses by driving double rows of wooden posts into the ground. These posts supported a hipped roof and screens made from woven hazel rods known as wattle. The screens were covered in daub, a mix of dung, clay and straw, which, when dried, would have been an effective, breathable, but water- and draught-proof, wall. The houses may have been insulated with a layer of earth sods, reeds or straw. An example of one of the rectangular

buildings and of a circular building have been reconstructed and now serve as Lough Gur's heritage centre.

From the heritage centre, follow a looped walk to visit some of the archaeological sites in the area. The first stop is 'the Spectacles', where there are the foundations of a number of buildings and field systems dating to the early medieval period. Follow the path beyond the Spectacles, climbing ever higher to get spectacular views over Lough Gur and the landscape that has drawn people to the shores of this small lake for thousands of years.

The remains of a *crannóg* can be seen in the lake, and the ruins of two Desmond castles are visible on the shore. The island near the eastern shore is named Garrett Island after the third Earl of Desmond, Gerald (or Garrett) Fitzgerald. He disappeared in 1398 and according to legend he is doomed to live under the lake. He emerges fully armed and dressed in his finery at daybreak one day every seven years, mounted on a phantom white horse. He rides across the lake and leads a fairy host. He is compelled to repeat this until his horse's silver shoes wear away. Folklore and mythology abound at Lough Gur, with legends of a lost city beneath its calm, enchanted waters.

When you have finished your visit to Lough Gur itself, it is a short drive up the road to the cashels of Carraig Áille. These well-preserved early medieval stone ringforts have quite spectacular views, and are well worth the short climb up the hill. Another short drive from Carraig Áille is a wonderful example of an Early Bronze Age wedge tomb. The tomb was excavated in 1938, and artefacts such as prehistoric pottery, flint and human remains were discovered.

Further along the road is Teampall Nua ('New Church'), a church thought to date to the seventeenth century. It replaced an older chapel used by the Earls of Desmond.

Perhaps the most evocative and atmospheric of Lough Gur's treasures is the Grange Stone Circle, located on the west of the lake and very easily accessible from the Limerick–Killmallock Road (R512). This stone circle is enormous, measuring nearly 50 metres (160 feet) in diameter. It is a near-perfect ring of 113 contiguous stones (i.e. all the stones are touching). The entrance is marked with the tallest stones and aligned with the rising sun of the summer solstice.

SITE MAP 7

LOUGH GUR

Coordinates: Lat: 52.522279, Long: -8.519878

Grid reference: R 64716 41330

Opening times: Lough Gur is open daily from January to end November. See www.loughgur.com for more information about specific opening hours.

Entry fee: Please visit www.loughgur.com

Facilities: Coffee shop, gift shop, toilet facilities, exhibition centre, guided tour of the site

Car parking: Large car park on site

Directions: From Limerick, follow the R512 (Kilmallock Road) south out of Limerick city for about 21km. Continue through Ballyneety and after about 8km take the left directly after Reardon's Pub. Continue on this road for about 2km to the large car park and heritage centre. The site is well signposted.

Nearest town: Limerick, 20km to the north, and Bruff, 7km to the south

79 | KILMALLOCK
COUNTY LIMERICK

Settlement in Kilmallock began around 600, when St Mocheallóg founded a monastery on a hill approximately 2km north-west of the current town. This monastery gave the town its name, as Kilmallock derives from the Irish *Cill Mocheallóg* ('the Church of Mocheallóg').

Kilmallock is one of Ireland's best-preserved walled towns, and contains a wealth of medieval buildings and features. Perhaps most impressive of this array of medieval architecture is the magnificent Dominican priory that sits on the banks of the River Loobagh. The priory was founded in 1291, though it was extended

Above: Kilmallock's Dominican priory
Right: Medieval sculpture in the Dominican priory in Kilmallock

and altered over the centuries. It contains some of Ireland's best examples of medieval architecture, such as the ornate five-light east window. A large number of sculptures of human heads (possibly representing benefactors of the priory) can be discovered throughout the buildings.

The priory was founded with the support of the powerful Gilbert Fitzgerald. His tomb lies in the sanctuary beside the high altar of the priory, an honoured place reserved for the founders of monasteries. The Fitzgerald family is entwined with the story of Kilmallock. This Anglo-Norman family dominated southern Munster for nearly three centuries. From their base in Kilmallock, the Fitzgerald Earls of Desmond (Desmond derives from *deas Mumhan*, meaning 'south Munster') controlled Limerick, north Kerry, north and east Cork and west Waterford, becoming almost de facto sovereigns of this vast area. Like many other Norman families, they intermarried with the native Irish and adopted Irish language and customs. The priory was suppressed during the Dissolution of the Monasteries ordered by King Henry VIII in 1541.

Although the Dominicans retained a presence here for a further two centuries, the position of the monastery was never secure in the turbulent times that followed. The priory was still home to a

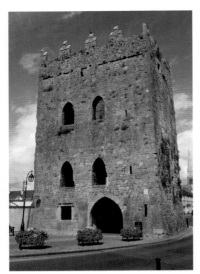

King's Castle at Kilmallock

community of monks in 1645 during the Confederate Wars, when it was visited by the Papal Legate, Cardinal Runnicini. Tragically, in 1648 it was attacked by the parliamentary forces of Lord Inchiquin and two monks were put to death in front of the altar. However, despite these shocking events, monks continued to live and work here until well into the eighteenth century, often under the threat of religious persecution.

As well as the impressive priory, Kilmallock has a number of other medieval buildings to discover. King's Castle is one of the most notable. This fine example of an urban tower house dates to the fifteenth century. It is likely that it was originally built as the fortified home of a wealthy merchant or noble. Some of the other medieval buildings include the remains of a sixteenth-century stone mansion house, the medieval collegiate church of Ss Peter and Paul and of course the well-preserved stone walls that surround the town.

KILMALLOCK   SITE MAP 7

Coordinates: Lat: 52.399562, Long: -8.574676

Grid reference: R 60888 27703

Opening times: Open all year round

Entry fee: Free

Facilities: Coffee shop, tourist information point and toilets in the town

Car parking: Parking throughout the town

Directions: Kilmallock is located in the Ballyhoura region, east of the N20. From Cork/Limerick, travelling on the N20, exit onto the R518, following signs for Bruree/Kilmallock. Continue on the R518 through Bruree and to Kilmallock.

Nearest town: Bruff, about 9km to the north, and Charleville, 9km to the south-west

Darby's Bed in County Limerick

Darby's Bed (also known as Duntryleague Passage Tomb) is the remains of a passage tomb, situated near the summit of a steep hill just outside the village of Galbally in County Limerick. The tomb dates to around 3000 BC, and was once covered by a stone cairn or earthen mound. All that remain visible today are the large upright stones, known as orthostats, that once lined the passageway and the capped chamber of the passage tomb. The entrance to the tomb faces north-west, possibly in alignment with sunset at midsummer. Though today the planted forest obscures much of the vista, it is clear that this tomb once commanded spectacular views over the landscape.

DARBY'S BED

The Neolithic tomb is steeped with legends and folklore, and the tragic lovers Diarmuid and Gráinne are said to have sheltered for a night inside this tomb when they were fleeing Fionn Mac Cumhaill.

DARBY'S BED SITE MAP 7

Coordinates: Lat: 52.407033, Long: -8.325066

Grid reference: R 77880 28429

Opening times: Open all year round

Entry fee: Free

Facilities: None

Car parking: Limited car parking available close to the site

Directions: From Galbally village square, head north-west and follow the signpost marked 'Duntryleague Cairns and Passage Tomb'. Follow this small road for approximately 2km to come to a small gravelled car park on the right with a wooden sign marked 'Megalithic Tomb'. Park here and walk along the path up the hill. The tomb is on the left. It is around 500 metres and quite a steep climb, so comfortable boots are recommended.

Nearest town: Galbally, about 2km to the east

Ferns Castle

St Maodhóg, better known as St Aidan, founded a monastery at Ferns in the seventh century. The monastery suffered a number of Viking raids in the ninth century, but survived to become an important religious centre. It was selected as one of the five diocesan centres in Leinster during the Synod of Rathbreasail that divided the country into dioceses and parishes in 1111.

The powerful Uí Cinsealagh, ancestors of the MacMurchadas (known today as MacMurroughs), made Ferns their base. They became Kings of Leinster in the eleventh century. A ringwork castle was constructed on the site where Ferns Castle stands today. It was

The reputed grave of Diarmait MacMurchada

most likely an earth-and-timber fortification and was the seat of the MacMurchadas until it was burned in 1166. In the years that followed the Anglo-Norman invasion, William Marshal constructed a fine stone castle on the site of the destroyed fort. This was a symbolic statement: by claiming the royal site of the Kings of Leinster, Marshal was reminding the people that he was linked to the family, following his marriage to Diarmait MacMurchada's granddaughter Isabel de Clare. He constructed the castle as a square block with four corner towers, though today only two of the towers survive. One of the towers is well preserved, and it is possible to take a guided tour to see the interior, as the castle is now managed by the OPW which runs an interpretative centre on site. There are three floors in the tower. On the first floor is the chapel with a vaulted and ribbed ceiling and trefoil windows, which may date to the thirteenth century. Excavations carried out on the castle in the 1970s revealed a large rock-cut ditch that surrounded the site, with evidence for a barbican and drawbridge.

Perhaps the most famous MacMurchada king was Diarmait MacMurchada. Diarmait was King of Leinster from around 1132.

A significant supporter of Church reform, he was responsible for the foundation of a number of monasteries, abbeys and religious houses in the south-east, including Killeshin in County Laois (Site 37) and All Hallows in Dublin. Diarmait became embroiled in a bloody feud with Tigearnán Ua Ruairc, the King of Breifne (roughly, the modern counties of Leitrim, Cavan and parts of Meath). This was exacerbated when Diarmait abducted Ua Ruairc's wife Dervogilla (though some say Dervogilla was rather keen to be abducted). In revenge, Ua Ruairc burned Diarmait's fort at Ferns in 1166. When the High King of Ireland, Ruaidrí Ua Conchobair, supported Ua Ruairc by banishing Dairmait, he fled Ireland. The Norman King of England, Henry II, allowed him to seek support amongst his barons and knights. In south Wales he received the support of Richard de Clare, Earl of Pembroke, known as Strongbow. The two men came to terms, with the understanding that Strongbow and his Norman forces would help Diarmait to defeat his enemies, in return for Strongbow being named as Diarmait's successor as Lord of Leinster and being given his daughter Aoife's hand in marriage. After the Normans invaded in 1169, both men kept their word. Diarmait died soon after in 1171, and his grave is marked in the graveyard of Ferns by the broken shaft of a high cross, decorated with intricate fretwork. It is said that the cross was broken during the Cromwellian invasion in the seventeenth century. Fragments of four other high crosses were also discovered in the graveyard and have been put back together to show how they once stood. These probably date to the tenth or eleventh centuries.

In the thirteenth century, a cathedral was built on the site of the ancient monastery by the first Norman Bishop of Ferns, John St John. This cathedral was burned in 1575 but was restored in 1577. The ruins of buildings associated with the medieval cathedral lie to the east of the present building. Here you can see the remains of what was once a large building with tall lancet windows, which may have been a separate choir constructed for the Augustinian canons. In 1817, a new cathedral was built on the site for the Church of Ireland community, and is one of the smallest cathedrals in Europe. Inside the cathedral you can see the thirteenth-century tomb effigy of John St John.

The remains of the Augustinian abbey at Ferns

South-east of the cathedral are the remains of the Augustinian abbey that was founded in 1150 by Diarmait MacMurchada. Diarmait was supposed to have sought shelter within this abbey as he awaited the arrival of the Normans. This abbey was dissolved in 1539 and its lands reverted to the Crown. All that remains of it are the north wall of the chancel, the nave and an unusual belfry tower, which is square at the base up to the roof level of the church and circular above. It contains a staircase and gave access to a gallery over the nave. It may be indicative of the transition from detached round towers to belfries being incorporated into churches. You can also see St Mogue's Cottage, an eighteenth-century building that was originally the priest's accommodation and is now used for community activities and training.

East of Ferns you can find the small nave-and-chancel church of St Peter's, believed to be a sixteenth-century construction. A twelfth-century Romanesque window in the south chancel wall was probably taken from another church nearby. St Mogue's Well is near to the church. Legend states that when St Mogue was building the monastery his followers complained bitterly that there was no water. St Mogue instructed them to dig at this very spot and the well was miraculously discovered. The well also incorporates fragments of earlier church buildings.

FERNS   SITE MAP 6

Coordinates: Lat: 52.590773, Long: -6.499128

Grid reference: T 01702 49882

Opening times: Ferns Castle is open from mid May to end September. The cathedral and abbey site is open all year round.

Entry fee: Free

Facilities: At the castle there is an exhibition, toilets and car park

Car parking: Car parking at Ferns Castle and at the cathedral

Directions: Ferns Castle is in the centre of Ferns. Ferns is located on the N11, the main Dublin–Wexford road.

Nearest town: Enniscorthy, about 12km to the south

The exterior of Enniscorthy Castle

The town of Enniscorthy developed around an Anglo-Norman manor that was granted to Robert de Quincy, who was married to Strongbow's sister Basilia. He died soon after the marriage, and Basilia married the famous Anglo-Norman warlord Raymond le Gros. It is possible that he erected a motte and bailey as the first fortification close to the site of the present castle, which was built on the east-facing slope of a rock outcrop that overlooks the Slaney River. The lands were later transferred through marriage to Philip de Prendergast in 1198, before the manor passed to the Rochfort family. The castle was recorded as being 'destroyed by the Irish' in 1326. The Gaelic-Irish MacMurchada family took possession of the town some time in the fifteenth century. The castle in its present form is thought to date to the late sixteenth century, when Sir Henry Wallop acquired the lease for the town. Its design, with four corner towers, is similar to that of Ferns Castle, though it is much smaller. Some of the distinctive late sixteenth-century features include square-headed doors, windows and fireplaces as well as gun loops. One of the unique features of the castle is the sixteenth-century depiction of a halberdier painted on the wall of the dungeon.

The poet Edmund Spenser, author of *The Faerie Queene*, leased the castle in 1581, though it seems he never actually lived there as he believed the region to have become too dangerous and unsettled. The castle was surrendered to Cromwell in 1649. Almost 150 years later, Enniscorthy would again be the setting for conflict during some of the fiercest fighting of the 1798 Rebellion, which took place in the streets of Enniscorthy and on Vinegar Hill on the opposite bank of the Slaney. The story of the rebellion and its aftermath can be discovered in the nearby National 1798 Rebellion Centre.

The castle has become the home of the Wexford County Museum. The ground floor has an introduction to the castle's history from its earliest origins to the twentieth century. The first floor is dedicated to the Roche family, who were the last occupants of the castle: Henry J. Roche, his wife Josephine and their five children lived here until Dodo (Josephine) Roche could no longer manage the castle in 1953. The Roche family were in the brewing industry, and were considerable landowners in the region. You can see many fascinating mementos and pictures of their life. Other exhibitions in the castle include a history of the 1916 Rising (outside of Dublin, Enniscorthy

A sixteenth-century depiction of a soldier or halberdier in the dungeon of Enniscorthy Castle

was the largest urban area to be taken by rebels, and the last place to surrender) and a profile of local woman Eileen Gray, the famous furniture designer and architect.

ENNISCORTHY CASTLE   SITE MAP 6

Coordinates: Lat: 52.501436, Long: -6.567107

Grid reference: S 97284 39844

Opening times: The castle is open all year round. Please see www.enniscorthycastle.ie for specific opening times

Entry fee: Please visit www.enniscorthycastle.ie

Facilities: Craft and gift shop, toilets and tourist information point

Car parking: There is no car parking at the castle but there is plenty of parking throughout the town

Directions: The castle is located in the centre of Enniscorthy

Nearest town: Wexford, about 24km to the south, and New Ross, 37km to the south-west

---

83 | NEW ROSS & THE ROS TAPESTRY COUNTY WEXFORD

The Norman town of New Ross was founded by a charter of William Marshal in 1207. He established the town to serve as a trading port on the River Barrow at a point that was navigable for large ships entering from the Irish Sea. The town flourished, and great quantities of grain, wool, timber and other goods were brought downriver to New Ross to be exported to England, Wales and France. Wine was one of the most important imports into New Ross from the continent, and the town and its burgesses grew wealthy through the trade. Marshal founded St Mary's Church in *c.* 1220. One of the largest medieval parish churches in Ireland, it was built in the Early English Gothic style, and it contains a number of fine examples of

St Mary's Church, New Ross

The Ros Tapestry

medieval sculpture. A nineteenth-century Church of Ireland church was constructed on the site of the nave.

The Ros Tapestry is a superb community-led initiative that depicts the tale of the Norman arrival in Ireland in a series of beautifully embroidered tapestries. The illustrations were created by Countess Ann Griffin Bernstorff, who first painted the scenes. They were then painstakingly stitched by over 150 volunteers from New

Ross, Wexford, Kilkenny, Waterford, Carlow, Offaly, Wicklow, Cork, Bristol and Essex. Many of the panels were stitched at the locations of the historic events depicted in them. The project began in 1998 and now fifteen large panels have been placed on permanent display in a dedicated exhibition on the Quay of New Ross. Panels depict scenes such as the Normans' first landing in Ireland at Bannow Strand, the life of William Marshal and his marriage to Isabel de Clare.

The Ros Tapestry is a unique and moving achievement. It is a wonderful testament to the skill and craftsmanship of all involved in the programme, and tangible evidence of the volunteers' pride and passion for their history.

On the Quay opposite the Ros Tapestry exhibition you can find the Dunbrody Famine Ship Experience. The ship is a reproduction of a three-masted barque, typical of the type of ship that transported Irish emigrants to America in the 1840s.

THE ROS TAPESTRY   SITE MAP 8

Coordinates: Lat: 52.391629, Long: -6.949746

Grid reference: S 71634 27423

Opening times: Open from April to December (10 a.m. – 5 p.m., closed Sundays)

Entry fee: Please visit www.rostapestry.ie

Facilities: Toilets, guided tours of exhibition

Car parking: Car parking available at the Dunbrody Famine Ship

Directions: The Ros Tapestry Exhibition Centre is in a blue building on the Quay in New Ross almost directly opposite the Dunbrody Famine Ship.

Nearest town: The tapestry is in New Ross

84 DUNBRODY ABBEY
COUNTY WEXFORD

Dunbrody Abbey

Dunbrody Abbey was founded by Hervey de Montmorency in 1182. He served as Strongbow's administrative officer of the Lordship of Leinster. The abbey was consecrated in 1201 by the Bishop of Leighlin, a man named Herlwyn, a nephew of de Montmorency. The abbey was founded on the low-lying plains near the Campile River. It was a Cistercian foundation and a daughter house of St Mary's Abbey in Dublin.

The abbey is a fine example of Cistercian Gothic architecture. The chancel and transepts of the abbey were possibly the first to be constructed, followed by the nave. The abbey was substantially modified in the fifteenth century, and it is likely that the crossing tower was added at this time. Within the south transept, the night stairs (which allowed easy access to the monks' dormitories for evening prayers) still stand. Antiquarian illustrations from the eighteenth century show an ornate window in the western wall of the church, but unfortunately this wall and window collapsed in 1852. Today you can still see the cloisters, with possible traces of a lavabo that were discovered during archaeological excavations in 2007. The eastern range of the abbey houses the ruins of the sacristy, the chapter house and an undercroft, which is positioned to the south. Beyond these claustral buildings are the remains of a gatehouse and a chapel. All of the fine dressed stone within the abbey was imported from Dundry, near Bristol in England – more evidence of the wealth of the abbey at the time.

Historical records point to repeated bouts of conflict and ill feeling between the monks of Dunbrody and nearby Tintern Abbey (Site 85), with bitter disputes over land. Local legend relates that the abbot of Dunbrody held a monk from Tintern in a cell for three days, and robbed him of his money and two horses.

The abbey was dissolved in 1536, and its lands were granted to Sir Osbourne Etchingham in 1545. He transformed parts of the abbey into a three-storey manor house. Today you can see evidence of his fine residence in the mullioned windows, chimneys and fireplaces. This house was abandoned in the seventeenth century for a new house that was built nearby to the east.

DUNBRODY ABBEY   SITE MAP 8

Coordinates: Lat: 52.283853, Long: -6.960056

Grid reference: S 70993 15145

Opening times: The abbey is open from mid May to September. Tours may be arranged in advance. Please see: www.dunbrodyabbey.com for more details.

Entry fee: Please visit www.dunbrodyabbey.com

Facilities: Maze, pitch and putt, craft shop and tea room

Car parking: Car parking available

Directions: Dunbrody Abbey is located off the R733. From New Ross, travel south on the R733 for about 15km and the abbey will be on your right.

Nearest town: New Ross, 15km to the north, and Ballyhack, 5km to the south

Tintern Abbey, County Wexford

Tintern Abbey was reputedly founded in 1200 when the powerful Norman knight William Marshal set out on his first visit to Ireland after his inheritance as Lord of Leinster. On the voyage, his ship was struck by a storm off the east coast and was close to foundering. He vowed to God that if he safely reached shore he would found an abbey wherever he landed. He managed to get ashore at Bannow Bay in County Wexford, and kept his vow, granting 3,500 hectares to the Cistercian Order to establish an abbey. Hence, Tintern was occasionally called 'Tintern de Voto' or 'Tintern of the Vow'. As the Earl of Pembroke, William Marshal was also the patron of Tintern Abbey in Monmouthshire in Wales. He brought monks from Monmouthshire to settle in his new foundation in Wexford, which they named Tintern in honour of their original home.

Tintern was a wealthy and powerful Cistercian foundation, thought to be the third wealthiest Cistercian abbey, after Mellifont (Site 4) and St Mary's in Dublin. Tintern followed the standard

Tintern Abbey viewed from the bridge

layout for all Cistercian abbeys in Ireland, based on the mother house of Mellifont. The cloisters were positioned at the south and were surrounded by a range of domestic and spiritual buildings, with a cruciform church to the north.

Like most other Irish monastic sites Tintern became private property after the Dissolution of the Monasteries in the 1540s during King Henry VIII's reign. The lands were granted to Anthony Colclough, an army officer. He and his descendants made extensive changes and modifications to the abbey to change it from a Cistercian place of worship into a fashionable but fortified home.

One of the most identifiable features of Tintern is the castellated bridge over the head of a stream and tidal inlet, which dates to the eighteenth century. Nearby are the remains of a large limekiln which shows some of the more industrious activities needed on a large estate of the seventeenth and eighteenth centuries.

Tintern was granted to the Irish state in 1959 by Marie Colclough. Along with the abbey, the Colcloughs also donated a walled garden that dates to the early nineteenth century. The local community and Hook Tourism have carried out enormous restoration works in recent years, and the gardens today attest to their hard work and vision. They recreated the elegance of the garden as it would have appeared in 1838 based on cartographic information. If you are visiting Tintern, a visit to the walled garden is also recommended.

TINTERN ABBEY   SITE MAP 8

Coordinates: Lat: 52.237039, Long: -6.837950

Grid reference: S 79367 10087

Opening times: Tintern Abbey is open from the start of April to end September from 10 a.m. to 5 p.m. Last admission is 45 minutes before closing time.

Entry fee: Please visit www.heritageireland.ie/en/south-east/tinternabbey/

Facilities: Guided tours of the site, tea rooms, exhibitions, toilets

Car parking: Large car park at the site

Directions: To get to Tintern Abbey from New Ross, travel south on the R733 for about 5km. Continue straight onto the R734. At the crossroads with the R733, turn left. Take the first right off this road (signed for Tintern Abbey) and continue on this road until reaching the site.

Nearest town: New Ross, about 16km to the north

---

86 | LOFTUS HALL
COUNTY WEXFORD

The first reference to a hall at this location dates to 1591, when an Alexander Redmond was recorded as owning a hall with surrounding lands. It is quite possible that this earlier hall was similar in design to that of nearby Slade Castle, a tower house and fortified hall. This earlier hall came under attack in 1642 by forces loyal to the Crown during the Irish Confederate Wars, led by a group of 100 men under the command of Thomas Aston. The elderly Alexander Redmond barricaded himself inside along with his two sons and a few loyal men, fewer than ten defenders in total. The attackers had brought cannon with them but this proved ineffectual and many soldiers

Loftus Hall, County Wexford

absconded to pillage the surrounding countryside and nearby farms. Irish Confederate forces that were nearby came to assist the Redmonds and drove off the attackers. As they tried to escape by sea a great storm blew up and drowned many of the soldiers. A number of others were captured by the Confederate Army and executed. However, soon afterwards the Redmonds lost their hall and lands following the Cromwellian invasion. By 1666, Sir Nicholas Loftus had been granted the lands and hall, which he renamed Loftus Hall. He and his descendants made many changes to the hall, particularly in the early eighteenth century.

One of the most legendary incidents of Loftus Hall happened around that time. The tale tells that on the night of a wicked storm, a beleaguered ship landed at Hook Head and a young man rode to Loftus Hall seeking shelter. At that time Charles Tottenham (who had married into the Loftus Family), his second wife Jane Cliffe and his daughter Anne (from his first marriage) were living at Loftus Hall. They were all enamoured with the stranger, particularly young Anne. They played cards with the man and Anne accidentally dropped a card.

When she went to pick it up from under the table, she saw that the young man had cloven hooves instead of feet. She screamed. The man leapt up, disappeared through the ceiling in a puff of smoke and was never seen again. He left behind him a pungent smell of sulphur and a hole in the roof that was impossible to repair. Anne had a life of tragedy. It is said that after that incident she would not eat or sleep. She became so uncontrollable that her family locked her in the Tapestry Chamber and called on their Protestant ministers, but when they failed to help, the family turned to the local Catholic priest, Fr Thomas Broaders, to carry out an exorcism. It seemed to help Anne, and afterwards the family became a champion of Catholic causes. Poor Anne died at just thirty-one years of age. Local legend says that she still haunts Loftus Hall to this day, one of several ghostly apparitions and hauntings for which Loftus Hall still holds a dark reputation.

The building was pulled down in 1870, and the present building was constructed. Nothing remains of the earlier incarnations of Loftus Hall or Redmond Hall, though the walled garden to the north-east may date to the 1680s.

LOFTUS HALL   SITE MAP 8

Coordinates: Lat: 52.148630, Long: -6.910016

Grid reference: S 74561 00180

Opening times: Loftus Hall is open daily from February to August, and at weekends in September and October. Please see: www.loftushall.ie for information about specific opening hours.

Entry fee: Please visit www.loftushall.ie

Facilities: Coffee shop, gift shop, toilet facilities, interactive guided tour of parts of the house

Car parking: Large car park on site

Directions: Loftus Hall is located on the Hook Head Peninsula. Drive south from Duncannon along the peninsula towards Hook Lighthouse. The house will be on the right.

Nearest town: Duncannon, about 12km to the north, and Slade, 2km to the south

LOFTUS HALL

Hook Lighthouse, County Wexford

Hook Lighthouse is one of the oldest operational lighthouses in the world. This iconic and unique monument was constructed by the powerful medieval magnate William Marshal in the early thirteenth century, some time between 1210 and 1230.

The tower was maintained and operated by the monks of St Saviour's of Rinndeuan, a monastery founded by a Welsh monk called St Dubhán in the fifth century. He is believed to have started the practice of lighting a warning beacon at Hook Head. This tradition was continued through the centuries by his monks until William Marshal had the lighthouse constructed. It is from Dubhán that the peninsula got its original name, *Rinn Dubháin*, before being incorrectly anglicised to Hook Head.

The tower of the original thirteenth-century lighthouse stands around 25 metres (66 ft) tall, and a large beacon fire would have been lit on top of the tower in the medieval period. The lighthouse was maintained without interruption until around 1641, but it was described in 1657 as 'a former lighthouse', suggesting it had fallen out of use for a period.

It was restored in 1671 by Robert Readinge, who encased the light in glass, and it was powered by coal. The lighthouse keeper and his assistant, together with their families, would have lived in the first and second floors of the building in quite cramped conditions.

In 1791 the large lamp of the lighthouse was powered by whale oil, and the lighthouse was under the control of the Ballast Office. By the middle of the nineteenth century, new houses were constructed for the lighthouse keepers, and the distinctive black-and-white stripes became the identifier of the lighthouse. In 1867

The stunning views from Hook Lighthouse

the tower was handed over to the Commissioners of Irish Lights, which still operate it to this day.

The lamps were converted first to gas, then paraffin and finally, in 1972, electricity. In 1996 the last lighthouse keeper left Hook Lighthouse, when the operation was automated. Today the lighthouse is a fascinating and unique place to visit, and the experience is made all the more rewarding by the gorgeous scenery of County Wexford and the Hook Head Peninsula.

HOOK LIGHTHOUSE SITE MAP 8

Coordinates: Lat: 52.124729, Long: -6.929040

Grid reference: S 74561 00180

Opening times: Open all year. Please see www.hookheritage.ie for specific opening hours

Entry fee: Please visit www.hookheritage.ie

Facilities: Toilets, gift shop, restaurant, guided tours of lighthouse

Car parking: Large car park on site

Directions: Hook Lighthouse is at the very tip of Hook Head. Travel south through Hook Head to a T-junction. Turn right here and follow the road to the lighthouse.

Nearest town: Slade, about 2km to the north, and Duncannon, about 15km to the north

The gatehouse into Lismore Castle, County Waterford

Situated close to the River Blackwater, Lismore is a charming and historic town. The name Lismore comes from the Irish *Lios Mór* meaning 'great fort'. The origins of the town begin with a monastery founded in 636 by St Carthage (also known as St Mochuda). The monastery became a prominent centre of learning in early medieval Ireland. Lismore was recognised as a diocesan centre by the Synod of Rathbreasail in 1111, as part of the wider Irish Church reforms.

Hagiography tells us that St Carthage came to Lismore with 500 followers, after he was expelled from the monastery of Rahan in County Offaly following a dispute over the dating of Easter. One of the many miracles he is credited with is the resurrection of the Queen of Munster and her son after they had been struck by a bolt of lightning. Just two years after his arrival in Lismore, Carthage died. However, he left a potent legacy: his flourishing monastery.

Today little remains to be seen of the original monastery. The first buildings would have been constructed of timber, but had been replaced with stone by the twelfth century. A large fire swept through Lismore in 1207 and destroyed much of the town along with the church. After it was reconstructed, the church was again destroyed in 1600 during the turmoil of the Nine Years' War. A new cathedral was commissioned by Sir Richard Boyle in 1633 and dedicated to St Carthage. The cathedral has been renovated and altered numerous times since its construction. The ribbed ceilings, stained-glass windows and spire were all added in the early nineteenth century. In the cathedral there is a fine example of a sixteenth-century tabletop tomb. The tomb commemorates John McGrath and his wife Katherine Prendergast (d. 1557) and depicts religious scenes such

Lismore Castle

as Christ in the Tomb with St Gregory celebrating Mass, the twelve apostles, and Ss Catherine, Patrick and Carthage. English novelist William Thackeray visited Lismore and St Carthage's Cathedral in 1842 and described: 'the graceful spire of Lismore, the prettiest I have seen in, or I think out of, Ireland'.

When the Anglo-Normans arrived here in 1185, Prince John had a castle constructed on the site where the present Lismore Castle stands, on a bluff overlooking the River Blackwater as it surges below. The castle was attacked a number of times in its history, though it was often rebuilt by the Bishops of Lismore who resided in it.

Lismore and its castle were attacked during the Desmond Rebellion of the late sixteenth century, and subsequently the town fell into a state of neglect. It was granted to the Elizabethan adventurer Sir Walter Raleigh in 1590; however, he sold the lands soon after to Sir Richard Boyle. His son was the famous pioneering scientist Robert Boyle, known as the 'father of modern chemistry'. Robert was born at Lismore Castle in 1627. The Boyles continued to try to restore the castle, though it eventually began to fall into decay and neglect. In the early eighteenth century, William Duke of Devonshire married Lady Charlotte Boyle, heiress of the Boyles' vast estates in counties Waterford and Cork. In the early nineteenth century, William Spencer Cavendish (known as the Bachelor Duke) carried out extensive remodelling of the castle. During this work, the Lismore Crozier and Book of Lismore, which had been lost for

A view of the gardens of Lismore Castle

centuries, were rediscovered. The crozier, thought to date to around 1100, was found hidden in a blocked-up doorway of the castle. Today you can see it on display in the National Museum of Ireland on Kildare Street, Dublin. The Book of Lismore was probably compiled in the early fifteenth century and references the lives of Irish saints, particularly Brigid, Columba and Patrick, as well as the *Acallam na Senórach* (Tales of the Elders) with stories from the Fenian Cycle.

Despite the extensive renovations, parts of Lismore Castle still retain many seventeenth-century features, such as musket loops and wall walks. The castle is famous for its idyllic gardens, which date back to the time of the Boyles. These gardens are open to the public, and are a wonderful place for a walk. You can even encounter a surprising piece of history, as two large fragments of the Berlin Wall stand in the leafy tranquility of the gardens.

The town grew in the shadow of the castle throughout the seventeenth, eighteenth and nineteenth centuries. Its fine archi-tecture and streetscapes made it a worthy recipient of becoming one of the listed 'Irish Heritage Towns'.

The story of Lismore can be further explored in the superb Lismore Heritage Centre, located within the handsome nineteenth-century courthouse. Just a few kilometres outside the town are the Towers of Ballysaggartmore (Site 89).

LISMORE　　　　　　　　　　　　　　　　　SITE MAP 9

Coordinates: Lat: 52.137282, Long: -7.932562

Grid reference: X 04573 98466

Opening times: Open all year round

Entry fee: Entry fees are charged at Lismore Castle for access to the gardens. Please see: www.lismorecastlegardens.com for more information about prices and opening hours.

Facilities: Coffee shops, tourist information point at Lismore Heritage Centre, toilets

Car parking: Parking available in the town, just off the N72

Directions: Lismore is situated on the banks of the River Blackwater. The N72 (which connects Fermoy and Dungarvan) is the main road through Lismore and all sites in the town are within walking distance of one another.

Nearest town: Cappoquin, about 7km to the east

89 | THE TOWERS OF BALLYSAGGARTMORE
COUNTY WATERFORD

These towers were commissioned by Arthur Kiely-Ussher around 1835. He had inherited over 8,000 acres of land in the area and quickly gained a reputation for being a harsh landlord. It is said that his wife had become deeply envious of Strancally Castle, built by Arthur's brother John Kiely, and hectored Arthur to build a residence to outshine that of his brother.

Plans for an extravagant mansion were drawn up and work began on the long and winding carriageway, with an ornate gate lodge. They then constructed an elaborate bridge over a small stream, with large

The Gate Lodge at Ballysaggartmore, County Waterford

towers flanking each side of the bridge. However, their grandiose ambitions quickly outstripped their funds. They ran out of money soon after completing the bridge. They spent their days in Ballysaggartmore House (burned in 1922 and demolished after the Second World War), and must have felt despair as they travelled along their stunning carriageway that would never lead to the mansion they had so desired. A contemporary account deriding the extravagance of some of the gentry in Ireland at the time noted that: 'the crowning folly of them all, at Ballysaggartmore in Waterford, huge gates, then an even larger bridge, then for economy a smaller bridge and then at last, no house for there was no more money, the derelict demense lies heavily overgrown, enclosed and silent ...'

It is hard to feel much sympathy for the Kiely-Usshers. Arthur was a cruel and avaricious landlord during the Great Famine, and evicted large numbers of tenants who could not pay their rents. He demolished their homes and replaced them with livestock that could bring in better revenue. A group of desperate tenants even tried to assassinate him. They failed in their attempts and a number were sentenced to be transported to Tasmania in 1849.

The Famine was one of the most catastrophic events in recorded Irish history. In this area around Lismore alone, the population fell by over 50 per cent between 1841 and 1851. To spend so much money on an extravagance like the towers while the country starved

The elaborate bridge at Ballysaggartmore

is an indication of the nature of the Kiely-Usshers.

Despite its unjust and sad history, today the site is a pleasant place to walk. There is a fairly large car park and a number of interpretative panels. When you arrive follow the path up the slope to the right and loop around to the towers, first entering by the gate lodge.

There are a number of other sites nearby, and Lismore town itself is a good place to spend an afternoon, with plenty of cafes in which to refuel as well as a number of heritage sites including Lismore Castle (Site 88).

THE TOWERS OF BALLYSAGGARTMORE SITE MAP 9

Coordinates: Lat: 52.147132, Long: -7.970042

Grid reference: X 02457 99460

Opening times: Open all year round

Entry fee: Free

Facilities: Interpretative panels, picnic tables

Car parking: Large car park

Directions: Easy to find: take the R666 from Lismore heading towards Fermoy (signposted left after the bridge past Lismore Castle). The towers are well signposted on the right-hand side after about 3–4km.

Nearest town: Lismore, about 3.5km to the south-east

Gaulstown Dolmen, County Waterford

The Gaulstown Dolmen dates to some time around 3500 BC. It is situated in a wooded glade at the base of a steep slope known locally as Cnoc na Cailligh ('The Hill of the Hag'). It is one of the finest examples of a portal tomb in the region and well worth a trip.

To construct a portal tomb, large stones were placed upright in the ground to form a chamber. A mound of earth was built around the upright stones and this mound was used to haul the large capstone up on top of the uprights. The capstone was hauled up on rolling logs using ropes and then manoeuvred into place. The tomb was then generally covered with an earthen mound or stone cairn.

There are over 170 dolmens (also known as portal tombs) recorded in Ireland. Geographically they are more common in the northern half of the island, with some clusters in the south-east and in the west. Portal tombs are one of the earliest of Ireland's megalithic tomb types.

GAULSTOWN DOLMEN

Coordinates: Lat: 52.205780, Long: -7.210858

Grid reference: S 53934 06297

Opening times: Open all year round

Entry fee: Free

Facilities: None

Car parking: Very limited parking on the site of the road. Please do not block the gateway.

Directions: The dolmen is roughly 7km south-west of Waterford city. Follow the R680 from Waterford towards Kilmeadan. At Tramore crossroads (signposted for Tramore) turn left onto the R682. Continue along this road, driving through the first set of crossroads until coming to a second set of crossroads. Turn right here and continue down this road (driving straight across another crossroads). The site will be on the left. The tomb is signposted, but you can easily miss it as a large modern gate blocks the laneway to the site and makes it look like the entrance to a private residence. Access to the site is through a pedestrian entrance to the side of the gate. Follow the short path to reach the dolmen.

Nearest town: Waterford city, about 7km to the north-east

91 | MOUNT CONGREVE
COUNTY WATERFORD

Mount Congreve House was first constructed in the mid eighteenth century in the Palladian style, reputedly designed by the noted architect John Roberts, who was responsible for a number of the public buildings in Waterford city. It was the home of the Congreve family right up until the last member of the family, Ambrose Congreve, died aged 104 in 2011. The interior of the house was extensively remodelled in the 1960s when Ambrose inherited the estate. He worked mainly in London, managing a gasworks and petrochemical company, but would often return to his home on the banks of the River Suir, where he began to develop his great passion

Mount Congreve House, County Waterford
Inset: The classical temple in the gardens

for gardening. He had been inspired from an early age by family friend Lionel de Rothschild, who had developed one of the finest woodland gardens in the world at Exbury in Hampshire. Through his shrewd business acumen, Ambrose became wealthy and Mount Congreve was run on a lavish scale. It is said that Mount Congreve was the last Irish 'Big House' to employ liveried servants.

Ambrose began to clear the land for planting in 1955. He appointed the talented Herman Drool as Garden Director in the 1960s and the two worked together to create one of the world's greatest gardens. Ambrose believed in planting things together in a group rather than sparsely across the land, planting his trees alongside those planted by his ancestors from hundreds of years ago. When he retired in 1983, he focused on transforming his 110 acres into extensive gardens. He planted thousands more trees and shrubs, plants and flowers, including over 2,000 species of rhododendron, the largest collection in the world, throughout the parkland. He delighted in creating secret features and hidden vistas that are wonderful to discover. Within the gardens you can walk

A peacock butterfly takes a break in the tranquil gardens at Mount Congreve

along some of the many pathways to find a waterfall, a Chinese pagoda, a classical temple, a wildflower meadow, a bluebell walk and a charming (and extensive) walled garden.

Ambrose was celebrated in his lifetime for his skills and services to horticulture. He was awarded thirteen gold medals for his garden at the Chelsea Royal Horicultural Society Garden Show, and in 2001 he won the gold medal for a 'Great Garden of the World' from the Botanic Gardens of Boston, Massachusetts. Ambrose passed away while attending the Chelsea Flower Show in London. As Ambrose and his wife died without children, the house and its extensive gardens were bequeathed to the state. Today they are a delightful place to enjoy a walk at any time of the year, a living testament to the genius and hard work of Ambrose, his colleagues and his forebears.

MOUNT CONGREVE   SITE MAP 8

Coordinates: Lat: 52.240730, Long: -7.219056

Grid reference: S 53789 09829

Opening times: Mount Congreve is open from March to October, Thursdays to Sundays and bank holidays.

Entry fee: Please visit www.mountcongreve.com

Facilities: Toilets, coffee shop, garden shop. Tours of gardens are also available for an extra charge and must be booked in advance. Please see: www.mountcongreve.com for more information.

Car parking: Large car park at the site

Directions: Mount Congreve is close to Waterford city. From the city, follow the R710 ring road to the Old Kilmeadan Road Roundabout. Take the first exit off this roundabout and follow the Old Kilmeadan Road for about 3km. The entrance to the gardens will be on the right.

Nearest town: Waterford city, about 8km to the north-east

Waterford is Ireland's oldest city. Its name comes from the Old Norse *Veðrafjǫrðr* meaning 'Windy Ford' (the Irish name *Port Láirge* translates as Lárag's Port). Since its foundation by Vikings, Waterford has played a hugely important role in Ireland's story and today you can experience 1,000 years of history by visiting the three museums that make up the Waterford Treasures in the Viking Triangle.

The first of these sites is Reginald's Tower, one of the finest surviving examples of medieval urban defence in Ireland. The story of Reginald's Tower begins with the Viking adventurer Ragnall, who constructed a defensive base (known as a longphort) where the tower stands today. Ragnall was the grandson of the feared Ivar the Boneless, and by establishing his longphort at Waterford he created the foundations for the city. It quickly developed into an important trading hub, and Waterford became a vital part in an expansive network that connected Ireland to far-flung and exotic places like Baghdad, Greenland, Russia and Byzantium. Waterford grew in wealth and prestige, and gradually the Viking raiders became entwined with the Gaelic-Irish population through alliances and marriage, forming a culture known to historians and archaeologists today as Hiberno-Norse.

The peace of Waterford was not to last and the city was taken following a siege by the Anglo-Normans in 1170. The Normans held the leaders of the city captive in Reginald's Tower, but released them following an intervention by their Irish ally Diarmait MacMurchada, King of Leinster. The leader of the Normans, Richard de Clare (known as Strongbow), married King Diarmait's daughter Aoife in Christchurch Cathedral in Waterford, strengthening the alliance between the Norman invaders and the Irish kingdom of Leinster. In 1171 King Henry II declared Waterford to be a 'Royal City', and took it into the direct control of the English Crown.

King Henry had the city refortified in the early thirteenth century, and it is likely that the wooden fort of Reginald's Tower was reconstructed in stone at this time. He had large stone walls constructed

Above: Reginald's Tower, Waterford

Right: Reflections of the past at Reginald's Tower

to surround and protect the city, with a number of defensive gateways and towers added. Portions of these walls still survive; of the seventeen defensive towers that once protected Waterford only six still survive, with Reginald's Tower being the most impressive and best preserved.

Reginald's Tower was again at the centre of the action in 1495. Perkin Warbeck, a pretender to the English Crown, sailed up the River Suir and began to bombard Waterford to force it to surrender. The townspeople retaliated by firing cannon from Reginald's Tower and succeeded in sinking one of Warbeck's ships, defending the city with such ferocity that Warbeck retreated. In recognition of the determined bravery of the people of Waterford, King Henry VII gave Waterford the motto: '*Urbs Intacta Manet Waterfordia*' ('Waterford Remains the Untaken City').

However, the tower is not without its scars, and if you look high to the right-hand side of the entrance you can see a cannonball

The Great Parchment Book in Waterford's Medieval Museum

deeply embedded into the stone. This was fired during the siege of 1650, when the English Parliamentary forces returned to capture Waterford after Cromwell had failed to do so in 1649. Waterford was the last Irish city east of the Shannon to fall to Cromwell's forces.

From Reginald's Tower take a short walk up the Mall to the Medieval Museum. This is one of Ireland's newest and finest museums. It is thoughtfully designed and combines modern architecture with the medieval Choristers' Hall and fifteenth-century wine cellars. Spread across a number of floors, the Medieval Museum leads the visitor through Waterford's history from its foundation as a Viking longphort, through the medieval and Tudor periods, up to the seventeenth century. Among the many fascinating artefacts on display are the unique Great Charter Roll from 1373, the Cap of Maintenance (the only item of Henry VIII's wardrobe that still exists) and the Great Parchment Book (detailing 300 years of life in Waterford, this ends dramatically with the final entry during Cromwell's siege of 1649).

When you fancy moving forward in history, cross the courtyard to the Bishop's Palace Georgian museum. Some of the highlights include the oldest piece of Waterford Crystal in the world (from

1789) and a mourning cross commissioned by Napoleon's mother on the Emperor's death in 1821, as well as the uniform and sword of one of Waterford's most famous sons, the Irish patriot Thomas Francis Meagher, who introduced the modern tricolour flag to Ireland.

The Medieval Museum in Waterford

WATERFORD CITY   SITE MAP 8

Coordinates: Lat: 52.260487, Long: -7.105261

Grid reference: S 61070 12447

Opening times: The three Waterford Treasures museums are open daily all year. From 9.15 a.m. to 6 p.m. (5 p.m. from September to May) Monday to Friday, 9.30 a.m. – 6 p.m. (10 a.m. – 6 p.m. September to May) on Saturdays and 11 a.m. – 6 p.m. on Sundays and bank holidays

Entry fee: Please visit www.waterfordtreasures.com

Facilities: Guided tours of the site, coffee shop, exhibitions, toilets, gift shop

Car parking: Car parking available along the quays in Waterford city.

Directions: The Waterford Treasures museums are located in what is known as the Viking Triangle where there are many interesting historical sites to explore.

Nearest town: Tramore, about 12km to the south

The mines at Tankardstown, County Waterford

93 | THE COPPER COAST
COUNTY WATERFORD

Ireland has a long history of copper mining, and the copper mines at Ross Island in County Kerry and Mount Gabriel in County Cork are some of the oldest in north-western Europe, dating back thousands of years to the Early Bronze Age. The rugged coastline that stretches between Tramore and Dungarvan is known as the Copper Coast because of the extensive copper-mining industry that thrived here during the nineteenth century.

The focus of the mining industry along the Copper Coast was centred around Knockmahon from the 1820s to the 1850s. By 1840, Knockmahon was regarded as one of the most important mining districts in the entire British Empire. The nearby village of Bunmahon swelled with large numbers of workers, some of whom were experienced miners from the copper mines of Cornwall. With the influx of more than 2,000 people, over twenty pubs and inns

The rugged cliffs of the Copper Coast

developed to ply their trade in Bunmahon, and proved so successful that a Temperance Hall had to be established to provide alcohol-free entertainment in an attempt to keep the workers sober and reliable.

The mine at Knockmahon was closed down around 1850 as it had become susceptible to flooding. A new mine was opened to the east, at Tankardstown. A large, Cornish-style engine house was built here in 1860, to pump water from the bottom of the 256-metre (840-ft) mineshaft. A small steam engine was housed in the engine house, and it wound large cables up and down the shaft to raise the copper ore and lower equipment and materials down into the mine. The men accessed the mine by long wooden ladders that were housed in the large shafthead known as 'Heron's Shaft'.

The price of copper ore fluctuated over the next twenty years, but by 1879 the mine at Tankardstown was deemed unprofitable and operations ceased. Thousands of miners left this area, many of them emigrating to Montana to work in the large copper mines of Butte. The steam engines and machinery were sold for scrap, and the buildings began to fall into disrepair, despite occasional attempts to revive the industry.

In the 1970s, an action film about a Second World War prisoner-of-war camp, *The McKenzie Break,* was filmed on location here, and in one of the scenes a large truck was pushed into the main shaft, where it burst into flames. It still lies in the shaft today.

The Copper Coast Tourism Group was established in 1997 and was granted permission to join the European Geoparks Network. The area was declared a UNESCO Global Geopark in 2004. It is one of fifty-nine Geoparks in Europe, and the smallest one globally. It was granted EU Geopark status in recognition of its geological diversity and its nineteenth-century mining heritage.

The Copper Coast makes for a picturesque drive, and the site at Tankardstown is a haunting reminder of how this scenic and sleepy coastline once rang with the sound of machinery and the labour of thousands of men and women.

THE COPPER COAST   SITE MAP 8

Coordinates: Lat: 52.138981, Long: -7.343066 (Tankardstown Mines)

Grid reference: X 44966 98768

Opening times: Open all year round. Please see: www.coppercoastgeopark.com for further information about tours or visiting the Geopark visitor centre.

Entry fee: Sites are free to enter. There is an admission charge to the visitor centre.

Facilities: Visitor centre has toilets, coffee shop and exhibitions

Car parking: Car parking available in Bunmahon and at Tankardstown Mines

Directions: To get to the Copper Coast, travel to Bunmahon and if you have time, visit the Copper Coast Geopark Visitor Centre. Then travel east along the R675. Tankardstown will be on the left. The Copper Coast extends along the R675 as far as Annestown.

Nearest town: The Copper Coast is about 18km west of Tramore and 23km east of Dungarvan

The round tower and cathedral at Ardmore, County Waterford

Ardmore is believed to have been founded by St Declan some time in the fifth century, though there is little that dates to that early period visible on site. The earliest structure is the small building called St Declan's Oratory, which may date to the eighth century, and reputedly houses the grave of St Declan. The building was renovated in the eighteenth century, when a new roof was added.

The largest building on site is the ruin of the cathedral, which dates to the second half of the twelfth century. It consists of a long nave and chancel. A fine chancel arch, along with a number of typically Romanesque features, such as rounded doorways and windows, are visible. Inside the cathedral are two ogham stones, which provide more evidence of the early medieval phase at Ardmore. An inscription on one of the ogham stones has been

The Romanesque panels on the gable of the cathedral at Ardmore

translated as 'The stone of Lugaid, grandson of Nia-Segmon'. There are also a number of medieval grave slabs.

The cathedral was extensively modified in the seventeenth century, when large buttresses were added and the chancel enlarged. A series of early medieval sculptures set within Romanesque arcading can be seen on the western gable end of the cathedral – an unusual feature. The style of artwork and the Romanesque arcading certainly suggest it is from the time of the bishopric, around the twelfth to thirteenth centuries, but its position probably dates to

Ardmore's Cliff Walk

the early seventeenth century, when Ardmore underwent a series of renovations and alterations.

Ardmore's round tower is one of the most striking examples in Ireland. It is a little later than most, as it is believed to be twelfth century. It tapers to a height of 30 metres (98 ft) and has a doorway positioned about 4 metres (13 ft) above ground level. The round tower is unusual in its three distinct external rings, after each of which the wall is inset a little, which adds to the dramatic tapering effect.

With its scenic setting and number of interesting medieval buildings and features, Ardmore should be on everyone's must-see list in Munster. On a sunny day there are few sites to compare with it in Ireland. To get here, simply head into the village of Ardmore in County Waterford and follow the signs up the hill. The monastic ruins are situated on the lovely Cliff Walk of Ardmore, a trail of clifftop paths and laneways with breathtaking scenery and all the bracing sea air you could wish for. The full walk begins just beyond the car park of the Cliff House Hotel, before bringing you to the ruins of St Declan's Church. On a clear day the Minehead Lighthouse can be seen in the distance, along with the shipwreck of the *Samson*, a construction ship that was driven against the cliff in a storm in 1988 (all survived). The Cliff Walk also gives wonderful opportunities to discover a little of the natural heritage of Ireland's eastern coast. If you are fortunate you may spot dolphins or whales. Seabirds such as kittiwakes, sand martins, rock pigeons and choughs are all common sights (and sounds).

Follow the path and ascend Ram's Head for a wonderful vista that extends as far as Capel Island off the coast of Cork and beyond to Ballycotton Island. Two coastal lookout stations can be seen, as well as a tall tower that dates from the Napoleonic wars of the early nineteenth century. Further along the path you will encounter a stone structure built over a natural spring in the early twentieth century. Take the right-hand path at the fork and follow the boreen until the round tower comes back into view. Then follow the tower back to the monastery to complete the walk.

ARDMORE   SITE MAP 9

Coordinates: Lat: 51.948479, Long: -7.726223

Grid reference: X 18818 77427

Opening times: Open all year round

Entry fee: Free

Facilities: None

Car parking: Small car park at the side of the road

Directions: Located at the top of Tower Hill in the town of Ardmore. The coastal path is narrow and occasionally quite muddy, so good boots are essential.

Nearest town: In Ardmore village, about 15km east of Youghal

Doneraile Court, County Cork

Doneraile is a hidden gem, a lovely village with fine nineteenth-century architecture and a charming atmosphere. The village has many stories: in horse-racing circles it is famous as the finish line of the first steeplechase, a horse race that ran from the steeple of the church at Buttevant to the steeple of the church at Doneraile in 1752.

Doneraile Court, nestled in 400 acres of landscaped grounds, has been ranked by the Irish Georgian Society as one of the country's top ten period buildings and settings. It is thought that the core of the building was constructed in the late 1690s after an earlier castle and manor house had been burned down. A major reconstruction was undertaken in 1725, commemorated by a plaque over the doorway. This was overseen by the architect Isaac Rothery and was commissioned by Hayes St Leger, fourth Viscount Doneraile. One of the main developments in 1725 was the addition of the bow-ended façade that gives Doneraile Court such a distinctive look. Other additions were made in 1805 and 1820 when the porch was added. The house faces north as the family wanted to see sunlight over the planned vista in front of them every morning. The extensive grounds were planned to make it look as close to nature as possible with a vista that sweeps all the way up the skyline. There are clever design features hidden from view that help to create this managed

Box hedging in the gardens of Doneraile Court

pastoral scene. One such feature is what is known as a 'ha-ha' ditch, which ensured that deer were enclosed in a certain area without the need for large, unsightly fences. Deer were probably introduced to Doneraile in the mid seventeenth century and would have been hunted for sport. The deer died out on the estate in the early 1900s but species like fallow, red and sika deer were reintroduced in the 1980s.

One of the most famous incident at Doneraile Court occurred during the time of Arthur St Leger, the first Viscount Doneraile, who was a Freemason. There were no lodges or meeting halls in Ireland in the early years of Freemasonry, so meetings had to be held in secret in the houses of the Freemasons, and meetings were held regularly at Doneraile Court. On one occasion, Arthur's daughter Elizabeth had dozed off while reading in the library. Her father was unaware of her whereabouts and began the masonic meeting. Elizabeth, upon awakening, heard the proceedings of the meeting. As she tried to escape unnoticed, the lodge guard caught her. Women were (and still are) forbidden from becoming Freemasons, but on this occasion, the rule was overlooked as Elizabeth had already heard so much. The only option was to swear her in as a Freemason. Elizabeth was very proud of her association with Freemasonry. According to her obituary in the *Leinster Journal*, she was 'The only woman in the world who had the honour of being made a Freemason', which is true to this day.

Elizabeth was one of the foremost members of the family. Her son St Leger Aldworth inherited the estate from his uncle and resurrected the title Viscount Doneraile in 1785. The family continued to hold the title and live at Doneraile until the middle of the twentieth century. The eighth Viscount, Hugh St Leger, was a solicitor and sheep farmer who lived in New Zealand. He and his wife took up residence at Doneraile Court but when he died in 1956 the title died with him. A claim to the title was made in the 1960s by Richard St Leger, who spent a large sum trying to prove his lineage, as his ancestor was an illegitimate son of a nineteenth-century Lord Doneraile. Richard's case was considered tenuous. It was brought before the House of Lords but they ruled against Richard and the title is now in abeyance. Lady Doneraile, who continued to live in the house after the death of her husband, sold the house to the Irish Land Commission in 1969, and 400 acres of the 600-acre estate to the Forestry Commission, which set about opening the park to the public. Unfortunately, the house stood derelict for a number of years. Plans were proposed to take the roof off the building so it could be declared a National Monument but thankfully the Irish Georgian Society intervened and carried out extensive refurbishments. Doneraile Court is now under the care of the OPW, which, with the local community and support of Doneraile Development Association, Ballyhoura Development, the Irish Georgian Society and Cork County Council, has been working to return the grounds and house to their former glory. Doneraile Park has free entry for visitors and has charming tea rooms, which stock fine local produce.

DONERAILE PARK   SITE MAP 9

Coordinates: Lat: 52.219655, Long: -8.580855

Grid reference: R 60163 07774

Opening times: Open all year round

Entry fee: Free

Facilities: Tea rooms and toilets. Guided tours of the parklands are available. See www.doneraile.ie for more information about the tours.

Car parking: Large car parks at site

Directions: Doneraile Park is located at the northern end of Doneraile village, on the R581. To get to Doneraile from Cork, follow the N20 towards Limerick. Turn right onto the R581 at Newtwopothouse. Follow the road through Doneraile. The park entrance will be on your right.

Nearest town: Cork city, about 46km to the south-west, and Mallow, 12km to the south-west

96 | BRIDGETOWN PRIORY
COUNTY CORK

The path to
Bridgetown Priory in
County Cork

Bridgetown Priory is a well-preserved medieval priory on the western bank of the River Blackwater in County Cork. The priory was founded in the early thirteenth century by Alexander FitzHugh Roche, the Norman Lord of Castletownroche. He gave the site to the Augustinian Order, with 13 carucates of woodland, pasture and arable land. A carucate was a medieval unit of assessment, calculated by the area a plough team of eight oxen could till in a single season. One carucate very roughly equates to around 120 acres, suggesting that the original donation to the Augustinians at Bridgetown was approximately 1,560 acres. FitzHugh Roche also generously donated one third of his revenue from his mills and fisheries, and all tolls from the bridge that once crossed the Blackwater at the priory.

The Augustinian Order had started to flourish in Ireland after the Anglo-Norman invasions that began in 1169, and as well as the establishment of Bridgetown Priory the area suddenly sprouted more priories, friaries, abbeys and nunneries nearby in Buttevant, Fermoy, Ballybeg, Glanworth and Castlelyons. Bridgetown Priory was a wealthy and prosperous site for the first century after it was established. In the Papal Taxation of 1306 the value of Bridgetown was reckoned at the hefty sum of £40.

A number of the structures that make up Bridgetown Priory have survived in excellent condition, making it a fantastic site to explore. The early thirteenth-century church contains an internal wall that separates the nave (where the general congregation sat during Mass) from the choir (reserved for the monks and clergy). There are signs

IRELAND'S ANCIENT EAST

The interior of the church at Bridgetown Priory

of later medieval developments and modifications at the church, with a large two-storey residential tower added. There is an interesting fifteenth-century tomb of the Roche Family in the choir: part of the decoration includes an upside-down shield with a fish on it. Having the shield upside down indicates the death of the bearer, and the fish was the emblem of the Roche family, who were key benefactors of the priory. Above the tomb there is a well-preserved late thirteenth-century window.

Among the medieval buildings and features in the priory are a sixteenth-century chapel, a well preserved thirteenth-century grave slab, the calefactory (or 'warming house'; apart from the kitchen, the calefactory was the only other building in the priory allowed to have a fire), the priors' domestic quarters, a room thought to be the kitchens, a large refectory where the priors met for large communal meals and a vaulted passageway that leads to the cloister.

By the fourteenth century Ireland had fallen into a period of strife and warfare as the resurgent Gaelic Irish fought the Anglo-Normans for supremacy. Bridgetown suffered during this period, and by the time of the Dissolution of the Monasteries during King Henry VIII's reign in 1541 the site was noted as being largely in ruins, and its value only estimated at £13. The last prior at Bridgetown was given a pension, and the site was granted to the English soldier Robert Browne. The site was sold on a number of times before completely falling into ruin. Cork County Council began conservation works on the site in the late 1970s and now it is open to the public. The remains are extensive and you can easily find hours slipping by at this peaceful spot.

BRIDGETOWN PRIORY   SITE MAP 9

Coordinates: Lat: 52.149404, Long: -8.450306

Grid reference: W 69183 99814

Opening times: Open all year round

Entry fee: Free

Facilities: None

Car parking: Parking at site

Directions: Bridgetown Priory is about 12km west of Fermoy off the N72. About 2km south of Castletownroche, take a minor road to the west at Kilcummer. Then take the road to the south after half a kilometre. The site is well signposted.

Nearest town: Castletownroche, about 4km to the north

97 | LABBACALLEE WEDGE TOMB
COUNTY CORK

The tomb at Labbacallee near Glanworth in County Cork is Ireland's largest example of a wedge tomb, with a chamber that measures nearly 14 metres (46 ft) long. Wedge tombs are the most common of Ireland's megalithic tombs, and are most commonly found in the western half of the country. The name 'wedge tomb' simply refers to the wedge shape, as the height and width of the monument decreases from the front to the rear. Wedge tombs are the last of Ireland's megalithic tombs, and usually date to the Late Neolithic or Early Bronze Age.

Labbacallee was excavated by Harold Leask and Liam Price in 1934. They found that the burial chamber was divided into two parts: a long gallery and a small box-like feature at the eastern end. This eastern feature contained cremated remains, and the unburned

Above: Labbacallee Wedge Tomb, near Glanworth, County Cork
Below: The interior of Labbacallee tomb

but headless skeleton of an adult female. The skull was found in the gallery next to the skeletons of an adult male and child. Radiocarbon dating reveals that they appear to have been interred separately between 2456–1776 BC.

The name Labbacallee can be roughly translated as 'The Hag's Bed'. Folklore has always helped to protect some of Ireland's ancient sites and, at Labbacallee, local legend tells the story that long ago four men went during the night to dig for gold that they believed was buried inside the tomb at Labbacallee. As soon as they started to dig, a strange cat with fire erupting from its tail appeared. The men were terrified and dazzled by the blinding light coming from the tail of this hellish cat. They panicked and ran for their lives across the fields. In their confusion they fell into the nearby River

Funshion. One of the men drowned, but the others lived to pass on the warning not to disturb the ancient dead at Labbacallee!

There are a number of other great sites to see nearby, including Glanworth itself with its castle and friary, and the remarkable Bridgetown Priory (Site 96).

LABBACALLEE WEDGE TOMB   SITE MAP 9

Coordinates: Lat: 52.174152, Long: -8.334484

Grid reference: R 77126 02519

Opening times: Open all year round

Entry fee: Free

Facilities: None

Car parking: Limited car parking beside the site

Directions: From the M8, exit at Junction 13 (signed for Mitchelstown) and continue onto the R639. Travel down this road for 7km and turn right following signs for Glanworth. When you reach Glanworth, simply head south on the R512 and take the first left after the church. The site is about 2km down this road. It will be on the left-hand side behind a small stone wall. There is room to pull in off the road in front of the monument.

Nearest town: Labbacallee is about 3km south of Glanworth

---

98 | YOUGHAL
COUNTY CORK

Youghal in County Cork is a wonderfully historic town located on Ireland's south-east coast. There is much to see in the town itself, but one of the highlights is St Mary's Collegiate Church. It is one of Ireland's best-preserved medieval parish churches, thought to have been founded in the thirteenth century on the site of an earlier church that was destroyed by a storm in 1192. It was built in a cruciform shape, and was altered and added to a number of times throughout its history, thanks to patronage by some of Ireland's

Above left: St Mary's Collegiate Church, Youghal, County Cork

Above right: The interior of St Mary's Collegiate Church

Left: Richard Boyle depicted lounging on his tomb, St Mary's Collegiate Church, Youghal

most powerful families. One of the most prominent of these were the Boyles. Richard Boyle was born in Canterbury, England, in 1566. He arrived in Ireland in June 1588 with just £27 in his pocket. Thanks to his intelligence and charm, he rose through the ranks of society to become one of the wealthiest men in Ireland. Boyle purchased all of Sir Walter Raleigh's estates in Ireland, amounting to over 42,000 acres in counties Cork, Waterford and Tipperary, for the bargain price of £1,000. He was a progressive and forward-thinking man, and set up a number of industries and mines, and invested in building roads and bridges to connect his newly developing towns. In 1620 he became the first Earl of Cork, and later became the Lord High Treasurer of Ireland. Richard Boyle's son, Robert, was a highly respected scientist who became known as the father of modern chemistry. The Boyles are commemorated in the church by a remarkably ostentatious seventeenth-century burial monument. The monument depicts Richard Boyle reclining, with his two wives (his first wife died at a young age) praying at either end. Above him, his mother reclines, and a number of his children are also depicted.

Directly across from the Boyle tomb is the remarkable medieval tomb effigy of Richard Benet and his wife Ellis Barry. The tomb depicts the couple lying side by side, with a number of rather eerie stone skulls at their heads. More fascinating tombs dating from the medieval period to the nineteenth century can be discovered throughout the church, and it is easy to spend hours inside just reading the epitaphs. The tombs range from the extravagant, like Richard Boyle's, to the poignantly simple, like the memorial plaque of Henry Digby Wallis, a 29-year-old who was killed in action during the Great War at St Julien in Belgium in 1914, which states: 'He died as he lived, a very gallant gentleman.'

After visiting this atmospheric church, spend a little time around Youghal, where a wealth of medieval and historic buildings are to be seen, including the town walls and the impressive Clock Tower. The community, with the support of the Heritage Council, have created an easy-to-follow and well-interpreted trail that makes for a rewarding and fun day.

YOUGHAL SITE MAP 9

Coordinates: Lat: 51.955334, Long: -7.852429

Grid reference: X 10526 77851

Opening times: Monday to Saturday: 10.30 a.m. – 4 p.m. (10 a.m. – 4.30 p.m. in summer), Sunday 12.30 p.m. – 4 p.m.

Entry fee: Free

Facilities: None

Car parking: Parking available throughout Youghal

Directions: St Mary's Collegiate Church is located at the end of Emmet Place in Youghal.

Nearest town: Midleton, about 30km to the west

The barrel of one of the large naval guns at Camden Fort Meagher

Positioned on a headland known as Ram's Head at a strategic point defending the entrance to Cork Harbour, Camden Fort Meagher is one of Ireland's best examples of a coastal artillery fort. This site was first fortified in the sixteenth century. However, most of the buildings and defensive features that can be seen today date to the 1860s, when a significant programme of construction and refortification was undertaken by the British army.

The fort covers an area of 45 acres, 65 per cent of which is underground, in a series of tunnel networks and chambers. During the First World War, Camden Fort Meagher was used as a naval base to protect the western approaches to Britain. The fort was protected from the sea by gun defences and steep slopes. It was defended from the land by a deep moat that surrounds the fort on three sides. The moat reputedly took 500 men forty years to dig. It is said that convicts (who were housed on Spike Island, located nearby in the harbour) were used to excavate the moat.

Other features of the fort include the guardroom and lock-ups where unruly soldiers were jailed for disobedience or unlicensed leave.

Unlike Spike Island, Camden Fort Meagher was never used as a prison and the lock-up was used only to discipline soldiers. The Casemate Buildings have been conserved and these billets or rooms were used as dormitories for thirteen soldiers in peacetime or twenty-two during times of war. The rooms were very basic with just enough room for a bed, a footlocker, a shelf and a hook. These billets now hold exhibitions of what the fort was like prior to conservation works and another exhibition features military paraphernalia.

Perhaps the most spectacular feature of the site is the network of tunnels and labyrinths under the fort. The impressive magazine, which can be accessed by visitors, was used to store ammunition, and every precaution was taken to prevent a catastrophic explosion. The soldiers working in the magazine had a separate flannel uniform and felt-lined shoes (rather like modern Ugg boots), which they wore when working to minimise the risk of sparks or static from their regular uniform or hobnailed boots. The room was lit by candles kept in glass cases in the wall, which could only be lit from a lamp passage surrounding the room. The temperature in the magazine remains constant at around 10° Celsius. Also within the magazine is a spiral staircase. Its function was to allow soldiers quick access to the munitions store, and the winch used to lift goods out of the magazine can still be seen beside the staircase.

The fort was occupied by the British army until 1938 when it was handed over to the Irish Free State as part of the settlement following the Anglo-Irish Trade War in the 1930s. Éamon de Valera (then Taoiseach) came to the fort for the handover and had breakfast in the Officers' Mess. The Irish army was based at the fort until the 1940s. The fort then became used as a training ground for the FCA (Reserve Defence Forces) and the Slua Muiri (Naval Reserve Defence Forces). Following a review in 1989, the fort was officially handed over to Cork County Council. The council, with a group of dedicated volunteers, set about the conservation of the site, and the volunteers conduct informative and engaging guided tours through the summer months.

CAMDEN FORT MEAGHER　　　　　　　　　　SITE MAP 9

Coordinates: Lat: 51.808688, Long -8.279086

Grid reference: W 80959 61789

Opening times: Every Saturday, Sunday and bank holiday from 12 p.m. to 5 p.m. from the end of May to mid September

Entry fee: Please visit www.camdenfortmeagher.ie

Facilities: Guided tours, tea rooms and toilets

Car parking: Large car park

Directions: From Cork city, take the N28 to Carrigaline. At Carrigaline, follow the signs for Crosshaven. When you reach Crosshaven, continue to the roundabout. Take the second exit and then turn left immediately onto the Camden Road. The site is at the end of this road.

Nearest town: Just outside the village of Crosshaven, approximately 20km south of Cork city.

100 | BLARNEY CASTLE
COUNTY CORK

Blarney Castle is undoubtedly one of Ireland's most popular historical sites. The castle is a late medieval tower house with a five-storey extension that was was added in the late sixteenth or seventeenth century. The castle is built on a stony limestone outcrop overlooking the confluence of the Martin and Blarney Rivers. It is thought that it was first built by Cormac Láidir MacTaidhg in the 1480s to protect his lands. The castle was the seat of the powerful MacCarthy family who were Lords of Muskerry, one of the leading

Blarney Castle

families of medieval Ireland. They lived in the castle until they lost their lands in the aftermath of the Williamite Wars. The castle we see today would have looked remarkably different back in its heyday. Instead of somewhat drab grey and brown stone, the castle was covered with lime plaster, bound together with horsehair and painted white. It was described at the time in the Annals of the Four Masters: 'Cormac, the son of Teige, son of Cormac Oge MacCarthy, Lord of Muskerry, a comely-shaped, bright countenanced man, who possessed most white washed edifices, fine built castles, and hereditary seats of any of the descendants of Eoghan More'. Blarney Castle was captured by Cromwell's forces in 1646. It was later restored to the MacCarthy family, before it was finally confiscated following the Williamite Wars of the 1690s. The castle and lands were granted to the Jeffeyes family before they passed to the Colthurst family in 1846, who remain the owners to this day.

The term 'blarney', meaning to charm, flatter, persuade and cajole, is derived from Cormac MacCarthy of Blarney Castle. In 1602 he managed to avoid the confiscation of his lands by the English Crown by sheer force of persuasion, flattery and eloquence. He cajoled Sir George Carew (Lord of Munster under Elizabeth I) so volubly and determinedly that he was permitted to keep his lands.

A view of the battlements of Blarney Castle, looking towards Blarney House, a nineteenth-century mansion that is open to visitors in the summer months

Queen Elizabeth is supposed to have declared: 'This is all Blarney; what he says he never means.'

Visitors can be bestowed with the same eloquence by kissing the Blarney Stone. The stone is set high on the inside wall of the tower, and whosoever kisses it is said to be granted 'sweet persuasive, wheedling eloquence'.

BLARNEY CASTLE SITE MAP 9

Coordinates: Lat: 51.929047, Long: -8.570651

Grid reference: W 60747 75343

Opening times: Open all year round

Entry fee: Please visit www.blarneycastle.ie

Facilities: Tea rooms, toilets, garden walks

Car parking: Parking at site

Directions: Blarney Castle is located in the village of Blarney and is well signposted

Nearest town: Cork city, about 8km to the south-east

BLARNEY CASTLE

SITE MAPS

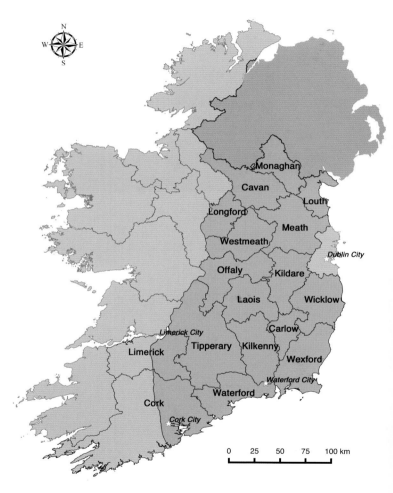

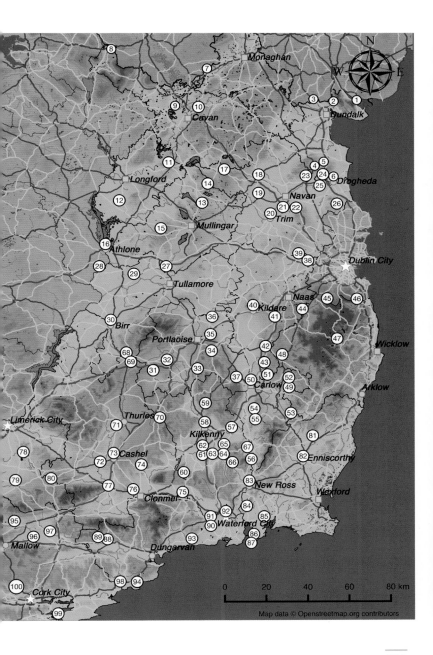

Site Map 1

Map data © Opensteetmap.org contributors

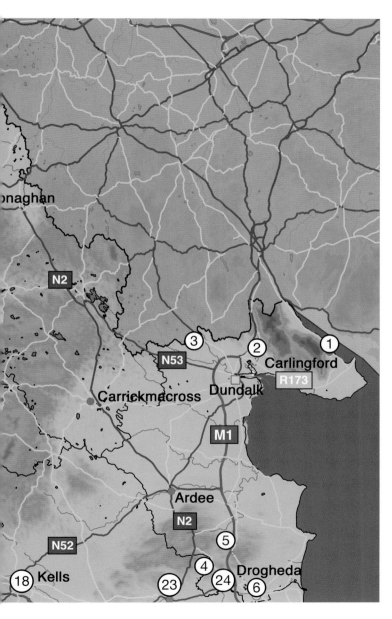

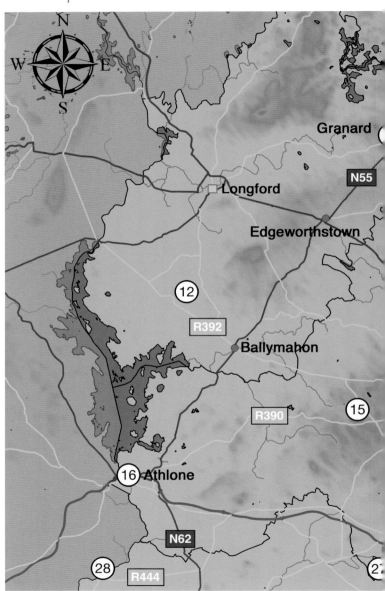

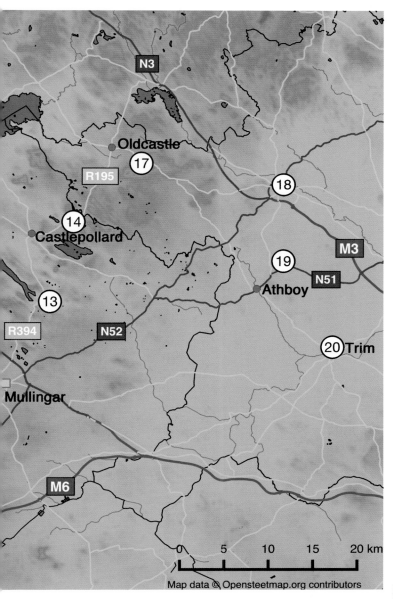

Map data © Opensteetmap.org contributors

Site Map 3

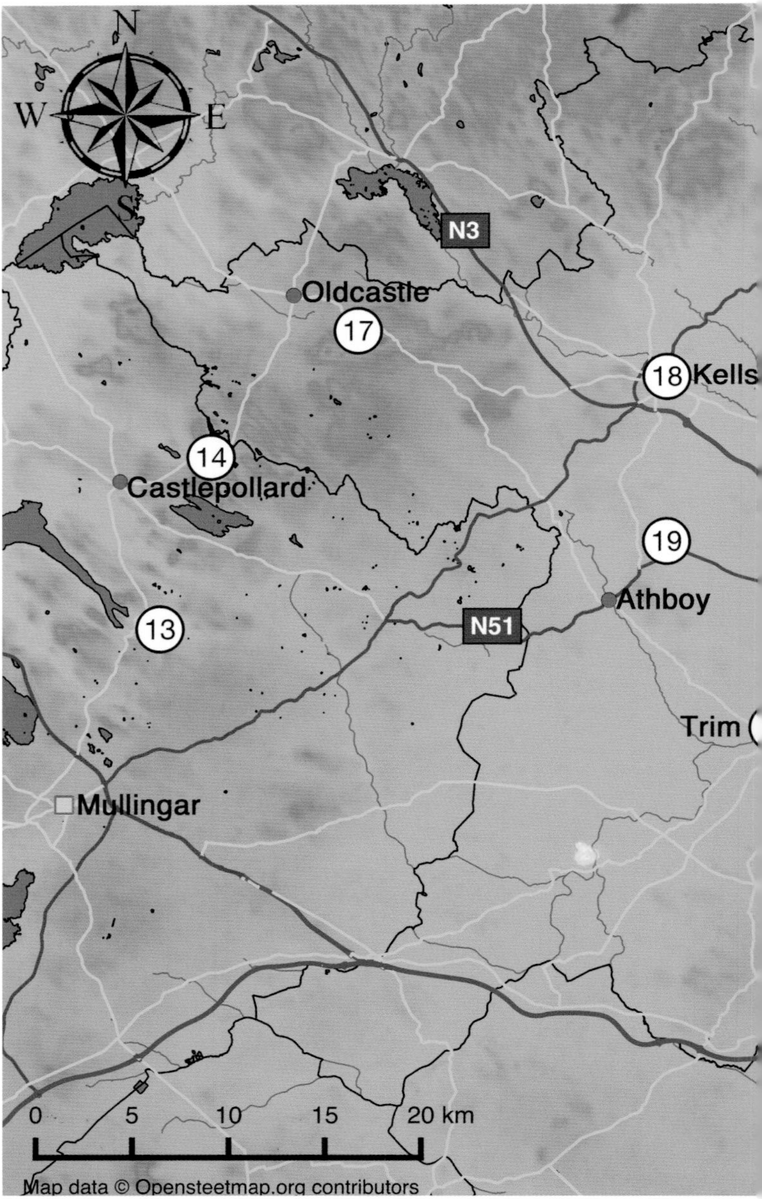

N3

Oldcastle
17

18 Kells

14
Castlepollard

19

Athboy

13

N51

Trim

Mullingar

0   5   10   15   20 km

Map data © Opensteetmap.org contributors

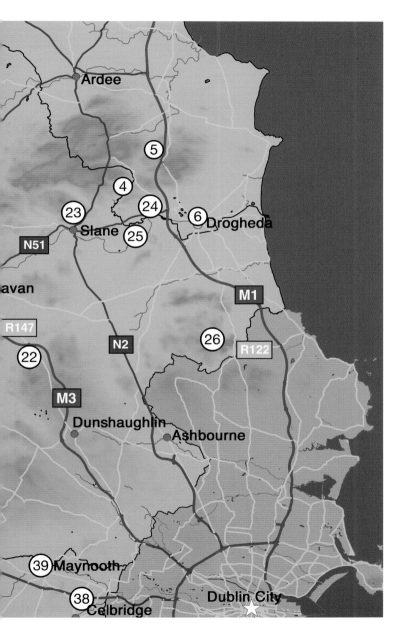

Ardee

⑤

④

㉓ ㉔

N51 ●Slane ㉕

⑥ Drogheda

avan

M1

R147

㉒ N2 ㉖ R122

M3

Dunshaughlin ●Ashbourne

㊴Maynooth

㊳ Dublin City
Celbridge ★

Site Map 4

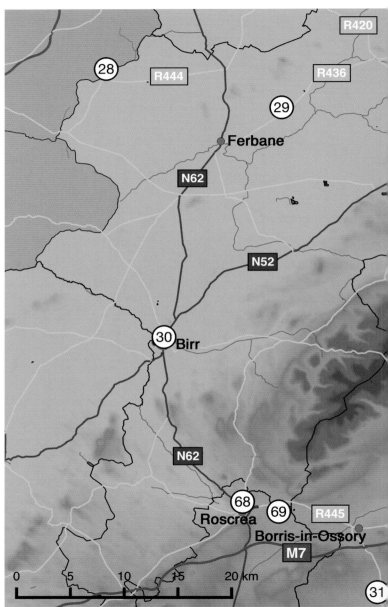

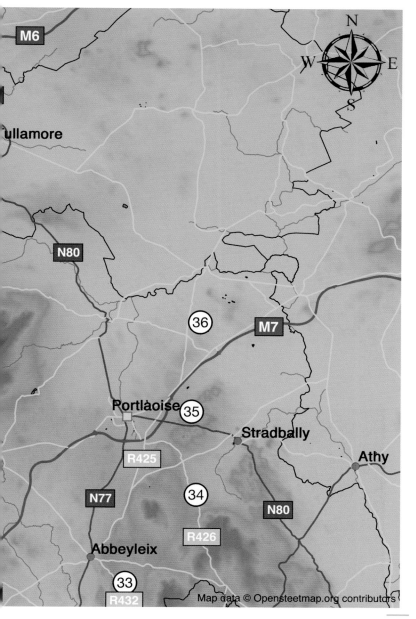

M6

ullamore

N80

36

M7

Portlàoise 35

Stradbally

Athy

R425

N77

34

N80

R426

Abbeyleix

33

R432

Map data © Opensteetmap.org contributors

Site Map 5

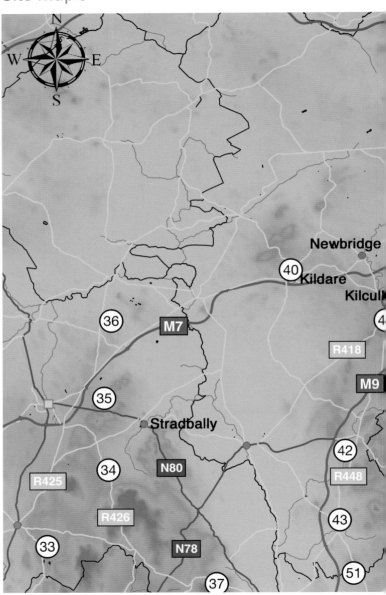

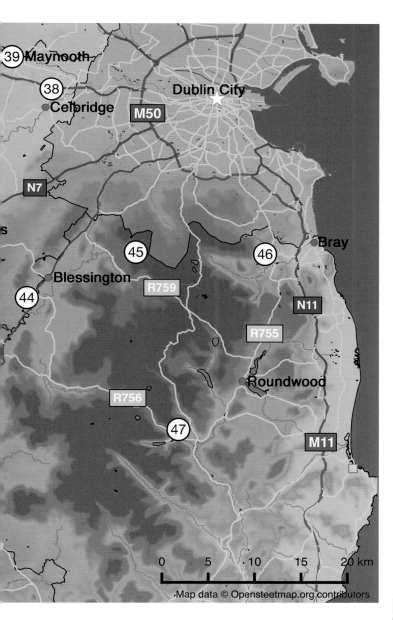

Site Map 6

Map data © Opensteetmap.org contributors

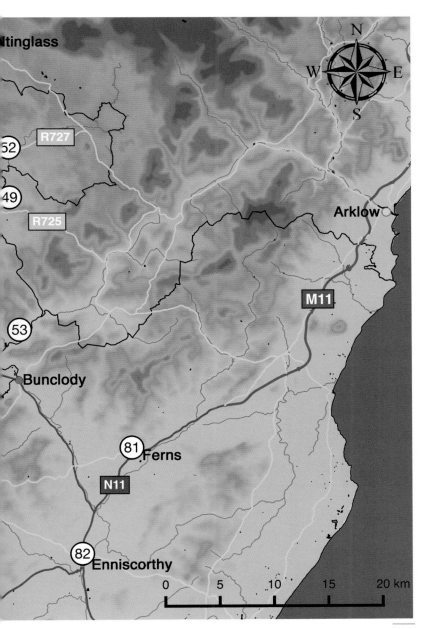

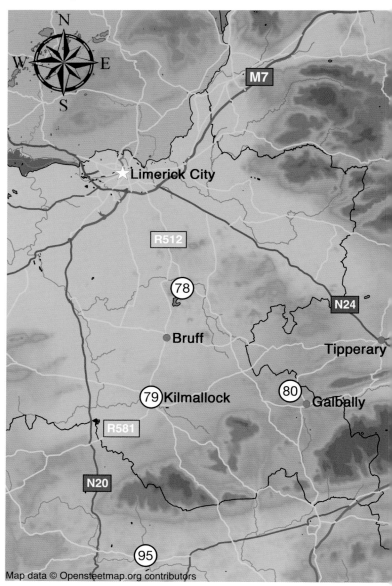

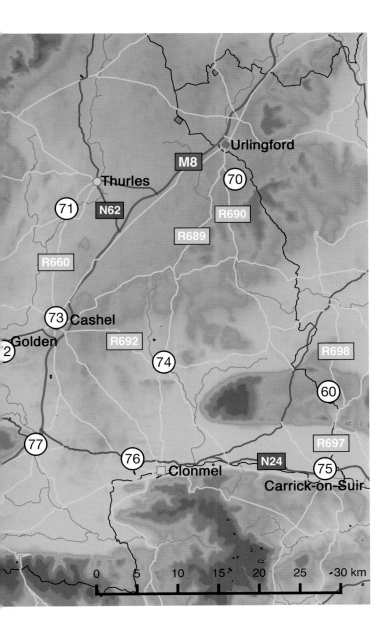

Site Map 8

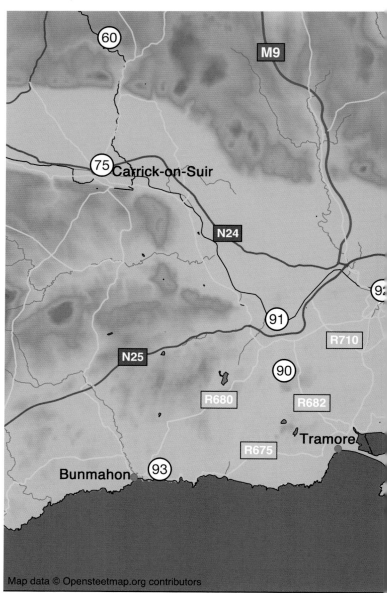

Map data © Opensteetmap.org contributors

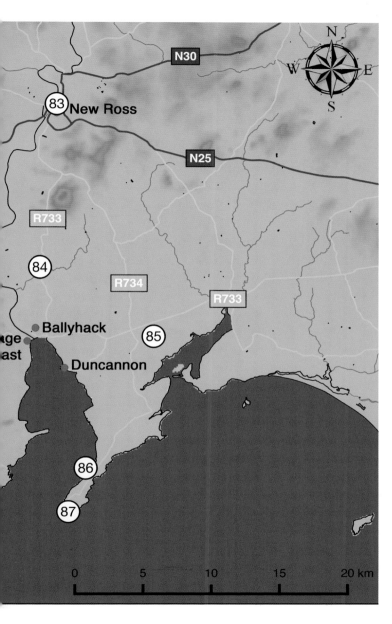

Site Map 9

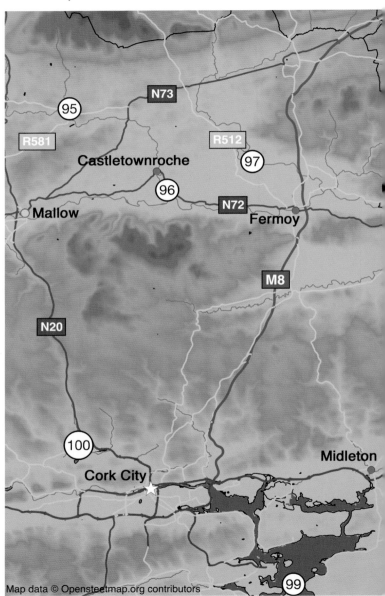

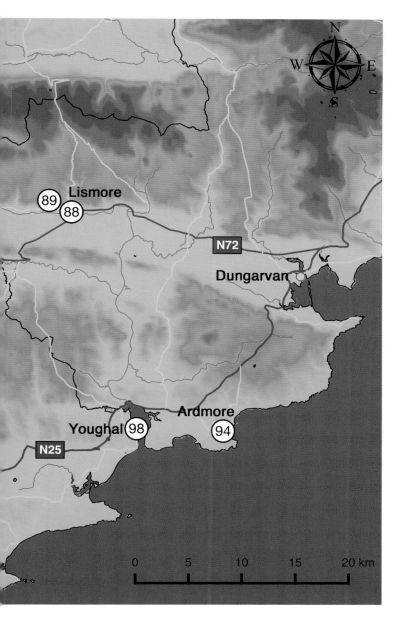

GLOSSARY

aisle: A side division, usually in relation to the nave of a church.

anchorite: A person living in isolation for their faith.

antae: Projections of the side walls beyond the eastern and western gables of early medieval Irish churches.

apse: The semicircular, or occasionally polygonal, end of the chancel of a church or cathedral.

bailey: A defended enclosure, usually in association with a motte. It often protected the ancillary structures related to the fort.

barbican: An external defensive structure, usually attached to the gate of a castle or walled town.

barrow: Circular ditched enclosure, often with an earthen mound in the centre, which covers a burial. Usually dates to the Bronze Age.

base batter: A sloping face on the exterior of castle walls, town walls or occasionally churches.

bawn: A fortified, walled enclosure that usually relates to a later medieval castle or tower house.

Bronze Age: (2400 BC – 500 BC approximately). The era of the introduction of metallurgy. Large copper mines were established in places like Mount Gabriel, County Cork. Initially copper was worked to make flat axes; the later introduction of tin led to increasingly elaborate bronze tools and weapons. Gold working became common, and burial rites changed to more individual focus in barrows and cist graves rather than communal burial monuments.

bullaun: A large stone with one or more circular depressions carved into it. Often related to early medieval monastic sites; they may have served as holy water fonts, or may have had a more practical purpose similar to a large pestle and mortar for grinding herbs or minerals.

burgage plots: Land and buildings in a town held in tenure by a noble or lord and rented out.

cairn: A man-made drystone mound, often covering the chambers of a megalithic tomb.

calefactory: A comparatively comfortable room within a medieval monastery, warmed by a fire.

cashel: A stone-built circular enclosure, usually dating to the early medieval period. A variation of a ringfort.

chancel: The eastern end of a church, usually where the altar is located.

chapter house: The building or room in a monastery where the monks assembled for meetings and readings.

choir: The area of a church reserved for monks, friars or clergy. Usually located close to the chancel.

cist: A stone-lined grave or chamber, usually dating to the earlier part of the Bronze Age.

cloister: A covered passageway forming a square in medieval monasteries.

corbelled roof: A stone roof constructed from horizontally laid rows of stones with each row projecting inwards more than the row below.

court tomb: A megalithic tomb type that usually features a large courtyard area in front of a covered gallery that contained human remains, often in two or more chambers. The galleries or chambers were originally covered with a large cairn of small stones or earth.

crossing tower: A tower, often housing a belfry, marking the point where the nave and chancel meet. Usually in association with medieval churches.

cruciform: In the shape of a cross.

curtain wall: The exterior defensive wall of a medieval castle.

cursus: A large prehistoric monument consisting of two parallel embankments.

Dissolution of the Monasteries: A set of administrative and legal processes between 1536 and 1541 by which Henry VIII disbanded Catholic monasteries, priories, convents and friaries in England, Wales and Ireland, and appropriated their income and estates.

dolmen: See portal tomb.

donjon: See keep.

early medieval: (500 AD – 1100 AD approximately). The period that saw the emergence of increasingly powerful regional kingdoms, occasionally ruled over by a High King. Gradual Christianisation of the country, leading to the establishment of monasteries across Ireland. Viking raids begin from the ninth century onwards.

gable: The pointed end wall of a building.

garderobe: A toilet (or latrine) usually built into the wall of a medieval castle or stone building.

glacial erratic: A large boulder carried by glacial ice and deposited at a distance from its point of origin.

Gothic: A twelfth- to thirteenth-century architectural style with features such as pointed arches, rib vaulting and flying buttresses.

high cross: A tall stone cross, often elaborately decorated with geometric designs or biblical depictions. Usually in association with early medieval Irish monastic sites.

henge: A large circular enclosure, usually comprised of earthen banks and ditches, and thought to have had a ceremonial function.

intramural: A passageway or feature within the walls of a building.

Iron Age: (500 BC – 500 AD approximately). The period most associated with Ireland's large ceremonial centres or 'royal' sites like Tara, Uisneach and Rathcroghan. Broadly feudal system based on a series of tribes ruled by regional kingship. Later in the period sees increased interaction with Roman Britain, leading to development of Christian communities by the fifth century.

keep: The central tower of a castle, often houses domestic quarters.

kerbstones: A line of stones surrounding a megalithic tomb. Sometimes decorated, kerbstones helped to keep the mound or cairn in place, as well as marking the boundary of the tomb.

lavabo: A washing place for medieval monks or friars, usually located close to the refectory of medieval monasteries.

lintel: The stone immediately above a door or passageway.

longphort: An Irish term applied to the fortified encampments of Viking raiders in the ninth century.

machicolation: A defensive feature, appearing as a stone structure projecting from a wall, usually positioned over an entrance. It allowed defenders to drop stones, etc., onto an attacking force.

Martello tower: A circular tower usually positioned on the coastline or riverside. Constructed as a defence by the British army in the wars against Napoleonic France in the early nineteenth century.

medieval: (1100 AD – 1607 AD approximately). This period saw a greater connection between Ireland and the rest of Europe, beginning with Church reforms and followed by the Anglo-Norman invasion of the later twelfth century. The end of the medieval period could be considered to be the Dissolution of the Monasteries in the mid-sixteenth century, or the Flight of the Earls in 1607, as both marked a pivotal change of Irish society.

megalithic: Derives from *mega* meaning big and *lithic* meaning stone. A blanket term that refers to the many different types of large prehistoric stone tombs.

moat: A deep ditch filled with water. Usually associated with medieval fortifications.

motte: An early Norman fortification. Appears as a tall earthen mound that served as the foundation for a wooden or stone tower. Often accompanied by a bailey.

murder hole: Similar in purpose to a machicolation. A hole or aperture, usually positioned above a passageway or gateway, through which defenders can drop large stones, etc., onto the heads of the attackers.

nave: The main body of a church.

Neolithic: (4000 BC – 2400 BC approximately). This era saw the introduction of agriculture and animal husbandry. More permanent settlements were established, and burial rituals became more elaborate in the form of megalithic tombs.

ogee-headed: A decorative window design dating to the medieval period.

Ogham: An early Irish script that usually dates to the early centuries AD. It consists of a series of horizontal or diagonal strokes crossing a vertical central line.

orthostat: An upright stone, usually in reference to the upright structural elements of a megalithic tomb.

Pale (the): The region under the effective control of the English Crown during the later medieval period. Contained parts of Louth, Meath, Dublin and Kildare.

palisade: A defensive structure consisting of a wooden fence.

passage tomb: The largest and most elaborate of the megalithic tomb types. Usually consists of a stone-lined passageway leading to a burial chamber. The passageway and chamber are then covered with an earthen or stone mound. Sometimes a mound may cover multiple passages and chambers. The most famous example in Ireland is Newgrange in County Meath.

Pattern day: An Irish Roman Catholic tradition that refers to the devotions that take place within a parish on the feast day of the patron saint of the parish, or on the nearest Sunday, called Pattern Sunday.

Penal Laws: A series of harsh and repressive laws that originated in the seventeenth century and were imposed in an attempt to force Irish Roman Catholics and Protestant dissenters (such as Presbyterians) to accept the reformed denomination as defined by the English state-established Anglican Church.

piscina: A stone basin in which clergy ceremonially washed their hands and communion vessels.

plantations: Land confiscated by the English Crown where the original inhabitants were replaced with English and Scottish Protestant settlers.

portal tomb: A megalithic tomb type typically consisting of a simple chamber formed of upright stones, with a large capstone. The monument was then possibly covered with a cairn of small stones or a mound of earth. Also known as a dolmen.

portcullis: A defensive gate in the entrance or gateway of a castle or fortification. Usually consisting of a large wood and metal grille that can be lowered into position in times of danger.

rag tree: Strips of cloth or rags tied to the branches of a tree (usually positioned next to a holy well or church site) as part of a healing ritual. As the cloth unravels and rots so the disease or ailment is believed to fade away.

rath: See ringfort.

refectory: The dining hall of a medieval monastery.

ringfort: (Also known as rath). A roughly circular enclosure surrounded by one or more ditches with banks of earth or stone. Usually dating to the early medieval period, ringforts are one of the most numerous archaeological sites in the Irish landscape. The enclosures often defended houses and other ancillary structures. When the enclosure is constructed of stone it is often termed a cashel.

Romanesque: A style of architecture and art originating on the continent that became popular in Irish churches in the twelfth century. Architectural features include rounded arches, elaborate decoration and depictions of human heads, foliage and animals.

rood screen: A church feature, usually containing a crucifix, that separated the nave from the choir.

round tower: Iconic and uniquely Irish, round towers were tall, slender towers of stone primarily used as belfries.

sacristy: A building associated with a church or monastery, where vestments and communion vessels are kept.

sedile (plural sedilia): A seat within a medieval church for a priest, abbot or bishop.

Sheela-na-gig: Small sculptures of nude females (and occasionally males) exhibiting their genitalia. Their purpose is subject to debate: some believe they were a way of warding off evil spirits, others that they were a warning against the sins of the flesh.

solar: The private chamber of a medieval house or castle.

souterrain: A tunnel-like stone passageway, usually dating to the early medieval period. Mainly found in association with ringforts or monastic sites. Thought to have been used for storage or possibly refuge. May feature chambers and multiple passageways.

togher: A wooden or stone trackway across boggy or marshy ground.

transepts: The side arms of a church, running north and south from the main church building.

trefoil: A decorative feature typically dating to the thirteenth century.

Urnes: Elaborate artistic style usually consisting of stylised animals interwoven into tight patterns of Scandinavian origin.

wedge tomb: The most numerous of Ireland's megalithic tombs, and most commonly found in the western half of the country. The name refers to the simple wedge shape, as the height and width of the monument decreases from the front to the rear. Wedge tombs are the last of Ireland's megalithic tombs, and usually date to the Late Neolithic or Early Bronze Age periods.

USEFUL WEBSITES

www.abartaheritage.ie

www.archaeology.ie

www.buildingsofireland.ie

www.discoveryprogramme.ie

www.excavations.ie

www.heritagecouncil.ie

www.heritageireland.ie

www.historicgraves.com

www.irisharchaeology.ie

www.irishwalledtownsnetwork.ie

www.megalithicireland.com

www.monastic.ie

www.museum.ie

www.nationalarchives.ie

www.nli.ie (National Library of Ireland)

www.pilgrimagemedievalireland.com

www.thestandingstone.ie

www.timetravelireland.blogspot.ie (author's blog)

www.voicesfromthedawn.com

BIBLIOGRAPHY

The Annals of Clonmacnoise: being annals of Ireland from the earliest period to AD 1408, translated into English, AD 1627 by Conell Mageoghagan, ed. D. Murphy (Royal Society of Antiquaries of Ireland, Dublin, 1896)

Annals of the kingdom of Ireland by the Four Masters from the earliest period to the year 1616, ed. and trans. John O'Donovan (7 vols., Dublin, 1851; reprint, New York, 1966)

The Annals of Lough Cé: a chronicle of Irish affairs, 1014–1690, ed. W. M. Hennessy (2 vols., London, 1871; reflex facsimile, Irish Manuscripts Commission, Dublin, 1939)

Andrews, J. H. 1986. *Irish Historic Towns Atlas, Kildare*. Dublin: Royal Irish Academy

Barrow, G. L. 1979. *The Round Towers of Ireland: A Study and Gazetteer*. Dublin: Academy Press

Barry, T. (ed.) 2000. *A History of Settlement in Ireland*. London & New York: Routledge

Barry, T. 1988. *The Archaeology of Medieval Ireland*. London: Routledge

Blake, T. & Reilly, F. 2013. *Ancient Ireland: Exploring Irish Historic Monuments*. Cork: The Collins Press

Bhreathnach, E. 2014. *Ireland in the Medieval World AD 400–1000*. Dublin: Four Courts Press

Brindley, A. 1986. *Archaeological Inventory of County Monaghan*. Dublin: Stationery Office

Brindley, A. & Kilfeather, A. 1993. *Archaeological Inventory of County Carlow*. Dublin: Stationery Office

Buckley, V. 1986. *Archaeological Inventory of County Louth*. Dublin: Stationery Office

Buttimer, N. Rynne, C. & Guerin, H. 2000. *The Heritage of Ireland*. Cork: The Collins Press

Carroll, J. Harrison, S.H. & Williams, G. 2014. *The Vikings in Britain and Ireland*. London: The British Museum

Clyne, M. 2007. *Kells Priory, Co. Kilkenny: Archaeological Excavations by T. Fanning & M. Clyne*. Dublin: The Stationery Office

Cochrane, A. & Meirion Jones, A. (eds). *Visualising the Neolithic*. Oxford: Oxbow Books

Cooney, G. 2000. *Landscapes of Neolithic Ireland*. London: Routledge

Cooney, G. & Grogan, E. 1994. *Irish Prehistory: A Social Perspective*. Dublin: Wordwell

Corlett, C. & Potterton, M. 2009. *Rural Settlement in Medieval Ireland*. Dublin: Wordwell

Craig, M. 2006. *Classic Irish Houses of the Middle Size*. Dublin: Ashfield House

Craig, M. 1982. *The Architecture of Ireland from the Earliest Times to 1880*. Dublin: Eason and Son Ltd., London: Batsford

Crowley, J., Smyth W. J. & Murphy, M. 2012. *Atlas of the Great Irish Famine*. Cork: Cork University Press

De Valera, R. & Ó Nualláin, S. 1972. *Survey of the Megalithic Tombs of Ireland*, vols. 1–6. Dublin: Stationery Office.

Discovery Programme, 2014. *Late Iron Age and 'Roman' Ireland*. Dublin: Wordwell

Doherty, C., Doran, L. & Kelly, M. (eds) 2011. *Glendalough, City of God*. Dublin: Four Courts Press

Dooley, T. 2007. *The Big Houses and Landed Estates of Ireland, A Research Guide*. Dublin: Four Courts Press

Dooley, A. & Roe., H. 1999. *Tales of the Elders of Ireland–A New Translation of Acallam na Senórach*. Oxford: Oxford University Press

Duffy, S. 2013. *Brian Boru and the Battle of Clontarf*. Dublin: Gill & Macmillan

Duffy, S. 2000. *The Concise History of Ireland*. Dublin: Gill & Macmillan

Edwards, N. 1990. *The Archaeology of Early Medieval Ireland*. London: Batsford

Farrelly, J. & O'Brien, C. 2002. *Archaeological Inventory of County Tipperary Volume 1: North Tipperary*. Dublin: Stationery Office

Fitzpatrick, E. & Kelly, J. 2011. *Domestic Life in Ireland, Proceedings of the Royal Irish Academy, Section C, Vol III*

Fitzpatrick, E. & O'Brien, C. 1998. *The Medieval Churches of County Offaly*. Dublin: Stationery Office

Glin, K. & Peil, J. 2010. *The Irish Country House*. London: Thames and Hudson

Grogan, E. & Kilfeather, A. 1997. *Archaeological Inventory of County Wicklow*. Dublin: Stationery Office

Grose, F. 1791. *The Antiquities of Ireland*, 2 vols. London: S. Hooper

Gwynn, A. & Hadcock, R.N. 1970 (Reprint 1988) *Medieval Religious Houses of Ireland*. Dublin: Irish Academic Press

Halpin, A. & Newman, C. 2006. *Ireland: An Oxford Archaeological Guide*. Oxford: Oxford University Press

Hamlin, A. & Hughes, K. 1997. *The Modern Traveller to the Early Irish Church*. Dublin: Four Courts Press

Harbison, P. 1970. *Guide to National and Historic Monuments of Ireland*. Dublin: Gill & Macmillan

Harbison, P. 2003. *Treasures of the Boyne Valley*. Dublin: Gill & Macmillan.

Herity, M. & Eogan, G. 1977. *Ireland in Prehistory*. London: Routledge

Jones, C. 2007. *Temples of Stone: Exploring the Megalithic Tombs of Ireland*. Cork: The Collins Press

Kelly, E. P. 1996. *Sheela-na-Gigs: Origins and Functions*. Dublin: Country House

Kelly, F. 2015. *A Guide To Irish Law*. Dublin: Dublin Institute for Advanced Studies (Reprint)

Kelly, F. 2000. *Early Irish Farming*. Dublin: Dublin Institute for Advanced Studies

Kilfeather, A. & Grogan, E. 1997. *Archaeological Inventory of County Wicklow*. Dublin: Stationery Office

Lalor, B. 1999. *The Irish Round Tower*. Cork: The Collins Press

Leask, H.G. 1944. Ballymoon Castle, County Carlow. *Journal of the Royal Society of Antiquaries of Ireland* 74, 183–90

Leask, H.G. 1951. *Irish Castles and Castellated Houses*. Dundalk: Dundalgan Press

Leask, H.G. 1960 (Reprint 1967 and 1990). Irish churches and monastic buildings, vol. II. *Gothic Architecture to A.D. 1400*. Dundalk: Dundalgan Press

Leins, I. 2015. *Celts, Art and Identity*. London: The British Museum

Lynch, A. 2010. *Tintern Abbey, Co. Wexford: Cistercians and Colcloughs*. Dublin: Stationery Office

Lyttleton, J. 2011. *Blarney Castle, An Irish Tower House*. Dublin: Four Courts Press

Manning, C. 2013. *Clogh Oughter Castle, Co. Cavan: Archaeology, History and Architecture*. Dublin: Stationery Office

Manning, C. (ed) 2003. *Excavations at Roscrea Castle*. Dublin: The Stationery Office

McBride, A. 2015. *Tipperary Folk Tales*. Dublin: The History Press

McBride, A. & Sheehan, J. 2014. *Carlow Folk Tales*. Dublin: The History Press

McMahon, S. & O'Donoghue, J. 2009, *Brewer's Dictionary of Irish Phrase and Fable*. London: Chambers Harrap Publishers Ltd.

McNeill, T. 1997. *Castles in Ireland: Feudal Power in a Gaelic World*. London: Routledge

Moore, M. 1999. *Archaeological Inventory of County Waterford*. Dublin: Stationery Office

Moore, M. 1995. *Archaeological Inventory of County Wexford*. Dublin: Stationery Office

Moore, S. 2007. *Archaeological Monuments in County Longford*. Longford: Longford County Council

Murtagh, H. (ed.) 1994. *Athlone: Irish Historic Towns Atlas, No. 6*. Dublin: Royal Irish Academy

Newman, C. 1997. *Tara: An Archaeological Survey*. Dublin: Royal Irish Academy

Nicholls, K.W. (ed.) 1994. *The Irish Fiants of the Tudor Sovereigns during the Reigns of Henry VIII, Edward VI, Philip & Mary, and Elizabeth I*, 4 vols. Dublin: Éamonn de Búrca for Edmund Burke Publisher

Nolan, W. & Simms, A. (eds) 1998. *Irish Towns: A Guide to Sources*. Dublin: Geography Publications

O'Brien, C. 2006. *Stories from a Sacred Landscape, Croghan Hill to Clonmacnoise*. Dublin: Mercier Press

O'Brien, C. & Sweetman, D. 1997. *Archaeological Inventory of County Offaly*. Dublin: Stationery Office

O'Brien, J. & Guinness, D. 1992. *Great Irish Houses and Castles*. London: George Weidenfeld & Nicholson Ltd.

O'Brien, J. & Harbison, P. 1996. *Ancient Ireland: From Prehistory to the Middle Ages*. London: George Weidenfeld & Nicholson Ltd.

Ó Carragáin, T. 2010. *Churches in Early Medieval Ireland*. London & New Haven: Yale University Press

Ó Cróinín, D. 1995, *Early Medieval Ireland, 400–1200 AD*. London: Longman

O'Donovan, P. F. *Archaeological Inventory of Cavan*. Dublin: Stationery Office

O'Keeffe, T. 2001. *Medieval Ireland: An Archaeology*. Gloucestershire: Tempus Publishing Ltd.

O'Keeffe, T. 2015. *Medieval Irish Buildings: 1100–1600*. Dublin: Four Courts Press

O'Keeffe, T. 1992. 'Romanesque architecture and sculpture at Ardmore' in C. Nolan, T. P. Power and D. Cowman (eds), *Waterford – History and Society*, 73–104. Dublin: Geography Publications

O'Meara, J. (ed.) 1951. *Gerald of Wales – The History and Topography of Ireland*. London: Penguin

Ó Riain, P. 2011. *A Dictionary of Irish Saints*. Dublin: Four Courts Press

O'Sullivan, M. 2005. *Duma na nGiall, Tara, The Mound of the Hostages*. Wicklow: Wordwell

O'Sullivan, M. 1993. *Megalithic Art in Ireland*. Dublin: Country House

Powell, E. 2007. *The High Crosses of Ireland, Inspirations in Stone*. Dublin: The Liffey Press

Raftery, B. 1994. *Pagan Celtic Ireland: The Enigma of the Irish Iron Age*. London: Thames and Hudson

Roche, R. 1995. *The Norman Invasion of Ireland*. Dublin: Anvil Books Ltd (Reprint)

Ryan, M. (ed) 1994. *Irish Archaeology Illustrated*. Dublin: Town House and Country House

Scott, A. B. & Martin, F. X. (eds) 1978. *Expugnatio Hibernica: The Conquest of Ireland by Giraldus Cambrensis*. Dublin: Royal Irish Academy

Stalley, R. 1987. *The Cistercian Monasteries of Ireland*. London & New Haven: Yale University Press

Stout, G. 2012. 'Bective: Medieval Cistercian abbey', in I. Bennett (ed.) *Excavations 2009: Summary accounts of archaeological excavations in Ireland*, 164–5, No. 637. Dublin: Wordwell

Stout, G. 2002. *Newgrange and the Bend of the Boyne*. Cork: Cork University Press

Sweetman, D. 1999. *The Medieval Castles of Ireland*. Cork: The Collins Press

Sweetman, D. Alcock & O. Moran, B. 1995. *Archaeological Inventory of Co. Laois*. Dublin: Stationery Office

Waddell, J. 2014. *Archaeology and Celtic Myth*. Dublin: Four Courts Press

Waddell, J. 2000. *The Prehistoric Archaeology of Ireland*. Wicklow: Wordwell

Wallace, P. F. & Floinn, R. (eds) 2002. *Treasures of the National Museum of Ireland*. Dublin: Gill & Macmillan

Westropp, T. J. 1903. 'Notes on the antiquities of Ardmore'. *JRSAI*, 33, 353–80

Wilde, W. 1850. *The Beauties of the Boyne and its Tributary, the Blackwater* (2nd ed). Dublin: McGlashan

INDEX